The Story of Success

The Story of Success

FIVE STEPS TO MASTERING ETHICS IN BUSINESS

LEIGH HAFREY

OTHER PRESS
NEW YORK

617 56029

Permission to print excerpts from the following is gratefully acknowledged:
- From *The Country Bunny and the Little Gold Shoes* by DuBose Heyward and Marjorie Flack. Copyright © 1939 by DuBose Heyward and Marjorie Flack Larsson. Copyright renewed 1966 by Hilma Larsson and Barnum and Jennifer Heyward. Reprinted by permission of Houghton Miflin Company.
- From *A Man for All Seasons* by Robert Bolt, copyright © 1960, 1962 by Robert Bolt. Used by permission of Random House, Inc.
- Three excerpts from pp. 2, 32, 38, 40 from *Cheaper by the Dozen* by Frank B. Gilbreth, Jr. and Ernestine Gilbreth Carey. Copyright © 1948, 1963 by Frank B. Gilbreth Jr. and Ernestine Gilbreth Carey. Reprinted by permission of HarperCollins Publishers Inc.
- Various extracts from *Two Lovely Beasts* by Liam O'Flaherty. Copyright © The Estate of Liam OíFlaherty 1948. Reproduced by permission of PFD (www.pfd.co.uk) on behalf of the Estate of Liam O'Flaherty.
- *The New York Times Magazine*, "Scenes from a Marriage," August 12, 2001, pp. 44ff.
- Dialogue from *Shall We Dance?* used by permission of Miramax Films.
- "Analect 1.14," "Analect 12.16," and "Analect 2.4" from *The Analects of Confucius*, translated by Simon Leys. Copyright © 1997 by Pierre Ryckmans. Used by permission of W. W. Norton & Company, Inc.
- "Letter from Birmingham Jail," in *Why We Can't Wait*. Copyright © 1963 Martin Luther King Jr. Copyright renewed 1991 Coretta Scott King. Reprinted by arrangement with the Estate of Martin Luther King Jr., ℅ Writers House as agent for the proprietor New York, NY.

Production Editor: Robert D. Hack
This book was designed/set in Albertina MT by Rachel Reiss.

10 9 8 7 6 5 4 3 2 1

LIBRARY OF CONGRESS CATALOGING-IN-PUBLICATION DATA

Hafrey, Leigh.
  The story of success : five steps to mastering ethics in business / by Leigh Hafrey.
    p. cm.
  Includes bibliographical references.
  ISBN 1-59051-120-4 (hardcover : alk. paper) 1. Business ethics. 2. Business ethics in literature. 3. Business ethics in motion pictures. I. Title.
  HF5387.H34 2005
  174'.4—dc22

2004027359

Contents

Acknowledgments

This book wouldn't have been possible without the hundreds of people in business, law, medicine, architecture, law enforcement, the arts, and many other walks of life who willingly talked with me about ethics in seminars, workshops, lectures, and casual conversations on airplanes, in restaurants, parks, and at holiday parties. I hope that *The Story of Success* begins to capture the spirit of their contributions; they have convinced me that human nature, however fallible, also contains the good that men and women across the ages and all cultures have hopefully ascribed to it.

A few specific thanks are in order: to Ramona Naddaff, for encouraging me to write *The Story of Success* and making the requisite publishing connection; to my family—Sandra, Nathaniel, Ben, and all the Hafreys and Naddaffs beyond our nuclear unit—who asked periodically and without too much probing, "So, how's the book?"; to Judith Feher-Gurewich, my publisher, who was willing to take a chance on this project; to Rosemary Ahern, my editor, for her light pencil; to Michelle Fiorenza, my assistant at MIT Sloan, for her logistical support; and to John Bethell and Ed Steinfeld for reading portions of the manuscript. Without you, too, there would have been no book.

Thus in the beginning all the world was America, and more so than that is now; for no such thing as money was anywhere known.

—JOHN LOCKE,
THE SECOND TREATISE OF GOVERNMENT

CHAPTER 1

The Importance of Story

Placing the Person and the Organization

The Subject

This book is about story and the ethical role storytelling plays in our lives—particularly our lives in organizations. So let me begin with a tale from an unusual workplace. I borrow it from a participant at one of my Stories for Leaders seminars, a principal in a West Coast marketing consultancy. He recalled an exchange he had with a salesperson, or "counselor," at a cemetery with which he was working at the time. I include his editorial notes in parentheses:

A guy calls me for a pre-need arrangement. (That's what they call buying your funeral before you die.) *He says on the phone, "How fast can I choose the plot, buy the casket, and pay for everything?" I tell him we can do it immediately. He shows up in an hour. The guy is only 45 years old and looks reasonably healthy. I take him up the hill to our latest property.* (That's what they call a gravesite.) *I tell him what the opening and closing costs will be.* (Opening and closing costs means digging the grave and then shoveling the dirt back in after the burial.)

I then take him over to the casket room. He chooses the most expensive casket, measuring to see how well he will fit into it. He makes all his decisions. He then asks me for the paperwork. I tell him that it will take a few hours to prepare and that I will send it to him the next day. "No," he says emphatically. "I need it now."

I look at him: "May I ask why you are in such a rush?" "Yes, you may," he answers. "When I am done here, I'm going home to commit suicide." I look back at him and say, "I'm a commission salesman. The deal has to be in effect for seven days in order for me to receive my commission. I've just spent hours with you and if you commit suicide today, I won't get my commission."

The guy waited because of me. I got him help. He's still alive. And I got my commission.

Most of us have only passing interactions with cemetery counselors, and prefer it that way. We do not spontaneously locate our notions of ethical practice at the cemetery—in fact, we generally assume that when we have gotten that far, it's too late to redeem ourselves through virtuous acts. Yet cemeteries, too, need to be managed, and so this grave story speaks to questions that *The Story of Success* raises and hopes to answer for business and management. Here are those questions, starting with the specifics of the story and expanding to the larger philosophical issues that they imply:

- Why did the client tell the counselor what he intended to do?

- If the client was sufficiently in command of his senses to organize his own burial, was he really on the verge of suicide?

- Did the salesperson at the cemetery really have a seven-day waiting period before his commission kicked in?

- Can one indeed do well by doing good, a claim that ethicists and socially responsible businesspeople keep making and that this salesperson seems to have proven?

And last but not least, given the theme of this book:

- In business, how often do you hear stories as good as this one, whether you're a management consultant or an investment banker or a salesperson or the mailroom clerk?!

The Story of Success draws on 15 years of conversations with businesspeople, managers, and other professionals in the course of my teaching at Harvard Business School, at the MIT Sloan School of Management, and in occasional sessions for the Brandeis Seminars in Humanities and the Professions and the Aspen Institute, which offers one of the best-known executive education programs in America. Outside the academy, the book emerges from a host of informal exchanges, where the stock response to my stated occupation is, "Business ethics? Isn't that an oxymoron?"

There is no contradiction in terms here. Eager young MBAs, midcareer executives, and senior executives from small, midsize, and Fortune 500 corporations as well as leaders in nonprofit organizations disprove the skepticism expressed in that question. The same is true of doctors, hospital administrators, lawyers, judges, artists, architects, police officers, politicians, and civil servants for whom business and management may not be a primary focus, but who engage more or less consciously in business and management as they pursue their material and spiritual goals. In all these cases, people talk about ethics in the workplace directly and indirectly, addressing leadership and professional standards, the balance of family and work life, wealth, liberty, efficiency, community, democracy, and what it means to build a good society. This book emerges from the experience that, contrary to stereotypes even businesspeople hold about themselves, many people engage the business portion of their lives having thought long and hard about what they do; even in the face of daunting obstacles, they aspire to live and work by their principles. For them, doing business or managing an organization is all about values (one of which may be the bottom line, but not always and not exclusively). That is the subject of this book.

The Method

Although it is true that people who take the time to talk about or speculate on the nature of their work are probably predisposed to say things worth hearing, to tell stories worth remembering, the very act of storytelling brings with it an openness toward the world and a fundamental optimism. Everyone has a good story to tell, and the very act of storytelling generates energy around the teller's subject, bringing speaker and audience to life in a way that defines ethical engagement.

Storytelling is a communal experience, a communication that brings into being, however briefly, a community of two or more. The impetus, again, is values. At its most elementary, story is the vehicle by which one generation instructs the next in what the world is or might be. We use story to help clarify right and wrong for our children, who haven't yet experienced the world as we have come to know it. Our stories illuminate modes of inter-action so that others can judge whether they are experiencing appropriate or inappropriate, outdated or premature ways of get-ting along in a community. Storytelling is never just about the telling: it is always also about the conversation or interpretation, the conflict of views, the building of consensus. What do *we* think about this story? That question is always as important to us as the question of what *I* think about it; the *I* learns from the ex-change as much as the *we*, hearing oneself in the audience and correcting that self as the story unfolds. That's why the act of storytelling is so invigorating!

In an era that considers itself increasingly bereft of commu-nity, it is easy to fall for the argument that we no longer tell sto-ries the way people once did. There's no more village camp fire, no gathering of the elders, no ritual moment when the commu-nity elder instructs the young people in the wisdom of the com-munity. The argument has some validity: the physical trappings of that mythical golden age are gone, erased by modern technol-ogy and fueled by notions of progress. Yet the storytelling goes on. Parents and grandparents still read to their children and grandchildren; people still have conversations over dinner, even if the conversations occur in a fast-food restaurant instead of by the kitchen fire; TV characters are perhaps more frequently the subject of discussion than characters in a novel, but they draw just as much attention, and play much the same role for the col-lective imagination.

We argue, too, that in an increasingly globalized world, we find it difficult to say which stories really matter, which ones sketch the dominant spirit or view in a global society that is itself many different societies. One answer to the concern lies ready to hand: American consumer culture, the American notion of

entertainment symbolized for many by Disney, is already ho-
mogenizing global notions of what makes a good story. In this
view, we will agree on right and wrong in a very few years, if current commercial trends in entertainment continue. This view
makes many people unhappy. It is a new form of imperialism, or
an old form from a new, imperial source, and it brings with it all
of the negative connotations that such hegemony traditionally
carries, despite the possibility that it will bridge the gaps among
current cultures.

Yet another, more broadly acceptable counterargument also
lies ready to hand: in this view, "the empire strikes back." All of
the great, bygone empires are now assimilating the far-flung populations they once dominated, but in the assimilation process,
they are being significantly and irrevocably altered. Whatever the
imperial effect of British, French, Russian, Japanese, American,
and Chinese culture, the minority populations they encompass
have a say in how those cultures will evolve in the coming years.
This view doesn't deny the force of the dominant culture; it simply asserts that the end result will look very different from what
one might suppose today.

Stories allow us to chart that course, entertaining and educating simultaneously, drawing an audience in and pointing the way
for people, or inviting them to help us see the way. Globalization
and cyberspace may change the physical markers for this process,
but the process itself remains the same across time and space. The
skills by which we understand printed or filmed stories are the
skills we apply when we tell our own stories by the office water
cooler or the village well. We are probing for ethical standards in
all of these situations, and the juxtaposition of stories across cultures, increasingly a feature of our global society, keeps us testing
our standards for validity. That is the method of this book.

Five Steps to Ethical Practice

The Story of Success offers five views on ethical behavior in business and management. For good or ill, behaving ethically rarely involves transcendent moments, though it does involve deep-seated values. People often say that ethics only matters after one has assured one's survival; what is the good of ethical business practices, for example, if the business goes under? In response, one might ask—as this book asks—how we define "survival." Removing ethics from the realm of daily action may preserve our values, but it also makes them very hard to recall from their luxury status when we decide they are needed.

Ethical practice is as fundamental to our survival as food, clothing, and shelter, for reasons that the stories explored in this book make evident. Despite the metaphysical halo with which we are inclined to endow our values, ethical practice resembles other processes we consider routine, from cooking to running errands to fixing your car: you can't escape thinking about it, even if you choose to be unethical; you're never quite sure of the results of your actions; you may have to improvise the ingredients, at your own risk; other people may not like the result and will tell you so; and the effects on you and others can linger for years. Finally, behaving ethically rarely leads to anything more than personal satisfaction, which can make for low-income living. Here again, though, how we define "survival" matters.

Because of the quotidian nature of ethical decisions—even those that provoke major outcomes—the five approaches to ethics offered in this book are grounded in the specifics of a case or story. People, not principles, make ethical practice, and the stories explored here are about people—not just the characters in the stories, but the readers, listeners, and viewers who engage the stories through their own stories, which they share with one another. Faced with this plenitude and variety, I offer approaches rather than prescriptions, stories of lived experience rather than abstract theories and formulas. I offer essays in ethical practice, not prescriptions for it. I argue that the ground on which we stand keeps shifting, and that story allows us to adapt to changing circumstances without losing sight of that crucial ethical network— the individual in relation to him- or herself, to the community, and vice versa.

At the same time, we need to organize our experience, to help it make sense to us and to others. This is an ethical imperative, too, and we should understand it as such, even when we claim simply to be doing our job or living our lives. The five cases of this book outline a consistent framework to ethical practice, though any one of the five offers a valid point of access to the others. They are: 1) speak up, speak out; 2) see the big picture; 3) break the rules, make the rules, absorb the costs; 4) tell good stories; and 5) test for truth.

SPEAK UP, SPEAK OUT

Little is left to chance in the classroom experience at Harvard Business School. For first-year MBAs in particular, everything revolves around section culture. When I taught at HBS from 1989 to 1993, each incoming class was divided into nine groups of ninety students, and those numbers have varied little since then. Each section meets in a tiered amphitheater, in which the professor walks almost as an invited guest. The students are divided into study groups for early-morning and late-evening team learning outside the classroom. Inside the classroom, they have the opportunity at the beginning of the year to choose their seats, after which seating charts are made for the faculty, complete with head shots of the students, so that the instructor can plan in advance whom to call on, and call on that person by name from the first class, remember after the fact who spoke, and record both the rate and the quality of the participation, which contributes substantially to the grade. A whole culture has evolved around that seating, though the interpretation of what it means to sit in the "worm deck" or the "sky deck," for example, is subject to conflicting interpretations: the worm deck places students at the bottom of the inverted pyramid, a lowly position; but those same students also sit closest to the faculty, who stands in the pit. Students who sit in the "sky deck" can be seen as wanting either to avoid notice or to dominate the discussion from on high—antithetical aims. Those in the middle are the silent majority, but they have an obligation to speak.

In moderated case discussion—the dominant teaching model at HBS—the do's and don'ts of participation are explicit for both sides of the exchange: for the students, concision and an explicit recognition of classmates' contributions are a virtue, "logging airtime"—speaking for the sake of getting noticed—a sin. Faculty must invite a broad range of contributions, watching other students while the one called on is speaking, in order to spot or encourage student engagement and get the speaker to speak to the class, not the instructor. The instructor must lead the class to solid conclusions about the case before them, ideally without revealing an opinion: watching an expert faculty member lead a case discussion is like watching a conductor lead an orchestra. If you know the piece, you can anticipate when in the hour-and-a-half session the class will reach its crescendo, and how. For inexpert faculty, and for many of the MBAs, case discussions are terrifying.

Bobby* took managerial communication with me when he arrived at HBS in the fall of 1990. He was a sky-decker, but very definitely of the quiet, slightly retiring variety. He spoke softly, a problem when the speaker is sitting at the back and top of a large room, and he spoke with hesitation, a problem regardless of where one sits in a case discussion. I encouraged him to speak up during the oral presentation exercises that we scheduled that semester in communication. He did reasonably well in the course, and we went our separate ways.

Then, three semesters later, in his last semester at HBS, Bobby appeared in my section of "The Business World: Moral and Social Inquiry Through Fiction." This course was initiated at HBS by the child psychiatrist and Harvard faculty member Robert Coles, the author of the famous series of books titled *Children of Crisis* (1967–1977), relating stories Coles had gathered talking with children in the American South during the civil rights era. It was my first time teaching the course, an elective, and I was nervous. I remembered Bobby, and was delighted to see him the way any faculty member is delighted to see a student come back for further instruction.

I also remembered the slightly discouraged demeanor Bobby had previously brought to the classroom, and I quickly recognized that he had not changed. He made contributions as we moved into the semester, but he faded into the background, still sitting in the sky deck. As in all classes, certain students quickly distinguished themselves as spokespeople and thought leaders for the class as a whole. All my hard-won moderating skills

---

* Here and throughout *The Story of Success,* seminar participants are given pseudonyms or no names; where necessary to preserve their anonymity, distinguishing features have been altered or eliminated.

couldn't bring Bobby to a similar pitch. His first paper was competent, but it, too, didn't stand out. On paper and in person, he seemed interested but not very involved. He was the same hesitant, nice guy with a careful smile and a low, almost reluctant voice that he had been when he first arrived at the school.

Then, in the space of one week, his voice changed completely. Suddenly, he had the ability to project emphatically across the amphitheater. The new voice sounded a little unpracticed, a little rough, like a foal getting to its feet after birth, but still uncertain whether it can actually pull off its first run. Yet he did pull it off, moving from comment to comment throughout that class at the same new volume, and with the same new self-assertiveness. He was still sitting in the sky deck, but now a position that had once suggested withdrawal read as the choice of a dominant place, overlooking the rest of the class. His body language was partially responsible, because it had changed, too. He sat straighter, looked more alert even when he wasn't actually speaking, smiled more. Bobby suddenly had gone from being one of the stragglers in the class to a major player.

In the next class, the same thing happened. Again, Bobby spoke with authority and volume; his comments showed a new precision in his thinking. Down in the pit looking up at him, I knew I had missed something in the course of the semester. This was the sort of teacherly ignorance that the carefully managed classroom experience at HBS sought to eliminate. I was at a loss, though delighted; and then, finally, I read the paper he had submitted at the beginning of the first class in which his voice had changed, and I knew why it had changed.

Earlier in the semester, we had spent a couple of hours talking about a novel by Harry Mulisch, one of the Netherlands' greatest living fiction writers. The book, titled *The Assault*, had been published in English in the mid-1980s. It tells the story of Anton Steenwijk, a 12-year-old boy who sees his family killed by Nazi occupiers in Holland during World War II. Their deaths were part of the Nazis' retaliation for the assassination of a Dutch Fascist collaborator on the street outside their house, a nightmare scene in the middle of blacked-out Holland that ended for Anton with a glimpse of his mother attacking a German soldier with her fists, the sound of machine gun fire, his family's house burned to the ground, and then a night in a cell with a woman who didn't know him, but who comforted him in his confusion and distress.

The killing occupies the first third of the novel. The balance of the book details the ways in which, after the war, Anton makes a life for himself. He becomes an anesthesiologist; he marries twice, has children by both wives, and maintains good relations with all of them, as well as with his colleagues and friends. And yet, he is never fully engaged with any of these aspects of his apparently comfortable, successful life; he is himself anesthetized, living a muted life in constant, semiconscious fear of having his past resurrected. As he comments once in order to extricate himself from an animated political discussion at a party, "I've had my share" (*The Assault*, p. 61).

When I read Bobby's paper, I discovered that he had drawn a step-by-step parallel between 'Ton's life and his own. At the age of 14, Bobby came home to find that his mother had committed suicide. Like 'Ton, he withdrew into himself and into the normalcy that sometimes comes with focused achievement. His siblings teased him for wanting to live the norm: a house with a white picket fence, 1.3 kids, and a good, steady job. He could feel the teasing and recognize the justice of what his siblings were saying to him, but he couldn't resist his own deep-seated need for that stability.

In 'Ton's story, Bobby had found a restatement of his own case, and the immediate result was the new, more self-assertive Bobby. He finished the semester in that same, reincarnated persona, graduated from HBS, and I lost touch with him. When I e-mailed him twelve years later and reminded him of our connection, he was very friendly and commented that he had very much enjoyed the course. He initially remembered neither *The Assault* nor his paper, which I had mentioned in my e-mail, but by the time we spoke a day later, he had gone to Amazon.com to remind himself of the book, and said with a chuckle that he would be buying it.

He remembered being more a "bean-counter" than a "poet" during his tenure at HBS. He remembered sitting in the sky deck, and noted that, for those who had a fear of public speaking, as he did, one could refine sitting at the top of the room by sitting close to the door out of the room, which he also did. Still, he added ruefully, there was no leaving the room during class. Today, Bobby is at a private equity investment firm in New York City, the one to which he went after graduating. He noted that such career stability is unusual among his classmates—"I'm a little more risk-averse than others"—but that he likes the people with whom he works, and has found the job both challenging and very satisfying. He is married, a relatively new father, and lives on Manhattan's Upper East Side. During our conversation, he was animated and happy; what I heard in his voice was very much the Bobby of "The Business World" *after* he wrote the paper on *The Assault*.

Bobby's story and Anton's couldn't in many ways be more different, and one could argue that Bobby's forgetting both the novel and the paper that he wrote mark how little the moment mattered to him in the long term. Yet he commented, when we talked in the summer of 2004, that it had been very difficult to write the paper. He had talked little of his mother's suicide until then (twelve years later). He also noted that, even for the relatively conservative, number-crunching type that he was, the experience of case discussion at HBS had demonstrated the power of story: "Cases are stories, and even in accounting, an area where I had expertise before business school, the cases made the material come alive. I learned how accounting could affect your business decisions; I learned how to *use* accounting."

Bobby thought that the outpouring of grief at Ronald Reagan's death, which had just happened when we spoke, could be traced in part to all the love Reagan had generated through "his ability to turn things into stories." He was mildly critical of the political correctness he had detected at HBS, but noted that, in the debate over whether ethics could be taught, he came down on the affirmative side: "I thought, you really can teach ethics. You discuss a book in a group, and norms get shaped." And finally, he recalled his fear of public speaking: "Your heart races, and when your heart races, it's hard to talk." But, he added, "it was different in 'The Business World'; with *The Assault*, it was different." At that moment, he found the opening to speak up and speak out, and it gave him a voice that he still has today, the voice of ethical practice.

SEE THE BIG PICTURE

Ten years ago, Royal Dutch/Shell produced a brochure titled "Global Scenarios: 1995–2020." Based on two volumes of detailed analysis, the scenarios were the latest in a series of documents the oil giant had produced since the early 1970s, when the company adopted the U.S. military's use of scenario planning to anticipate future challenges to the organization. Scenario planners intend not so much to forecast future trends in the economy, global politics, or the arms race, as to inculcate flexibility of mind in managers within organizations. Scenario planners hope that, when managers have a full understanding of the array of possible developments over a specified period, they will respond more quickly and effectively to business challenges that present themselves. Like the case studies that mediate much of business education, scenarios are stories tailored to the needs of practicing managers and their organizations. They provide the focus necessary to deal with real-life complexity.

"Global Scenarios: 1995–2020" offered two possibilities for the coming quarter century. The first imagined the continuing success of late twentieth-century, U.S.-style capitalism, quick and improvisational and reliant on technology to sustain its successes. The second reflected the increasing clout of the Asian economies, and specifically the East Asian countries. It foresaw a rising global emphasis on networks and the coordinating role of governments, and a more monolithic appreciation for society and social good over the individual, individual creativity, and individual satisfaction. These scenarios reflect old stereotypes about Western vs. Asian cultures, the subject of manuals on cross-cultural business etiquette. They also capture the crosscurrents implicit in the complaint launched near the end of the century by Mahathir Mohammad, then prime minister of Malaysia, about the Western bias of the U.N. Universal Declaration of Human Rights. For Mahathir and his supporters, the declaration, which has provided the foundation for human rights discussions since its adoption and proclamation by the world body in 1948, places too much emphasis on rights and too little on responsibilities, the latter providing the foundation of the Asian scenario Royal Dutch/Shell planners articulated.

For a business organization, this *is* the big picture: global forces that express themselves in financial and cultural phenomena and that are only marginally within the control of individuals even at the top of organizations, whether these be local companies, multinationals, or nation-states. But business and other organizations must cope with complexity, just as individuals must do: Royal Dutch/Shell's first scenario contributes U.S.-style entrepreneurial nimbleness to individual or corporate action on the global stage (of which, more shortly), and its second scenario adds a notion of Confucian mastery or authority that is equally effective but culturally very different.

> 2.4 *The Master said: "At fifteen, I set my mind upon learning. At thirty, I took my stand. At forty, I had no doubts. At fifty, I knew the will of Heaven. At sixty, my ear was attuned. At seventy, I follow all the desires of my heart without breaking any rule."*
> (CONFUCIUS, THE ANALECTS,
> P. 6, TRANS. SIMON LEYS)

Although we might read this passage primarily as a progress report on self-discipline, issued rather ironically when it was really too late for Confucius to recant past sins (even the Master seems to have had a sense of humor), this fragment from *The Analects* refers equally to the forces that impose mastery on the individual. What is "the will of Heaven," and which "rules" does the Master invoke in his closing phrase? They may be larger, more transcendent forces than those imagined in "Global Scenarios," but their net impact remains the same. We impose order progressively, to deal with progressive levels of turmoil: working from his or her own comparatively narrow perspective, the individual finds it hard to understand fully the logic of a set of rules imposed by the larger society in which he or she has a place; at first glance, submission to authority seems the only viable response, and it is this logic that underwrites the more top-down social structures that we associate with "Asian" values.

Yet the progress of learning is also a process of educating, the self inserting itself into the larger world from which it learns. Over the past several years, I have taught seminars in business or managerial ethics in China, where MIT Sloan has several affiliated programs. On my initial visit, I offered the internationally focused business students, or IMBAs, the broadly cosmopolitan syllabus that I have offered most audiences. In the face of the students' persistent focus on adopting Western values as a road to success in the global marketplace, though, I began working specifically with Chinese materials, in juxtaposition with analogous texts from the Western canon. Though it may seem arrogant, I began teaching Confucius in China because I knew that, even as my IMBAs proclaimed themselves Confucian, they had read no more than a few pages of *The Analects* in middle school, and then primarily as an exercise in language study.

I sought a less monolithically corporatist reading of Confucius than my students advanced. As with much wisdom literature, his work has been adopted and adapted by countless rulers, and rulers' systems, to justify their authority. And yet, in the Master's notion of the gentleman, stripped of its antecedents in class privilege, lies the basis for an ethical practice that is deeply individual—that seemed a lesson worth imparting. To ground the East–West comparison at home, moreover, I juxtaposed with Confucius passages from Aristotle, the ancient Greek philosopher who wrote two centuries or so after the Master, on the other side of the globe. Both traditions make way for the individual and individual striving for perfection, yet both have a very clear concept of the power of the community to constrain the individual, even as it benefits him or her. How far is Aristotle from Confucius when he argues in the *Politics*:

> *The proof that the state is a creation of nature and prior to the individual is that the individual, when isolated, is not self-sufficing; and therefore he is like a part in relation to the whole. But he who is unable to live in society, or who has no need because he is sufficient for himself, must be either a beast or a god: he is no part of a state. A social instinct is implanted in all men by nature.*
>   ARISTOTLE, *POLITICS*, P. 1130

In *Nicomachean Ethics* Aristotle argues that a good life is not definitively so until it has been lived out completely:

> *For as it is not one swallow or one fine day that makes a spring, so it is not one day or a short time that makes a man blessed and happy.*
>   ARISTOTLE, *NICOMACHEAN ETHICS*, P. 10

This formulation puts the definition of happiness firmly in the hands of the community that survives us.

Suddenly, the dichotomy implicit in the scenarios Royal Dutch/Shell offers for 1995–2020 seemed less like alternatives and more like nearly indistinguishable halves of the same whole. In the spirit of continuous change that underlies today's American business model, one might wish to reject Aristotle as obsolete, irrelevant, or merely "old Europe," and yet his work has played the same tone-setting role in the West that Confucius does in the East—influence enhanced today by the fact that it goes largely unnoticed. Despite the origins of our modern democracies in ancient Athenian democracy, how far have we moved, in the ensuing two millennia, beyond ruling elites? We need only consider our largest corporations, which hold wealth and wield power equal to or greater than that of many nation-states and which are built, moreover, on hierarchies that are decidedly undemocratic, to realize that even our Western past is still very much with us, and it doesn't look that different from the supposedly authoritarian East.

In the climate of populist outrage we have experienced in the twenty-first century over corporate abuses in the United States, this truth may not sit well, but it reflects a reality of leadership that we know as well in the more individualistic Western countries. Hierarchies evolve to address the fact that some people have more information than others. Corporations represent one manifestation of this asymmetry. The decisions that get made in organizations can work to the disadvantage of the individual, even when the individual has the political or civil right to speak his or her mind. Yet if those decision-making powers get exercised with the intent to impart the benefits of better information to the community as a whole, to teach both the truth and the means of seeing the truth, the individual is not lost to the community. That, too, is ethical practice, and the role of the master in both the East and the West.

BREAK THE RULES, MAKE THE RULES, ABSORB THE COSTS

In June 2000 I moderated a seminar at the Aspen Institute titled "Leadership and Moral Decision Making at the Millennium." The seminar was a version of the flagship Aspen product, the Executive Seminar, that the institute had been offering to corporate executives since the 1950s, and that I had been co-moderating for five years. The topics were mainstream Aspen: rights, liberty, equality, and property—a subset of the larger corpus that also includes efficiency, democracy, leadership, and community—big topics for people with big responsibilities. The readings in each module also derived from the syllabus for the weeklong Executive Seminar: Aristotle, Hobbes, Kant, the U.S. Declaration of Independence, economists Milton Friedman and Arthur Okun, the Bible, and Karl Marx and Friedrich Engels.

The seminar differed markedly from the regular Executive Seminar, though, in the participants. While the institute had made its reputation since the 1950s by drawing the power elites from Washington, New York, and Chicago, bringing presidents and Supreme Court justices and Fortune 500 CEOs to the same table to discuss the issues of the day, this weekend in the Colorado Rockies was catering to a younger crowd, many of whom came from a new center of power and influence—the San Francisco Bay area. Launched by Gary and Laura Lauder, respectively a Silicon Valley venture capitalist and a philanthropist, the Socrates Society Future Leaders Forum was explicitly designed to renew the audience for the institute's offerings and to expand its reach into the digital economy. The 2000 forum was the fifth such event, and many of the people had attended before. The gathering was a reunion as much as a symposium, fueled by a shared place of origin for many, but also by a shared stake in the Internet boom.

As a measure of the forum's character, the company names on my list of seminar participants indicated that this was a different kind of Aspen event: most of them included tag terms like "Communications," "Online," "Interactive Media," ".com," "Solutions," "Labs." Among the more than one hundred participants and their families, there were numerous CEOs, managing directors, executive directors, as well as a software architect or two, and many venture capitalists investing in new media. Yet a quick glance around the room at the inaugural dinner would have suggested a crowd much lower on the traditional corporate ladder by virtue of their youth. At that dinner, and at all the events over those three days, there was a hubbub, an energy and enthusiasm that fed off the clear mountain air and the sunshine, the euphoria of people who know they are making a difference.

By July 2000, of course, the bloom was already off the dotcom rose, though how much so no one knew yet. One participant freely acknowledged that he had lost eighty percent of his net worth in the preceding six months, but he was still wealthy, at least on paper. What's more, many of the participants with whom I talked had developed a cult of failure. It was a mark of achievement to have burned through several million dollars, regardless of the outcome. There would always be more money, and your burn rate only indicated that someone had thought you had something worth investing in, and the skills to make it pay off. That, too, could go on your résumé, and factor into the next business plan. So the dark clouds on the horizon that summer still looked to some, at least, like a passing phenomenon.

It was an exhilarating experience, and the ensuing crash has done nothing to tarnish my personal memory of those days: confidence inspires confidence and enthusiasm generates enthusiasm, at least at first; but then it becomes necessary to probe the substance on which the confidence and enthusiasm build. Our conversations gave me the opportunity to ask questions and weigh the evidence for the attendees' euphoria, beyond their shared youth. As a group, they were well educated, having in most cases gotten a solid liberal arts undergraduate education, and in many cases advanced degrees. Their comments during our discussions of the canonic texts reflected their training and breadth of culture, and echoed responses I had heard in the regular executive seminar.

And yet, as we approached the end of the symposium, I realized to my astonishment that this group did differ from others with which I had worked. As we tested the often grim hypotheses regarding human nature, economics, and the levers of social order advanced by Hobbes, Friedman, Okun, Marx, Engels, and the anonymous writers of Genesis, it dawned on me that the people in the room did not believe in a central, underlying concept that united our authors. For the dot-com crowd, scarcity was a nonstarter. As they saw it, we had unlimited resources with which to work, and a permanent hold on the means of production. Nothing in their world indicated that life in nature, as Hobbes famously phrased it, was "solitary, poor, nasty, brutish, and short." We didn't have to worry about redistributing income, as Okun—one of the engineers of President Lyndon B. Johnson's Great Society—urged us to do: the new economy would take care of it. No one toiled in the sweat of their brow, as the Bible insisted; if you worked 18-hour days—and many in that room had, for prolonged periods of time—you did it because you loved what you were doing, you did it well, and you knew success was just over the horizon, if you didn't already have it in hand. Finally, you were never "alienated labor," *pace* Marx and Engels; you were in command of the means of production, and everyone else could be in command just like you, *at the same time.*

It was, as I've said, breathtaking. This group encompassed the masters of the universe, entrepreneurs for a new era, breaking with the most fundamental principles wise men had articulated over the centuries. Even looking at the event with a jaundiced eye, you couldn't help wanting this vision to triumph, it was so spectacularly optimistic, energizing, and fertile. I wondered at the time deliver on their earlier promise; and though it is hard to imagine the final form these rearrangements will take, they too represent a form of corporate social responsibility, the ethical commitment of the individual player to equity in a new economic game.

TELL GOOD STORIES

A few months after the attacks on the World Trade Center in New York City and the Pentagon in Washington, D.C., on September 11, 2001, Chris Stone and his wife, Anne Mackinnon, came to visit our family in Cambridge. We had become friends a year or two earlier, and kept in touch even though we saw one another relatively little; Chris, Anne, and their two daughters lived in New York. Shortly after they arrived at our house, Chris mentioned that the offices of the Vera Institute of Justice, the private non-profit of which he was then the director, looked out on the World Trade Center. He described how he and his staff had stood at the windows of the institute, watching people jump or fall from the two towers, singly and in pairs, for about half an hour. He was acutely aware during that time, he said, of the horror of what he was witnessing; but even more, he was conscious that his staff was looking to him for guidance, both logistical and emotional.

At about that point in his narrative, I left the room briefly to fetch something. When I returned, Chris patted me on the back, smiled sympathetically, and said these weren't easy things to discuss. The comment startled me, because I hadn't been aware of leaving the room in order to escape the image that he had called up for me. Later, I realized that I hadn't asked him what he did in order to meet his staff's need for leadership. It would have been a natural question, because my wife and I, as masters of one of the undergraduate residential houses at Harvard, had faced much the

who in the group was thinking about people on the other side of
the digital divide—What about the developing nations? What
about the vast majority of the world's population? Was it possible
to think of unlimited resources as one traveled through Africa or
parts of Central Asia? But I didn't ask those questions, partly because I didn't want to spoil the fun (for myself, too!), and partly
because I knew that the resources that would set us all free were in
many cases virtual, and that it wouldn't take much intellectual
acuity to factor that aspect of the new economy into an equation
benefiting those who had lost out in the old economy.

In retrospect, the missing ingredient to this intoxicating brew
was caution. We now have the advantage of short-term historical
hindsight, and know that the revolution was, at least in economic
terms, a bubble. It's hard to imagine that the exuberance the
Socrates crowd brought into the mountains with them would
have been so persuasive, had someone stood up at the inaugural
dinner and said, "These are the principles with which we are
breaking, this is how we are breaking with them, this is how our
new rules improve on the old, and this is what it will cost us in-
dividually and as a group to make the revolution happen." Such
pragmatism would have been a much harder sell, both within
and without the digital community, and would have made the
work they were doing much harder.

At the same time, chances are excellent that the underlying
principles of the digital revolution will ultimately prove sound,
and we will discover that we have lived through a revolution in
our economic and social arrangements. The change has yet to be
optimized or even fully articulated in a way that will make it available to all of us, but it has happened, and represents our future. If
the cowboy days are over, some significant percentage of those
who drove the change are back now, somewhat the wiser, to

same situation on September 11. We had 430 sophomores, jun-
iors, and seniors in our charge, as well as seventy to eighty staff
members; many of them had friends and family in Manhattan.
As the events of that day unfolded, we knew that they would
need care and attention, and, in some cases, crisis intervention,
and in the weeks that followed, we spent a lot of our time providing exactly that. So, comparing notes with Chris would have
been the logical thing to do, but I didn't do it.

Several years later, I finally made up for the oversight with an
e-mail query. This is what Chris wrote in response:

> Vera's offices occupy a full floor of the Woolworth Building, a block
> from the World Trade Center. At 8:45 A.M. on that Tuesday morn-
> ing, we had about thirty of our ninety staff at work. The sound and
> vibration of the first plane hitting the North Tower drew a small
> crowd to our rear windows from where we were looking at a gaping
> hole, billowing black smoke, and after a few minutes, people falling.
> The entire scene was difficult to take in, but it was the creeping real-
> ization that we were watching people fall that made the scene truly
> horrible. They were falling singly, and sometimes in pairs. There were
> never more than a few falling at once, but they kept coming. They
> were dressed in business attire. They were alive, but clearly only for a
> second or two after we saw them. One staff member turned to me
> and asked, "Those aren't people, are they?" And then just gasped and
> began to cry, without needing an answer.
>
> While the staff at that window did not need me to answer their
> questions about what they were seeing, I began to understand that most
> of them did want help in understanding how to respond to the death
> and destruction in front of us. In a sense, they were looking for leader-
> ship as much as or more than they were looking for information. Then
> the second plane came briefly into view before striking the South Tower.

You asked what I did to respond to that need for leadership. I did four things.

First, that morning, a few minutes after the second plane hit, I helped evacuate the floor. Because it was still the morning rush hour, people were arriving at work. I stayed as long as the police would permit me in the lobby of our building, talking to staff members and sending them back home. The towers were still standing and most people expected to be back at work the next day. When the police told us to leave lower Manhattan, we all went home.

By the time I got home, about forty minutes later, the first tower had fallen and the tragedy had been transformed. I did two more things at that moment. I started a phone tree to reach all of our New York City staff to make sure everyone was safe, and invited all of the Brooklyn residents to come to my house for a makeshift lunch the next day. At the same time, I telephoned a board member in a big midtown law firm to ask if we could relocate our management to his offices. It turned out, of course, that no one could accommodate all ninety of our displaced staff, but I started collecting spaces around the city where people could work with people who would be useful to them. For example, I got the New York Times to give us a set of offices on their editorial floor, normally used by columnists who were not coming in to work during the crisis, and I put our communications staff in those offices. I found space with a couple of private foundations, and so on. By Friday we were back in business, and on Saturday morning I personally led an expedition into the "frozen zone" to reclaim some equipment from our offices (the zone was still blockaded by National Guard troops). Our party had to climb the twelve stories in the Woolworth Building, since it was still without electricity.

The fourth thing I did was create a new project that was about the crisis. The New York courts are just a few blocks from the Trade Center, and there were thousands of prisoners who were supposed to have their day in court on September 11, 12, 13, and so on. I decided that Vera staff would document how the courts responded to the crisis and discern lessons for handling future emergencies. The resulting report on the administration of justice under emergency conditions documented how the courts responded, but also gave our staff a way to engage substantively with the tragedy using their skills.

Bottom line: I focused on getting people together and giving them a purpose connected to the tragedy. Getting people together was hard because the city was locked down for days and our offices were inaccessible for a month. Giving people a project connected to the tragedy was merely a matter of imagination. The two in combination kept spirits remarkably high. A year later, as we were preparing to mark the first anniversary of the attack back in our offices, our librarian came up to me to confess that she was feeling nostalgic for the days of that tragic week. Her memories were of the lunch at my house, the makeshift offices spread across the city, and the excitement of improvising an organization together.

Obviously, Chris's experience of September 11 has all of the qualities of a good documentary, an engaged observer's recollections of a terrible day in recent American history. But the "good story" here is the other story, the story he wove for his organization in response to 9/11. One could rewrite this narrative to give business school students the challenge of managing their staff in time of emergency: "A block from your offices, the World Trade Center is in flames; your staff is distraught and confused; what do you do?" Numerous other organizations had to adapt just as the Vera Institute did, so the challenge is not a unique one. Chris chose a particular set of responses: those may have been unique to his organization, and they, too, would be open to discussion and question in a classroom setting. But Chris's librarian has already supplied a convincing, if anecdotal, evaluation: for her, those days of trouble were a time of real and meaningful engagement. Chris led his staff by developing the story of their organization in relation to a catastrophe, a story that they could act out, and that kept them focused and engaged during the height of the crisis. Over the long term, at least one staff member found renewed commitment to her work and her organization.

Were his actions as a leader and manager fundamentally ethical? At the very least, the project on which he launched his staff after the attacks embodies the notion of corporate social responsibility. One could argue that, as the director of a nonprofit, Chris didn't face much of a challenge in finding the socially responsible thing to do under the circumstances. But that social responsibility takes two forms: (1) the organization's responsibility to its environment; and (2) the leader's responsibility to keep his organization functional, to ensure that all the members of the organization get the attention they need in trying conditions. The second mandate also feeds back into the first, in that employees to whose well-being the leader has devoted appropriate attention continue to function positively outside the organization, in ways that are constructive for the community as a whole. Managers who rise to that challenge do so in nonprofits and for-profits alike. They express their ethical practice in a simultaneous recognition of the needs of the individual and the needs of the community; balancing the two may be a matter of judgment, but that too is implicit in the notion of ethical practice.

TEST FOR TRUTH

One man's challenge to Enron, when no one else was asking any questions, is a very public case of testing for truth. By the end of the last century Houston-based Enron, founded in 1985, was by its own description one of the world's largest energy companies. It was the darling of investors, and observers of the business scene couldn't make enough of Enron's winning formulas, both externally and internally. It was admired for its innovative, dynamic culture and its financial success. It started by delivering energy, but later expanded into brokering energy futures. In 1999 it launched EnronOnline, a Web-based commodity trading site, which made it an e-commerce player. Enron reported revenues of $101 billion in 2000. When it declared bankruptcy in December 2001, the company wiped out the savings of thousands of its employees, even as its senior management apparently survived the filing unscathed. The bankruptcy filing also launched the death agony of Enron's auditor, Arthur Andersen, and began a scandal the complexities of which continue to unfurl.

For a long time, Enron had a "good story." People whose business it is to assess the competence of management teams and the viability of corporate strategies were still buying into it as late as the fall of 2001. But Richard Grubman, a managing director of Highfields Capital Management LP, in Boston, had raised a warning flag. Grubman cofounded Highfields in 1998 with Jonathon Jacobson, formerly of the Harvard Management Company, the university subsidiary that manages the Harvard endowment. Highfields started with $500 million from the university and $1 billion from other investors: today, it has about $6 billion under management.

On April 17, 2001, during a conference call that then–Enron CEO Jeffrey Skilling was holding with stock analysts and reporters, Grubman made what might have seemed a routine request. Grubman's exchange with Skilling, captured in the following transcript, has since become (in)famous:

OPERATOR: Richard Grubman of Highfields Capital.

GRUBMAN: Good morning. Can you tell us what the assets and liabilities from price risk management were at quarter-end, what those balances were?

SKILLING: We do not have the balance sheet completed. We will have that done shortly when we file the Q. But until we put all of that together, we just cannot give you that.

GRUBMAN: I'm trying to understand why that would appear to be an unreasonable request, in light of your comments about daily control of all your credits. I mean, you have a trading desk with a $21 billion matched book that's two times your book value, and you cannot tell us what the balances are?

SKILLING: I'm not saying we can't tell you what the balances are. We clearly have all of those positions on a daily basis, but at this point, we will wait to disclose those until all of the netting and the right accounting is put together.

GRUBMAN: You're the only financial institution that cannot produce a balance sheet or cash flow statement with their earnings.

SKILLING: Thank you very much, we appreciate that.

GRUBMAN: We appreciate that?

SKILLING: Asshole.

Perhaps because the two men so casually use the terms of their profession at the outset of this exchange, the end note is particularly jarring. Annotated versions of the transcript have Skilling chuckle as he calls Grubman a name, but whether he did so with jocular or hostile intent, Skilling's end to the exchange suggests that Grubman had touched a nerve, and that there was more to say. Four months later, Skilling resigned the CEO job he had taken on less than a year earlier.

Skilling has been quoted since as saying that he didn't appreciate Grubman's using the conference call "for some personal vested interest related to their [Highfields'] stock position," implying, observers hypothesized, that Grubman was looking for ways to drive down Enron's stock price. In another conference call six months later, Enron's chairman, Ken Lay, refused to answer Grubman's questions and accused him outright of driving down the share price. At the time of Grubman's exchange with Skilling, Highfields had already "shorted" Enron stock, a process by which an investor can make money betting that share price will fall—which it did. By some reports, Highfields made $50 million for Harvard in the process; if Enron had been as good as its story, Highfields could have reaped that benefit from the company's growth, not its collapse. In the end, Enron's share price was driven down not by skeptics like Grubman, but by its own fraudulent and deceptive behavior. As Grubman later noted, "We were merely spectators who had done a lot of homework."

As with everything else connected to Enron, even this apparently straightforward story of good and evil, competence and deception, has its complications. HarvardWatch, a student and alumni group that monitors and advocates greater transparency and accountability in corporate governance at the university, suggested in early 2002 that Grubman and Highfields were acting on insider information provided by then–Harvard Corporation member Herbert "Pug" Winokur, at the time also an Enron director. Winokur stepped down from his position at Harvard later that spring, citing the growing public distress over Enron; for its part, HarvardWatch conceded, as the *Chronicle of Higher Education* reported in May 2002, "that its suspicions [about Highfields] are based on circumstantial evidence, and that it has no smoking gun" (John Pulley, "Investing on the Edge," May 10, 2002).

When I asked Grubman to speak on a panel about professional standards in April 2002, he noted grimly that he might not be a good choice, given the negative press he'd been getting. The *Boston Globe* had picked up the HarvardWatch story, and he was feeling embattled. But Grubman and Highfields haven't just picked on Enron; a June 2002 article in *Folio Magazine* on the *Reader's Digest* deal for Reiman Publications noted, "Highfields is known as an activist shareholder, one that is not shy about jousting with company executives" (Joe Hagan, "The High-Wire Act," June 1, 2002); and a January 2004 article in the *Boston Globe* singled out Grubman as a praiseworthy troublemaker "most likely to throw a high hard one at an underperforming CEO's head" (Steve Bailey, "My Favorite Troublemakers," January 7, 2004).

Grubman himself is articulate, if also rather despairing, on the subject of corporate ethics. He claims that attention to business ethics follows a fifteen-year cycle, starting with a crisis that gets people riled up about the question, but gradually declining into indifference again until the next spike. He certainly didn't create the spike that became Enron, but he tested for truth during that April 2001 conference call, and anyone who was really listening would have realized that the Enron story had either outlived itself or been a lie from the beginning. Grubman spoke well at the panel discussion, despite his initial reluctance. His exchanges with Skilling and Lay never came up, but when I later mentioned that chapter of his recent past to one of the young finance specialists in the audience, he said with admiration in his eyes: "That was *him*!?"

Story and Ethical Practice

I mentioned in the story of Chris Stone and 9/11 that my wife and I had faced a similar, though less dramatic challenge on 9/11, in our capacity as masters of one of the undergraduate houses at Harvard. Each of the five stories demonstrating the steps of ethical practice bears directly on what we do as masters at Mather House, when we are not teaching and administering in other parts of our respective universities—Sandra at Harvard, I at MIT. As co-master, I have taken to heart these stories and others; they are a means of seeing clearly and fulfilling our obligations to the community we lead.

When we became acting masters in the fall of 1992, we were told by a number of our colleagues in the other twelve houses that our role as masters was to see to the well-being of the community, a job description that seemed then, and quickly proved, to mean simultaneously everything and nothing; it was an invitation to entrepreneurial engagement—breaking the rules and making the rules, however inadvertently—and we did a certain amount of that during the early years, absorbing the costs as we went. Confronting the vagueness of our received masterly wisdom, the Council of Masters and central administration later worked up a manual recognizing the multiplicity of our functions; but even that didn't particularly narrow our field of improvisation or initiative, which is a good thing if you incline to autonomy, as we did and still do.

The element of discipline and hierarchical position remains, though, as it does in the discussions I had with my Chinese IMBAs, around the notion of mastery itself—seeing the big picture. It is understood that the masters symbolize the academic and intellectual pursuits of the community to the community, even as we host the dinners, concerts, and study breaks that go with the job, even as we attend students' games, performances, and discussion groups, even as we write the letters of recommendation that support the students' applications for fellowships, graduate and professional schools, and first jobs. Those myriad interactions are fun, and a major benefit of the job, but they also steadily remind us of our primary commitment; just as our students produce, and produce at the highest level, so must we practice the discipline that brought us to Harvard in the first place. In business terminology, we always have to remember the bottom line: no one arrives at the university to become a master; you are first and foremost a professor or senior administrator, and your productivity will be measured by your performance in your field, where reputations are made and salaries earned. The "House Masters' Manual" is clear on this: building the world of the house is a spare-time, amateur engagement, secondary or tertiary to the professional commitment of a scholar.

At the same time, though, the mastership invites the self-discovery that ethical management and leadership can and should bring with them: the constant interaction that goes with presiding over a community of close to 500 people generates a better understanding of who we are and what we believe as individuals—our version of Bobby's "speak up, speak out." With that increased self-understanding, it becomes easier to know what you need to convey to the community in order to make it the happy, productive place it should be; or—and this recognizes the complexities of storytelling—it becomes easier to know which of the stories circulating in the community you want to encourage and enlarge. This is the noncrisis version of "tell good stories." Finally, perhaps more than at any other time, those crises give us an opportunity to "test for truth." Do our notions of how a community should manage itself hold up in times of trouble like 9/11, or in the spates of uncontrolled partying, or in the face of homophobia, racism, or the multiple forms of individual and small-group dysfunction that characterize life in a diverse environment?

This quick enumeration suggests that the five steps to ethical practice outlined above derive as much from my own managerial and leadership roles as from the many hours I have spent with people who run and work in more typical business organizations. My work as both practitioner and observer suggests that there is no typical business organization, no typical managerial challenge; if there were, we wouldn't need the notion of ethical practice, which covers the crucial judgments that go into every waking moment of our days. Caught between the diversity of our communities—an increasing reality in our globalized world—and the strictures of increasingly complex organizations, we turn to story because it has the power to anchor our actions in the specifics of the individual, even as it recognizes larger forces at work. Story is where enterprise and mastery meet, and where good stories help us to define both our problems and our solutions.

But what is a good story? It doesn't exactly fall off the tongue for most of us. The office water cooler and the village well test our success in expressing our views through story, and can generate as much anxiety as any experience of public speaking. Some stories are greeted with laughter, but that laughter may signify approbation or derision; some stories provoke tears, but those tears may be tears of sympathy, sorrow, or depression. Even the author may not know which will result from the telling of a particular story, unless he or she knows the audience well, and in that case the story belongs to the community before it has even been told. A good storyteller can confidently achieve personal ends as a result of that kind of knowledge, a possibility that reveals the danger implicit in the notion of a good story. After all, we use the phrase, "That's a good story!" with a mildly ironic tone, to suggest that we have just heard a lie.

We do have alternatives. Most cultures have a tradition of wisdom literature that can be regarded as the core of their ethical thinking. Lies are less of an issue there; when the material takes written form, though, it is often very esoteric, difficult to read, and even more difficult to parse effectively—think of *The Analects* of Confucius. The wisdom implicit in proverbs expresses this component of most cultures in popular form, but even proverbs have a hermetic quality that requires unpacking the material and the background and the personalities involved for one pithy line to make sense.

Another alternative lies for some cultures in religious writing and musings on or exegesis of core religious texts, on the one hand, such as the Jewish Talmud and Torah, and the corpus of law, now always written, that rules our daily interactions, on the other. For daily interactions in most environments that we cannot readily identify as monolithic—say, a congregation of a particular faith—the former category feels too committed to a particular world (or other-world) view to be useful in a secular and diversified environment; and the latter quickly takes us into an arcane realm of which we are—usually painfully—aware, but which we again consign to the skills of professionals. Part of the reason lawyers generate so much dislike as a profession lies in the fact that we as a society can't live without them.

At first glance, the story approach to ethics feels neither esoteric nor focused, a tradition with no antecedents and no visible future trajectory. In fact, the older traditions just mentioned rely heavily on example, analogy, and parable for their effect, and these ancient forms are rudimentary stories, used with the same intent that I set forth here for modern stories—to make difficult questions accessible to those who don't necessarily have the time or the schooling to delve into a centuries-old debate, and who are willing to be drawn into the world of the story. This book honors but modernizes these traditions; it stands apart in its argument for an approach to integrity, responsibility, and self-worth through our contemporary culture, where all of us feel we have something to say.

So which contemporary stories are good stories? What makes them good stories—relevance, entertainment, deep insight? Who decides that they are good?

Here, we move from the stories we have told in the introduction to the stories that occupy the bulk of this book. The five stories just presented to illustrate the steps of ethical practice are good examples of the challenges businesspeople, managers, and leaders face. They commemorate moments and specific challenges that many of us recognize, especially if we belong to the world from which they come. At the same time, as examples they are primarily vehicles for the present argument about ethics and the place of ethics in business and management. I have shaped them accordingly, and in so doing limited their reach. There are always shades of intention in storytelling. We have all heard about the author who has a particular ax to grind or a person to exalt or malign, but a good story is good precisely because it rises above these individual agendas to celebrate its own function as story.

Good stories make us alert, open to fuller perception and appreciation, ready to act on our renewed understanding of who we are and how we can proceed. They are not instrumental, not merely a guide to a specific action; they inspire us, and then our imagination and training come into play to help us achieve our goals. Through those stories, we are better able to find the examples or anecdotes, like the five just outlined above, that explain how to deal with our past, accept the burdens of leadership, redefine society's notions of its resources, bring our organization through a cataclysm, or get at the truth of a complex situation.

Good stories can be appreciated from many angles, because they contain elements that appeal to audiences from many different backgrounds, occupations, convictions, and eras. When a story has that breadth of appeal, the elements that go into its making become "truths." Truths are the grail of ethical practice, the object for which we quest and in the name of which we monitor our behavior, even though the goal may be nowhere in sight. A good story has the ability to overwhelm us, to capture our senses, to drive us to new discoveries and new horizons, even if that newness is in fact the reanimation of our consciousness of something we have already and perhaps always known.

Good stories allow us to talk outside our personal range of reference. They allow us to talk about the specifics of our lives, our work, our environment in terms readily available to people working with a different set of specifics, in the name of shared goals. That breadth of reference becomes the basis for a larger community, which is the reality of our lives. Ethics is about community, but we manage it and ourselves in it only by seeing clearly the successive circles within which we and others live, engaging the possibilities for expansion, and accepting the pressures for restraint. It is, as will become apparent in the stories that follow, hard work to be ethical; but that is the way we succeed at building the good society of which we all dream.

CHAPTER 2

Speak Up, Speak Out
Articulating One's Managerial Self

Faculty who teach the so-called softer skills in MBA programs recognize that managerial communication and organizational behavior or organizational processes are of little interest to the students—at least when they first arrive at business school. During the first semester or two, marketing, finance, economics, accounting—in short, the numbers-based subjects—draw the most interest. Then the first-year students return from their summer internships, the graduates come back to visit on campus from their work as investment bankers or management consultants, and the story changes completely: they suddenly realize that the people skills they learn in business school are the skills they need most, and that knowing how to work with people will make the most difference to them in building their careers.

If student testimonials weren't enough, formal studies confirm their insight. Executives and recruiters cite communication skills as the number one factor in the hiring and promotion of young businesspeople, and they matter from the very beginning of that career. When my colleagues and I teach managerial communication at Sloan,

we note that the skills students acquire in our classes will contribute to their success in other courses at Sloan, well before they
start their summer internships or post-MBA jobs. We co-teach
classes with the Career Development Office, which stresses the
need for both articulacy and good manners in the application
and interview process. We teach first-year students how to cope
with hostile or indifferent audiences, and we coach them in the
"elevator speech." An exercise in impromptu speaking, the elevator speech hypothesizes the job searcher's dream: by a lucky
coincidence, on going for an informational interview with the
human resources department at a firm for which you want to
work, you get on the elevator with a senior executive in the firm.
You now have forty-five to sixty seconds, before the elevator
reaches the executive's floor, to tell him or her who you are and
why you're there. What do you say?

Contrary to what these exercises may suggest, I know of no
MBAs with copies of Emily Post or Miss Manners in their back-
packs; still, the notion of etiquette or appropriate behavior lies
very close to the surface. The schools may prefer to view it as
"branding"—What does a good Sloan MBA look like, for the reputation of both school and individual?—but the exercises aim at
nothing less than socialization; and with that we come back to
ethical practice. It is hard to say at what point good manners become ethical behavior, given the centrality of social norms to
both; in both, regard for the other person plays a key role, and that
element is fundamental to our definition of ethical practice. Yet
etiquette without ethics is an empty gesture, form without meaning. Ethics as a subject contributes most to the MBA curriculum
precisely in that it adds substance and integrity to the notions of
effective communication and effective practice in organizations.

Once we address ethical behavior in business and management, communication becomes more than a matter of putting the right spin on a situation, and leadership goes beyond manipulating employees to achieve a desired personal or institutional end, regardless of their best interests. The connection between communication and promotability can be read simply as the ability to pander to the boss, until we factor in the element of values; then, even pandering becomes a judgment call rather than a character flaw, and we look for another word or phrase to describe it—"managing upward"? Finally, because most business decisions are at least partially data-driven, the self-awareness we can generate for communication and organizational behavior extends to the so-called hard disciplines. The numbers no longer speak for us or for themselves; we speak through them, and in doing so introduce an ethical element into those fields as well.

What is narrowly true of the MBA curriculum is broadly true for business: ethical practice adds the substance in the name of which we do business. But what does ethical business practice look like?

The first two of our "good stories," the core of this chapter, invite readers to think about what it means to manage, as a way of getting at what it means to manage ethically. Rather than offer a single tactical prescription for good management, the juxtaposition of DuBose Heyward's *The Country Bunny and the Little Gold Shoes* and Frank Gilbreth, Jr. and Ernestine Gilbreth Carey's *Cheaper by the Dozen* allows readers to draw out their own and others' principles of management through two clearly divergent models. Discussing these stories, managers "speak up" and "speak out" by confronting previously unarticulated notions of themselves, their present and future roles in organizations, and human nature in general. Business and management are pervasive in our lives; coming to terms with this fact grounds them and us in ethical practice.

Management and Mother's Milk

I had asked a friend with two young children if he could recommend stories about management. Without further explanation, he named *The Country Bunny and the Little Gold Shoes* (1939), a classic of American children's literature, written by a descendant of one of the signers of the American Declaration of Independence. Though he was white, DuBose Heyward is often associated with the African-American literary movement of the 1920s and '30s known as the Harlem Renaissance. Among other books about the Gullah people of South Carolina, he wrote the novel *Porgy*, which he later reworked, together with George and Ira Gershwin, into that classic of American musical theater, *Porgy and Bess*.

It is a long way from Catfish Row to management science. And yet, Heyward's *Country Bunny*, an amply illustrated twenty-minute read, routinely does more than any other text I use to reveal participant thinking about work, management, leadership, and, most importantly, the participants themselves. Its utility stems in part from surprise. In the bookstore I found the book packaged in a clear plastic envelope, accompanied by an audio-cassette for children who like to be read to, or who aren't quite far enough along to read to themselves. Managers participating in a seminar usually arrive grinning skeptically about what they refer to as "the bunny book."

Yet it is also a great adult community-builder, as I discovered in January 1997 at the World Economic Forum, where I ran a session on story as a means of talking about business and business ethics. The venue was the forum's annual Davos meeting where luminaries from business, government, and academia discussed how to overcome the divide between the haves and the have-nots of the global digital revolution.

The forum staff agreed that *The Country Bunny* would make an appropriately short, easily digestible text—if nothing else, a change of pace. By the afternoon before our evening session, though, the stack of copies for the participants at the seminar coordinator's stall had not significantly shrunk, and I began girding myself to face a two-hour discussion for which no one had done the work— assuming they came at all. My anxiety proved unfounded: the session was one of the most convivial that I have led using the Heyward text. I passed a copy of *The Country Bunny* around the table and asked each participant to read one page. Halfway through the book, we stopped and talked for half an hour, then repeated the process for the second half of the book. With a minimum of preparation but more real-life experience than most, these participants immediately got to the heart of the matter that informs *The Country Bunny*—how to balance individual ambition and social or family norms, how to mentor, how to parent, how to plan for succession within an organization. The snow lay thick on the ground outside our Swiss chalet, and everyone relaxed and seemed tacitly to agree that taking turns reading aloud from a children's book was the perfect way to spend the evening together.

But with their wealth of experience, the forum participants raised questions for which the text had only limited answers. After that session, I began pairing Heyward's work with *Cheaper by the Dozen* (1948), a memoir of family life written by two of the twelve children of Frank Bunker Gilbreth and his wife, Lillian Moller Gilbreth, among America's best-known management gurus during the first third of the twentieth century. The authors lovingly and humorously describe how their parents "managed" the family, judging that what worked in a large family would work in the factory, and vice versa. A best seller on publication and a steady seller since, especially with younger audiences, the book was made into a film starring Myrna Loy and Clifton Webb in 1950, and remade in 2003 with Steve Martin and Bonnie Hunt.

Cheaper by the Dozen is as far from a management manual as *The Country Bunny*, despite its central characters. Yet like Heyward's story it raises topics of direct import to managers, and like Heyward's story, it does so in an apparently innocuous but inevitable and fundamental way—this is management theory ingested at the breakfast table. After all the similarities, it is only when the two stories are set side by side that we realize *Cheaper by the Dozen* makes very different claims from Heyward's *Country Bunny* about how we manage, and these disagreements remain useful half a century later.

So You Want to Be an Easter Bunny

In the world of Heyward's Country Bunny, everyone wants to be one of the five Easter bunnies. These five are selected by the wise old Grandfather Bunny to deliver eggs to children the world over on Easter morning. The Country Bunny—a little girl bunny, we are told, with brown skin—shares this ambition, but the other bunnies quickly send her back to the country where they think she belongs.

Heyward elaborated the title of *The Country Bunny and the Little Gold Shoes* with the phrase, "as told to Jenifer." In a roomful of MBAs talking about the story, the phrase "glass ceiling" usually surfaces within a minute or two, as a quick commentary on the way in which the country bunny is denied success before she can even compete for it. As in real life, too, the gender picture quickly grows even more complicated: "The little girl Cottontail grew up to be a young lady Cottontail. And by and by she had a husband

and then one day, much to her surprise there were twenty-one Cottontail babies to take care of" (p. 6).

With that, the Mother Cottontail "stopped thinking," we are told, about becoming an Easter Bunny, and focuses on her children. When she judges that they have matured sufficiently, she assigns them chores: two do the washing, two the cooking, two the gardening, and so on. Everyone has a role to play.

Then, as luck would have it, one of the Easter Bunnies retires. At first, the Mother Cottontail "was sad because she thought that now she was nothing but an old mother bunny" (p. 12); still, she takes her little bunnies to the competition, where her offspring's perky ears and generally cooperative demeanor catch the eye of the Grandfather Bunny. He is looking for rabbits that are kind and wise and swift, the three criteria by which he chooses his Easter Bunnies. Looking at the family arrayed before him, he deduces that the Mother Cottontail has the first two qualities, and she then proves that she is swift as well by telling her children to scatter, then rounding them up. Poised to make her an Easter Bunny, the Grandfather hesitates at the thought of depriving these children of their mother. Who will run the house? But she explains that they have developed certain skills, and that they will run the house better than she, in her absence. The Grandfather replies, "You have proved yourself to be not only *wise*, and *kind*, and *swift*, but also very clever" (p. 20). And with that, he appoints her to be his fifth Easter Bunny.

What Are Children For?

As one might suppose with a group of ambitious young MBAs, the Country Bunny's lost dreams are a source of concern and are the topic that initially generates the most conversation. But the group invariably polarizes around the question of whether she has indeed lost her dreams, and how she comes in the end to fulfill them anyway. The two primary positions look like this:

Scenario 1: The Country Bunny finds she has twenty-one baby bunnies to tend, and abandons her dreams. She is conscientious, and does what she knows to be right—mothers must take care of their children, so she takes care of her children. She wants them to be independent, so she gives them chores, and sure enough they develop skills that allow them to run the house even in her absence. The Grandfather Bunny sees her and her happy children, and deduces that she has been a very good mother and will therefore be a very good Easter Bunny.

Scenario 2: The Country Bunny finds she has twenty-one baby bunnies to tend, but she refuses to abandon her dreams. As soon as she is able, she gives her children the skills they need to run the house in her absence, so that she can then go off and compete to become one of the Easter Bunnies. Moreover, she counts on her children to showcase her talents, making them quite deliberately into the competitive edge that will convince the Grandfather Bunny that she is a good manager.

With the managerial model in the background, scenario 1 raises questions about the skills the Country Bunny imparts to her offspring. What is the value of learning to be a sweeper, or a cook, or a gardener? Is the Country Bunny educating her children or simply training them? If the latter, what will they be fit for, once they are adults—sweeping, cooking, gardening? Invariably, some students will argue that the acquisition of such trades is in fact an excellent thing, a skill the individual bunny can fall back on. They also argue that the acquisition of even one skill sufficiently sets the pattern for later, individual development—especially if coupled with the role model that the Mother Cottontail offers by becoming an Easter Bunny.

The MBAs sometimes characterize scenario 2 as "cynical," because it suggests that the Mother Cottontail is using her children to get ahead. To borrow a phrase from Immanuel Kant, whose writings have had a massive influence on ethical thought in the post-Enlightenment West, she is using them as a means to her own ends, rather than treating them as ends in themselves. She wants to be an Easter Bunny, whatever the cost to her little bunnies' development. She places her interests first, and succeeds. Interestingly, in multicultural discussion groups, Caucasians—and specifically Americans—tend quite explicitly to argue for the primacy of the child's interests over those of his or her parents; Asians and Asian-Americans are much more likely to argue for the importance of the child serving the parents' interests, in knowing reciprocity for the parents' commitment to the child's well-being.

Scenario 2 also comes in a realistic version, often advanced by participants who are themselves the product of large families. The Country Bunny has no choice but to organize her offspring, they argue, because the family would be unmanageable on other terms. Role modeling figures prominently in this argument: though Mother Cottontail leaves her bunnies to accomplish her goals, she has given them something to live for—a claim that the idealists in the group refute by arguing that she does not in fact give them the means to become Easter Bunnies in their own right. Whereas she has the global skills to train each of them up to a certain level of competence, the story does not indicate that she gives them her own breadth of training and individual responsibility. Could she at least offer them job rotation, so that they really are independent, or is she content to see to it that they learn one job well, however simple it may be? The story doesn't say, but if so, their success seems determined—which is to say, constrained—by their allegiance to the social whole.

You Are How You Read

This discussion rarely makes converts to either scenario. The idealists tend to remain idealistic, the cynics cynical, and the realists think that they are mediating between the other two camps. The lesson here is not that one interpretation or the other has identified the truth of Heyward's book. Rather, repeated requests to students for evidence to support one position or another eventually reveal to everyone that much of what they get out of *The Country Bunny and the Little Gold Shoes* is no more than what they put in. We aren't told that the Mother Cottontail limits her young bunnies to one job and one job only. We are told that she goes off to the competition thinking that she is now "nothing but an old mother bunny," but we are also told that the Grandfather Bunny, on hearing how she has organized her family, compliments her on being "clever." Why not "foresightful," why not "dutiful," why not simply "a good mother"? Could he be acknowledging here that she has mapped out a good strategy for getting to her goals?

We don't know the answers to these and other questions that the text raises. And therein lies a major benefit to the use of this story: the holes in the narrative follow naturally from the quality of story itself; whatever the author intends, we fill in the gaps in our knowledge of the events, our vision of the characters, our assessment of the action, with details drawn from our experience and inclinations. The debate over the Mother Cottontail's intentions toward her offspring is invariably a debate about us—about our sense of the world and the way the world works.

To say that you believe the mother rabbit is using her children is to say that you have the imaginative range to conceive that possibility. It also allows the group to ask how you came to such an idea, and whether you really believe it. It allows you then to ask yourself the same questions, and wrestle with the possibility that, under similar circumstances, someone else used you in a similar fashion, or that you yourself might be capable of using your own children if the occasion presented itself. And if the occasion does present itself, would you feel you needed to justify your actions, and if so, what justification would you offer?

These debates are no different from the kinds of conversations that colleagues in a business organization have about themselves, but even more about their superiors. Too often, we work with the notion that employers are adults and employees are children, based on each group's relative access to information and the experience that they may have accrued in using it. In developed countries, employees are all of age, but that doesn't change the fact that we often feel we are treated as children, wherever we are in the hierarchy. The organization's need for interdependence and occasional subservience or declared dependence can feel to the individual worker—especially for Americans, who value freedom—like a child's lack of autonomy. Entrepreneurs often cite that deprivation as a motive for going out on their own, and the least productive interactions in large corporations stem from a local culture that appears to disenfranchise individuals. Both employer and employee will recognize the politics of resentment that ensues.

That these discussions imply an ethical standpoint should be clear. How we treat employees, how employees view themselves in relation to the organization—this is the stuff of leadership and the values that inform it, at every level of the organization. A workplace that allows its people to come to terms with their own views on the organization and the implications of their views for its productivity has already gone a long way toward empowering the work force collectively to do its best for the organization. But that is the world of the seminar; in the world of *The Country Bunny*, some things don't get discussed, they simply happen, as the second half of the story shows.

What's a Boss For?

By the midpoint in Heyward's story, the Mother Cottontail has demonstrated that she has all the qualifications for the position of Easter Bunny. As we discussed in the previous section, the cynical reader might argue that she used her children to put a particular spin on her candidacy, differentiating herself on qualities that, before the fact, seem irrelevant to the competition. Yet the wise old Grandfather Bunny quickly reveals that he has hired her with something special in mind, and that her children matter in a way that even the Country Bunny at her hypothetically most manipulative could not anticipate.

When she arrives at the palace of Easter Eggs, we are told, the four other Easter Bunnies recognize her as one of them, and don't scorn her funny country dress. They show her around; then, once darkness has fallen, the five of them set to work distributing the Easter Eggs. They work into the night, and the Country Bunny begins to flag and to think about going home. But just then, Grandfather Bunny calls her to him:

> When she went close, she saw that he was holding in his hand the loveliest egg she had ever seen. It glittered like a diamond. "Peek through and see what you shall see," he said; so she peeked through

the little hole in one end and she saw a beautiful scene with a sleigh, and a lake with people skating on the ice. And he said, "Because you have such a loving heart for children, I am going to give you the best but the hardest trip of all." [p. 25]

The Grandfather Bunny wants her to deliver the beautiful egg to a little boy who is sick on a mountaintop, far away across two rivers and three mountains. The Mother Cottontail sets out, initially with fair success. But as she approaches the mountaintop where the little boy lies in his cottage, she slips and tumbles back down the mountain. When she finally stops her fall, she finds that she can't get up again. Dawn is breaking, and the Mother Cottontail knows that she is about to fail in her mission; and then, the Grandfather Bunny appears by her side. "And he smiled at her and he said, 'You are not only *wise*, and *kind*, and *swift*, but you are also the *bravest* of all the bunnies. And I shall make you my very own Gold Shoe Easter Bunny'" (p. 35). With that, he pulls out a pair of tiny gold shoes and places them on the Mother Cottontail's feet. Suddenly she is off again. The shoes have the power of seven-league boots, and in a couple of hops the Mother Cottontail has reached her goal and delivered the special egg. Then she turns around, goes back to the palace, picks up the basket for her little bunnies, and returns to her home, which, as she expected, is spic and span, with all the little bunnies sound asleep in their beds. To this day, the Country Bunny's cottage can be told apart from all the rest by the pair of little gold shoes that hangs on her wall. It seems to be a happy ending, but what do those shoes signify, and just what did the Grandfather Bunny have in mind when he hired Cottontail?

Again, the story elicits multiple readings. The optimists read the shoes as a special insignia, showing that the Country Bunny has distinguished herself. However she got to the cottage on the mountaintop, she persevered—so the argument goes—and vindicated the Grandfather Bunny's faith in her. In a more jaded view, the gold shoes resemble the proverbial gold watch, a token for prolonged and faithful service, usually awarded late in one's career or at retirement. So has the Grandfather Bunny retired the Mother Cottontail after one Easter Eve? Is this a case of the glass ceiling after all, where, as professional women have maintained, the woman has to work twice as hard (the special egg) as any man in the office, and still does not make partner?

But does she deserve to make partner? From the manager's point of view, hiring the Country Bunny seems to have been a gamble, and a poor one at that; although she has the basic qualifications for the job, she lacks stamina, and when the going gets tough she requires direct assistance to finish it. If the Grandfather Bunny hired her on demonstrated performance—her twenty-one perky children—she fails to deliver when he gives her the special egg. So has he misjudged her? And does he compound that error by giving her the hardest task of all, when she was the newest of the Easter Bunnies? Though he seems to have hired her for skills above and beyond the requisite three, why would he subject her to a test at which she was more likely than the others to fail, based on her lack of experience? What conclusions might one draw from these results about the Grandfather Bunny's managerial competence?

Seminar participants from all backgrounds are quick to note that, whereas the Easter Bunnies voluntarily retire when they age and slow down, the Grandfather Bunny appears only to get older. No one in the story talks of a competition to replace him. Yet participants are quick to suggest that, when he notes qualities in the

Mother Cottontail beyond kindness, wisdom, and swiftness—she is clever, brave, and has "a loving heart for children"—he may in fact be laying out a plan for his own succession. She is sufficiently different from the others to have the potential for a different career path.

Students articulate this theory in the face of an equally evident possibility that Heyward intended the Grandfather Bunny to be a god figure—omnipotent, omniscient, immortal, and therefore in no need of a successor. In this view, the mission to deliver the special egg is meant as a test, an assessment not of the Country Bunny's ability to do the work of an Easter Bunny—that has already been determined—but to see if she might fulfill the criteria for an even bigger position.

Others leave the succession theory to one side, but still see the Grandfather Bunny as a manager testing a new employee and having the wisdom to step in and encourage her when she fails. According to this view, he knows he must challenge his employees, but also give them the support they need, regardless of their success or failure. From his point of view, stepping in to help her in her moment of need can only foster loyalty and recognition of his own competence.

Malice does have its day, though, in a related interpretation. Here, the Grandfather Bunny deliberately sets up the Country Bunny to fail, which then allows him to step in and show her that, without him, she cannot succeed. Here again, it is important to note that the text gives little direct evidence to support one theory over another. The Grandfather Bunny simply does what he does—his explanations are minimal at best, and participants in the conversation about the story fill in the rest, from their experience, their inclination, and their fantasies.

When a Mentor Is Not a Mentor

In each of these theses about the Grandfather Bunny's motivation and intent, the word *mentoring* always arises. Whether he intends the Country Bunny to succeed him or wishes to bind her to him as a loyal employee or cripple her self-esteem so that she won't become too ambitious, the Grandfather Bunny plays a mentoring role in relation to her. MBAs are particularly alert to this aspect of the story, as many of them have had work experiences in which their success depended in part on a mentor, whether assigned or unofficial. They are equally concerned about their immediate future, the first few years after they finish their professional degrees, when they know that their paths will be heavily influenced by senior managers.

So what is the value of the Grandfather Bunny's mentoring to the Mother Cottontail? The story offers more certitude here than it does about the Grandfather Bunny's motives. Though the book is dedicated to "Jenifer," the child at the end of the Country Bunny's odyssey is a little boy—a human boy, not a little boy bunny. Therein lies the moment that closes the loop on Cottontail's ambitions: she will be an Easter Bunny, but even in her moment of triumph she is a second-class citizen. The shift in categories of being—bunny to boy—puts success again just beyond her reach, and she must accept this truth with the willing humility that she has brought to the rest of her labors.

One could argue reasonably that *The Country Bunny* encourages team skills, that the Mother Cottontail's fatalism usefully tempers the arrogance of our MBA prodigies, even as she shares their ambition. Like her, they will make their way to the mountain on their own, but reach the top only by recognizing that they cannot do it without the rest of the world, and specifically their superiors. In this book, the price of fulfilling one's dream—a great or small one, depending on how you interpret the gold shoes hanging on the wall—is the realization that you didn't do it alone; indeed, that if you tried it alone, you would never succeed, because by yourself you are incomplete, and need therefore to cultivate and rely on others.

Yet most of us find it hard to verbalize this exchange: recognizing the cost of success as it is portrayed here is simply not an option for many rising managers, because it would cause them to question the very system that offers them that success, and their identity with it. The solution would be to anticipate a strain on personal standards or freedom, and think through a means of altering the system to obviate this sacrifice. But that is simultaneously frightening and labor-intensive, when the job itself already imposes a great deal of stress. The self-censorship goes well with a culture focused on an alignment of values and old-style organizational efficiency, but it clashes with the more recent idea that even organizational work ought to fulfill the whole person.

Away from the workplace, it is easier to alert MBAs to the pressure points they have encountered, or may encounter when they return to it. In a continuing education or executive seminar, one can draw out people's experiences and help them think about the trade-offs they have made—if they are in the room, they are probably inclined to do so anyway. Although many of these constituencies chafe at what they consider the "political correctness" of American business education—and this is true of both American and international students—they quickly recognize ways in which they are coming up against disenfranchising violations of those norms, sometimes on location and at the hands of their own classmates. The school itself then becomes a forum in which students can explore such obstacles and develop relationships that reproduce the disinterested mentoring they might hope to secure in the workplace.

The stories students tell in this environment illustrate the scope of the challenge they face, and we along with them. Either reflecting on their past experience or contemplating current clashes, students do speak up on the limits that other people, conditioned by organizational frameworks, impose on them. Here are a few examples echoing the Country Bunny's story—she clearly isn't alone, more than half a century later, on several fronts:

- A black student reflects on the fact that, during her time on Wall Street before coming to business school, she was invariably taken for a courier or low-level assistant when she went to other organizations, even though she was attending meetings significantly further up the hierarchy. She notes that her business dress should have made her role apparent, but people routinely could not look past the color of her skin.

- A very successful engineer and scientist muses ruefully that she has become the public face of a government agency, even though her scientific and technical training is as good as that of her male colleagues, and should keep her otherwise occupied.

- An MBA student comments happily that she feels "empowered" by the leadership roles the women in a film play, and the solidarity they feel among themselves. A male student steps in almost before the words are out of her mouth; well-spoken, confident, and possessed like her of a solid liberal arts education, he then mounts a relaxed, good-humored, but thorough critique of the film. The woman who has declared herself empowered doesn't utter another word during the session.

Are these moments the result of human nature, organizational expediency, or both? In each of these cases, the woman in question came up against external or internal constraints that limited her ability to do what she intended or was mandated to do. Though the Country Bunny's relationship to the Grandfather Bunny and the rest of the community seems to work out to everyone's satisfaction within the story, in a real-life context it illustrates the price we impose on individuals—including ourselves—in the name of social and organizational cohesion, as well as the benefits that may follow. Like the characters in each of these real-life stories, we may bear the trade-offs just enumerated, but with sufficient training, we may also be inclined to look or ask for managerial alternatives, perhaps even design them ourselves. To address the closing exclusion of the Mother Cottontail in *The Country Bunny*, we are not dutiful creatures waiting on a human being. We work as human beings with other human beings, which demands organizational solutions that our nature makes it possible to devise. That is why I started pairing Heyward's story with *Cheaper by the Dozen*.

Not All Stories Are Alike

Dad always practiced what he preached, and it was just about impossible to tell where his scientific management company ended and his family life began. His office was always full of children, and he often took two or three of us, and sometimes all twelve, on business trips. Frequently, we'd tag along at his side, pencils and notebooks in our hands, when Dad toured a factory which had hired him as an efficiency expert.

On the other hand, our house at Montclair, New Jersey, was a sort of school for scientific management and the elimination of wasted motions—or "motion study," as Dad and Mother named it.

Dad took moving pictures of us children washing dishes, so that he could figure out how we could reduce our motions and thus hurry through the task. Irregular jobs, such as painting the back porch or removing a stump from the front lawn, were awarded on a low-bid basis. Each child who wanted extra pocket money submitted a sealed bid saying what he would do the job for. The lowest bidder got the contract. [pp. 1–2]

So begins Frank Gilbreth, Jr. and Ernestine Gilbreth Carey's memoir of growing up with their parents and their ten siblings in early 1900s America. The book tells a cheery tale, full of each family member's affection and respect for the others. The two memoirists, albeit reluctant participants in some experiments, recognize all the arguments we have just reviewed for the Mother Cottontail's style of home management: it's hard enough to get one child out the door in the morning, so how to manage a dozen, if not with checklists, assigned tasks, and delegated supervision? The authors see nothing unusual here, given the unusualness of a family of twelve.

The passage just quoted also indicates that the Gilbreth parents have decided to do things differently. The Country Bunny did not take her little bunnies along when she went to deliver her share of the Easter eggs; in fact, her role in that distribution was predicated on the children staying home. In the Gilbreths' scheme, the children may have to work at home, but they also have at least an observer's role in the work done outside the home.

Chapter 5, "Mr. Chairman," takes this absence of boundaries between home and the workplace a step further: the Gilbreth parents decide to establish a family council, fashioned "after an employer-employee board" (p. 32) that Frank Gilbreth Sr. found so helpful in motivating factory workers.

In the case narrated here, Frank Sr.'s aim is to get the children voluntarily to take on chores in the family's new large house; the handyman and cook who have traveled with them can't cope anymore.

> *"The first job of the Council is to apportion necessary work in the house and yard. Does the chair hear any suggestions?"*
>
> *There were no suggestions. Dad forced a smile and attempted to radiate good humor.*
>
> *"Come, come, fellow members of the Council," he said. "This is a democracy. Everybody has an equal voice. How do you want to divide the work?"* [p. 33]

Needless to say, it's not a democracy: what the chairman wants, the chairman gets. But the method he has chosen quickly produces interesting results.

> *The next Sunday, when Dad convened the second meeting of the Council, we sat self-consciously around the table, biding our time. . . .*
>
> *Martha, who had been carefully coached in private caucus, arose.*
>
> *"It has come to the attention of the membership," she began, "that the assistant chairman [the mother, Lillian Moller Gilbreth] intends to buy a new rug for the dining room. Since the entire membership will be required to look upon, and sit in chairs resting upon, the rug, I move that the Council be consulted before any rug is purchased."* [p. 35]

Although the father fakes democratic process to achieve his own ends—ends he obviously believes are essential to the well-being of the family—the children quickly figure out how to make the system work for them. To Frank Sr.'s credit, he abides by the rules of the game he himself has set up: not only do the children get to specify the kind of rug they want, they also set the price slightly lower than their mother had estimated, and then vote to spend the balance on a dog.

The children's mother plays a crucial, mediating role in this resolution, one that makes her story yet another variant on the Mother Cottontail's, but with crucial and positive differences. A trained psychologist, Lillian Moller Gilbreth was very much her husband's colleague in his industrial engineering endeavors before he died in 1924; building on their initial, shared success, she went on to a hugely successful solo consulting and teaching career thereafter. The second volume of the Gilbreth memoir, *Belles on Their Toes* (1950; also made into a film in 1952), documents this period in the family's history, beginning directly after Frank Sr. has died. In order to maintain the couple's consulting practice, Lillian leaves the children to manage the house and themselves while she fulfills her husband's speaking engagements in Europe. The children cope as their parents might have hoped, but very much on their own terms; they secure those shaky start-up days for their mother, much as the little bunnies do for the Mother Cottontail.

The pair of books documenting the Gilbreth family's colorful history give us a measure of the long-term results generated by that early employer–employee works council. Once I started assigning *The Country Bunny* and the fifth chapter from *Cheaper by the Dozen* side by side, participants were quick to recognize the degree to which the Country Bunny's approach represents only one response to a large and potentially chaotic organizational scenario. The "democratic" solution to the assignment of chores recognizes equally the necessity of getting the job done, but it implies all the freedom that the Mother Cottontail's distribution of tasks does not. Again, the narrative doesn't give us much detail, but the notion of allowing the children to choose their tasks, or minding the children's innate abilities and inclinations in the assignment process, improves considerably on the relative autocracy of *The Country Bunny*, an autocracy that the Grandfather Bunny reproduces one level higher in the system.

One can fairly argue that, people being humans rather than rodents, the Gilbreth parents had had their children serially, and therefore had a range of ages with which to work. This fact of life alone makes a more participatory assignment process plausible, and it means in this case that a few members of the family council, while not fully fledged, still have enough maturity to game the parliamentary process to their own and their siblings' advantage. The Mother Cottontail, rabbit that she is, has had her babies all at once, which significantly limits her options—and minimizes the likelihood of a revolt.

These biological niceties aside, though, the two stories present scenarios for employer–employee relations that produce different results. Whatever Frank Gilbreth's short-term ambitions, whatever the industrial management model he hopes to apply, he has in fact set himself and his family goals that have little to do with following orders. Quite the contrary: his children are presented the challenge of thinking their way out of a situation, succeed in doing so, and are rewarded—however grudgingly—for their performance. They have within their reach the levers of power, as designated by the forces currently in control.

The Country Bunny's offspring are offered no equivalent choice. Whatever Mother Cottontail's intentions for them, the story records only the fulfillment of her ambition for herself, and for the children a net gain of skills acquired and applied for the greater good. The methodological difference is, finally, a difference between education and training: education for the Gilbreth children and training for the Country Bunny's little bunnies. The first formula implies a self-determination—at least long-term—that the second precludes; the first expresses a confidence in individual autonomy that actually threatens the training scenario, where the system relies on a coordination that only a few can assure.

Confronted with this pair of options, our free-thinking, autonomy-prone MBAs invariably opt for the democratic solution, though usually with the qualification that certain situations may justify the Country Bunny's approach. They also recognize that the Gilbreths' family council is at best an inefficient means of getting the job done, but short-term bottom-line efficiency doesn't necessarily translate into a long-term, full-cost accounting equivalent. While we cheer for the Country Bunny, her success doesn't obviously bring anyone with her, in spite of the team-building in which she has engaged, nor—if the gold shoes hanging on her wall are any indication—does her success necessarily give her long-term benefits. The Gilbreth children's memoir suggests a different and lasting legacy, as well as the means of achieving it.

Thinking About Human Nature

Two different managerial models are illustrated by these two books, in apparent indifference to the young audiences for which they were written. Their juxtaposition raises questions about the larger conceptual framework in which we view management. The two books suggest that we think of families as organizations and vice versa. But is this reasonable, either for the family or the organization? How do we define each of them? Where is there overlap, for social and behavioral purposes? Why do we insist on organizing ourselves and our lives according to such groupings, and is it ethical to apply one category of organization to another setting?

As we noted earlier, whether autocratic or quasi-democratic, the organizational processes set forth in the two stories assume that the "managers" of the family are the adults, and the employees or workers are the children. The Country Bunny mothers her twenty-one baby bunnies, but they do the work around the house. The Gilbreth parents parent their twelve children, and educate them in the process, but the kids are doing the chores. The Grandfather Bunny's elite group of Easter Bunnies may be adults as they distribute the eggs, but they are so far junior to him by virtue of his age that they might as well be a different category of creation.

One can look at this imposition of biology on a sociological framework from two perspectives: that of the corporation and that of the family. But in these family organizations there is no firing of employees; the closest we come is the Easter Bunny's retiring. Indeed, one could argue that the gold shoes keep the Grandfather Bunny's company family-like; he may mete out tough love, but he keeps his team intact by salvaging Mother Cottontail's mission. In that sense, none of these groups can be said to represent American corporate practice, where layoffs can be massive and have far-reaching implications for workers and their communities.

So, why can we so easily draw lessons about managerial technique from these literary families? The answer lies with models of management that attribute simple motives to people at the bottom of the economic ladder: if you're making minimum wage, the argument runs, how could you have a vision of the world that comes only with a full experience of it, and with the comprehensive vision of human interaction that management requires? Perhaps more than any other, the military command-and-control model inherited from pre-republican days expresses this hierarchical vision of humanity—the perennial military managerial necessity of directing and supporting large numbers of people yields a class-based and now archaic definition of what it means to be those people. The irony, of course, is that the U.S. military has invested vast amounts of time and money since the Vietnam War in reshaping its vision of how to manage large numbers of men and women and the materiel they need to carry out their organizational mission, but the rest of society seems not to have caught up with this reconception of the model.

From the family perspective, the question of biology and management immediately confronts us with the family as an economic unit. In agricultural societies, children provide hands to work, not just mouths to feed. Even as we leave behind more primitive forms of social organization, the economic value of off-spring remains present to everyone. Although *The Country Bunny* and *Cheaper by the Dozen* predate postindustrial America, the managerial premises they advance are still very much with us, as well as the means by which they are inculcated. When Heyward's "Jenifer" read or heard the story the author composed for her, she probably didn't say to herself, "I am being socialized to take my place in society, to do the work that will make my life meaningful in others' eyes." She didn't need to do so; all she needed was sufficient imagination to identify with the baby bunnies, or with the Country Bunny who had finally fulfilled her ambition—the work is there to be done, and the rewards in terms of social cohesion and personal meaning are clear. Again, with *Cheaper by the Dozen*, the lesson points to the importance of work. The son and daughter who wrote their memoir demonstrate the lesson of family love, but this book is unambiguously about work as well as family, and about a better way to run organizations.

Still, the younger Gilbreths' very act of memorializing their parents gives their discoveries human scope, and in so doing makes a slightly different declaration about the ethics of work. *Cheaper by the Dozen* is the story of a family: people are born, smile, weep, joke, argue, and die. With those elements built in, the challenge of effectively conveying simple work and complex management automatically takes a certain turn—the system comes to serve the individual and the ties that bind individual to individual, in all of their complexity, rather than the reverse. *The Country Bunny* animates the question of work and management, too, but Heyward's choice of animal over human, though possibly unthinking, is not coincidental. It, too, sends a certain message: we know that we are reading about the interaction among people, but their humanity is immediately constrained by the way in which they are portrayed, in both text and illustration, and the thematic work environment in which we see them only amplifies that constriction.

In both cases, the choice of story thus confronts us with the challenge of defining human nature, even as we talk or read about work. It forces a decision on our part about what constitutes informed or mature consent, and the degree to which we as individuals can exercise that consent in an organization, whether familial or corporate. That in turn implies management. These two very different stories about childhood and adulthood tell us, not so much that managers are adults and employees children, but that we choose our own personal and professional stories before we even know that we must do so. We then tell our own stories, and lead our own lives, in a way that bolsters our early choice—that is our individual exercise in management, apparently as natural as eating, sleeping, and breathing.

Business, Human Nature, and the News

The business manifestations of this process are all around us. The saga of Aaron Feuerstein and Malden Mills is perhaps the best-known recent example of the family model applied to business. Founded in 1906 in Malden, Massachusetts, Malden Mills had been in the Feuerstein family for three generations when much of its physical plant burned to the ground on December 11, 1995. By then, the company employed 3,000 people; it was a major employer in the depressed area around Lowell, Massachusetts, and had found recent success as the inventor and sole purveyor of Polartec® fleece, the material of choice for a wide range of winter and sports garments.

After the fire, Feuerstein could have walked away with the insurance money. Instead, he pledged to rebuild the plant, paid his employees their regular salaries through December, January, and February, and in March 1996 the plant was up and running again, with most of its original employees. In March 2002, "60 Minutes" did a twenty-minute segment on Feuerstein and Malden Mills, in which Feuerstein commented: "I also felt a responsibility for all my employees, to take care of them, to give them jobs." In other testimony, he linked that view to his religious faith, but he also explained it as good business. His judgment brought him private testimonials, financial contributions, contracts, and honorary degrees. True, neither Feuerstein's newsworthiness nor the private contributions kept Malden Mills in the black; by the time of the "60 Minutes" broadcast in 2002, the company had filed for Chapter 11 bankruptcy protection; in October 2003, though, the Feuerstein phoenix rose from the ashes yet again, restructured and reenergized.

Feuerstein's emphasis on a supportive relation to his people and the community in which he operates takes his managerial style beyond the range of mere paternalism to a broader view of what managers owe their fellow man, wherever they are in the corporate hierarchy. The mechanisms for accomplishing this goal are varied, don't necessarily come into play only in time of crisis, and can be more hard-headed than the Malden Mills story might suggest, without causing the manager or executive to lose the passion that Feuerstein clearly felt for his work and his people.

Alex d'Arbeloff, co-founder and long-time chairman and president of the automatic test equipment leader Teradyne, speaks regularly and convincingly of the importance of trust in all business relations, a trust that has brought him, his company, and the Massachusetts economy considerable benefit. His view is pragmatic, geared first to the operational level where employees and managers face their ethical challenges. At the fiftieth anniversary celebration of the MIT Sloan School of Management in the fall of 2002, d'Arbeloff gave a keynote address in which he set forth a number of test cases for ethical behavior in the workplace. These ranged from how to deal with the violation of nondisclosure agreements, to subtle forms of bribery, use of insider information, and nepotism. The instructional intent of d'Arbeloff's scenarios is part of the fabric of daily life in the company, and closely geared to Teradyne's code of conduct: when employees are asked to think them through, they understand in a deep sense how the company's code builds around ethical principles. Ronald Reagan introduced the phrase "Trust, but verify" as the basis for U.S.–Soviet relations on arms control. There is an element of that in the Teradyne solution to building ethics into everyday practice. As a formula, it combines elements of both the Grandfather Bunny's and the Gilbreth parents' approaches—and that, too, is an option for budding or growing managers.

Further to the skeptical end of the spectrum, Andy Grove, the former CEO and now chairman of the board at microprocessor manufacturer Intel, showed his view of human nature and human interaction when he published *Only the Paranoid Survive: How to Exploit the Crisis Points that Challenge Every Company and Career* (1996). The book offers other terms for "paranoia," including the less fraught notion of "worry." Moreover, Grove is working most eagerly at defining critical moments in the life cycle of businesses, what he calls "inflection points," when the circumstances under which a company is operating suddenly change. The notion approaches a firm-specific version of the better known "paradigm shifts" introduced by Thomas Kuhn and since used in every conceivable field: Kuhn argued, in *The Structure of Scientific Revolutions* (1962), that scientific disciplines undergo periodic overhauls or shifts as new facts, methods, and materials become available; this counters the stereotypical view of science as a steady if difficult progress toward immutable truth.

Yet neither Grove's alternative phrases nor his serious theoretical focus can undo such statements as this, included in the preface to *Only the Paranoid Survive*: "I believe in the value of paranoia. Business success contains the seeds of its own destruction. The more successful you are, the more people want a chunk of your business and then another chunk and then another until there is nothing left" (p. 3). The fact that Grove's phrase has become a quotable quote suggests how deeply it resonates with people in contemporary U.S. business culture, and not just in the high-tech arena that Grove calls home. While it could be regarded as a plausible view of the competition, the only viable means of success in a white-hot field, it has the potential to bleed into in-house operations, which may partly explain why Intel under Grove initially temporized over a flaw in their hugely successful Pentium chip in 1994.

The story plays a prominent role in *Only the Paranoid Survive*, published just two years later, and Grove tells it well. He argues that the Pentium chip crisis was indeed an inflection point for the company, a moment when Intel had to come to grips with its own phenomenal growth and the consequences of its very successful marketing campaign, "Intel Inside." Having made the company a high-profile winner, he now had to accept the burden of responsibility that goes with making the occasional, but still high-profile, mistake. Curiously, aside from the general tone of storm and stress that characterizes his book, Grove hardly mentions the paranoia of the title and preface in the rest of the text. To the contrary, he argues that he took from the Pentium incident the lesson that, in business, success goes to those who are open to change and solicit input from a range of players—customers, lower-level employees, the press, and so on. As a long-term formula, combining openness with paranoia would seem at best an uncomfortable solution.

At the skeptical far end of the spectrum, any manager who micromanages is telling us that he or she doesn't trust the employees to rise above childhood to do the work that needs doing. Off the skeptical far end, Jeffrey Skilling's name-calling episode, mentioned in Chapter 1, was widely regarded at the time as proof that he didn't have the stuff to be CEO, whatever the condition of Enron. That response is reassuring in itself, because it suggests that across a wide range observers were galvanized to come down on the same side in favor of a more mature, humane understanding of corporate relations, both internal and external, as expressed by the people at the top. As Morley Safer put it when he introduced the Feuerstein piece on "60 Minutes," "When it comes to doing business, there are two extremes: there's the Enron way, and there's the Malden Mills way."

Here, we enter the realm of the sound bite, with everything the term suggests in the way of shallow interpretation. At the same time, the power of sound bites lies precisely in their intimation of larger truths: they are like the dangling end of a thread that, once pulled, can unravel a very large cloth. Feuerstein's caring, d'Arbeloff's trust, Grove's paranoia, and Skilling's evasion all reveal something profound about them and the organizations they oversee. To talk intelligently about management or managerial leadership, to lead in our own name, we need to follow these threads to their conclusion. That is where story comes in, and our persistent, compulsive reliance on storytelling.

In their differences, *The Country Bunny and the Little Gold Shoes* and *Cheaper by the Dozen* illustrate the power of story to give us not incidental observations but a holistic presentation—worker, task, and management all carefully coordinated. We can accept or reject the package, but we know that it is indeed a package. How you see mankind affects how you see our activity; how you see our activity—our work, our managerial choices—tells us how you see mankind. The fiction of some people as eternal children and others as eternal adults, whether by inclination or socialization, fits one theory of the way the world works, but only one.

The Moral of the Story

With the question of an identity or difference between family and corporation, we have moved firmly into the realm of ideology. How do we construe the social whole? We also need to ask, did our authors intend these lessons? One could argue that neither Heyward nor the Gilbreth children intended any indoctrination. On the surface, neither *The Country Bunny* nor *Cheaper by the Dozen* actively seeks to convert the reader, however vulnerable, to its point of view. It says simply, here life is, in all its complexity. See the connections, see the implications, and make what you will of it. We then read ourselves into the story, filling holes in the evidence, building logic bridges where none may exist. We do this with greater success in stories that capture our view of the world, and as with most aspects of our lives, we remember our successes best.

Moreover, the only story that captures the complexity of a single human being is the individual's own life story, which may prove at best incompletely coherent. Ideological package or no, to read is to mix and match, to tailor each new narrative statement to the reality that we know. One can like both *The Country Bunny* and *Cheaper by the Dozen*; I do. Wittingly or unwittingly, we stitch together a garment of people's stories in which to clothe ourselves; we do so as a concession to our place in the family, the community, or the society, even though we hardly know that we are doing so, especially in the early years.

This process of acculturation works against the other process of finding oneself in story, or a story, but the two create a loop in which we are constantly redefining ourselves and our place, a redefinition that releases us from predilections that would otherwise confine us. The notion that we change over time, that we adjust our nature to meet changes both external and internal, makes the premise of this book possible. If we do not change, reweave, reconstruct, and recount our stories, we cannot discover new ways of being and managing. Story serves that need for definition and redefinition; that is its promise here.

Yet the reinvention of oneself is fraught with peril, both for the individual and the society. It isn't so much that we fear change as that we can't anticipate where the change will lead us. One could argue that the other rabbits' initial rejection of the Country Bunny was just such an attempt to avoid the pressure of redefining their society's norms, and that Frank Gilbreth, Sr., feared the redefinition of his family implicit in the children's insistence that democratic process be honored, because he didn't know where it would take him.

The two responses illustrate two different ethical positions on the threat or promise of change: the moral of the story is that story is always moral, even when it claims simply to present the world. When we tell a story, about elites, due process, love, or death, we are making sense of the world, and that sense-making automatically gives rise to notions of right and wrong. We can choose to avoid making sense by allowing others to dictate the rules, or by arrogating to ourselves the power to make the rules in the absence of input from our families and other affinity groups. But that is simply a morality that has failed, because it voids the notion of exchange—communication—implicit in the word *community*.

The act of storytelling implies both speaker and audience—roles that may be exchanged in the course of the narrative. In that dynamic among participants, storytelling emerges as an ethical act, an articulation of norms among and by all. It isn't always easy to situate the time or place at which that articulation takes place, the ethical moment when the norms get crafted, and yet that place and time exist for all of us, sometimes in multiple iterations. That is why it is important to speak up and speak out, as the various examples drawn from both life at Sloan and life in the larger business community will have demonstrated. At the very least, the lesson here might be, "If I can't say what I'm thinking or doing, should I be thinking or doing it?"

Beyond these methodological issues, *The Country Bunny and the Little Gold Shoes* and *Cheaper by the Dozen* teach us lessons about business and management themselves. In their specificity as children's literature, the two books suggest that we engage in the debate about how we manage our business organizations and ensure their viability well before we have the vote. In fact, we have probably taken a stand on these matters by the time we get to kindergarten—we speak out on them even as we are learning to speak. But if that is so, what happens when we return to such materials as practicing, adult managers? If we have unconsciously imbibed opinions on this complex subject early in life, what crisis of identity may ensue when we excavate the past? Or conversely, can knowing where we have stood on professional practice from our early childhood make any difference to us, now that we have engrained those views through years of repeated, albeit unconscious use, and if so, how?

Everything just said about story in our lives applies to our use of story in management. We have our predilections, whether they are inculcated at an early age by our experience of our environment or adopted by natural inclination. Speaking up and speaking out does not allow us to rewire ourselves; it simply helps us to recognize the possibilities for business managerial competence that we have been given, or have given ourselves, and places them alongside others' ways of seeing the same problems. Speaking up and speaking out is about self-assertion, but it is also about uncovering our shared, human essence. At the very least, business management is second nature to us, absorbed from our environment at an early age; these two stories suggest it is part of human nature, and thereby ties it into everything else we do, making business ethics inevitable—not a contradiction in terms.

CHAPTER 3

See the Big Picture

Professional Norms, Mastery, and the Teaching Organization

All too often, discussions about ethics end with an agreement that our ethics are situational; that is, we will do one thing under a given set of circumstances, and call it ethical, while we might do just the opposite under other circumstances, and consider that ethical, too. This "flexibility" is the despair of many who would like to believe that ethics turns on a few universally applicable notions that are constant across time, culture, and geography. Others believe that the same flexibility is the essence of ethical—as opposed to law-abiding—behavior, and reveals the imagination and creativity that characterize ethical practice.

We have seen the importance of story to an understanding and application of ethics in management, but we have yet to talk in any detail about what it means to be ethical, what ethics themselves are (or even whether ethics is singular or plural), a system or a set of intuitions geared to—here, another troublesome phrase—our "moral compass." We have used the word *integrity*, and we have talked about the importance of seeing other people's points of view and by extension recognizing the place of business management in the larger society, in order to ground ethical practice. Storytelling, and the discussion with one's audience of the story told, makes these recognitions possible, assuming that one speaks up and out, and that one listens.

This chapter situates business or managerial ethics in a specific place in society: the realm of professional standards. The debate continues to this day about whether business is a profession like law and medicine, even as we issue ever more degrees that certify professional standing in business administration, and talk with ever more assurance about the leadership role businesspeople play in today's global economy. This chapter argues that business is and must be a profession if we are to ground it in ethical practice. At the same time, that net gain in commitment to society, coupled with the increase in social status that accrues to business—historically one of the big benefits of this arrangement to the professional—comes at a price. When we speak of leadership in business, we seem often to be talking at cross-purposes to the notion of a firm code of conduct. After all, goes the argument, leaders need to be flexible enough to do whatever it takes to get results; establishing a firm code of conduct will impede that freedom, and therefore diminish businesspeople's leadership ability.

The argument here is that we must have it both ways—professional norms and leadership flexibility—or we will have no ethical practice at all. To illustrate the point, we turn to director Ang Lee's film *Crouching Tiger, Hidden Dragon* (2000). Set in nineteenth-century Qing Dynasty China, *Crouching Tiger, Hidden Dragon* is a beautifully filmed historical drama about a legendary sword and the people whose lives it affects. As such, one might argue that the film has little bearing on the matter of ethics today. But Lee's film makes concrete for us, in temporal and geographic terms, the question of ethical relativism. What could nineteenth-century warriors and mandarins have in common with twenty-first-century China, America, Europe, and our still much-debated emerging global society? Surely people then behaved according to a completely different set of norms—look at their costumes and the natural and social setting in which they move!

Yet the lives of Lee's characters, borrowed from an even older Chinese literature, illustrate that, while ethics may be situational, professional ethical practice originates at a specific point in society, and that this point is the same point for every society. For all its apparent otherworldliness, *Crouching Tiger, Hidden Dragon* does a better job of defining professional commitment today than most texts that directly target the subject, and it does so in terms that emerge from and are appropriate to both Eastern and Western cultures, thus giving it precisely the universality we seek in our discussions about ethical practice.

This chapter traces the relations among Ang Lee's characters in *Crouching Tiger, Hidden Dragon,* with an eye to the social geography that these relations imply, developing lessons about the professional realm in which ethical action takes its root and from which it spreads to influence the society as a whole. That broad reach gives substance to the notion that one must see the big picture in order to fulfill one's commitment as a professional. It also suggests that "mastery," a key concept offered us in *Crouching Tiger,* echoes and amplifies current managerial views of the learning organization, and applies directly to our goals. With Lee's film as a framework, we will articulate the notion of the teaching organization, explore initiatives to instill professional standards in the corporate sphere, and apply those initiatives to such political challenges as executive compensation in America today; for in the end, ethical business practice—the balance of business rights and responsibilities—factors directly into the way we govern ourselves and our future.

"The New Chinese Girl"

Before I went to China to teach *Crouching Tiger, Hidden Dragon* for the first time, I knew that the film had not been a hit on the mainland. For audiences accustomed to martial arts prowess in the traditions of Jackie Chan and Jet Li, the kung fu of *Crouching Tiger* didn't make the grade. The same criticisms had been leveled at the film in the United States, too, but that didn't stop people from flocking to see it, or prevent the Academy of Motion Picture Arts and Sciences from awarding it the Oscar for Best Foreign Film.

I had my own ideas about the Chinese resistance to Lee's film, based on what I had heard from Chinese students with whom I was working through the MIT China Management Education Project. The project had launched international MBA programs at three major Chinese schools—Tsinghua University in Beijing, Fudan University in Shanghai, and Lingnan College at Zhongshan University in Guangzhou—where English was at least intermittently the language of instruction; hence the "international" tag to the students' MBA.

Candidates for these programs had to have relatively good English language skills to gain admission, and generally hoped to land jobs with multinationals, both in and outside of China. As a result, they were attuned to what they perceived as culture clashes between China and the global but U.S.-dominated economy. During my first visit to the three schools, several students had commented on the need for China to abandon its "Chinese values" and adopt more Western ways. We had conversations about what Chinese values the students hoped to give up, an exchange that left me with the sense that we were really talking in covert terms about a process both public and already well underway—China's transition to something like a market economy, with a potential loss in prestige and authority for the Chinese Communist Party.

With those conversations in mind, I led off each of the six classes for which I taught *Crouching Tiger* by asking the IMBAs why they didn't like it. As I expected, each of the groups talked about the poor quality of the fighting, and the preposterously exaggerated flying that Lee had his characters do. I had heard, too, that Mandarin-speaking audiences found the accent of one of the actresses—Malaysian-born, but ethnically Chinese Michelle Yeoh—difficult to accept: Yeoh had apparently had to learn all her lines in Mandarin as a foreign language, and her performance suffered accordingly, at least for those whose mother tongue she was using.

Asking about Yeoh's accent probably qualified as leading the audience, but it seemed to me a fair question, and produced the same response each time—grins and nods of recognition or admission. In each of the six sessions, though, it also almost immediately led to someone in the class saying with great emphasis: "This is not a Chinese film." And with that comment, of course, we were suddenly brought to the heart of the students' programmatic debate about the values necessary to help their country enter the global economy and give them their place as managers and businesspeople in the transition.

If *Crouching Tiger* is not a Chinese film, I asked my students, then what is it? It is set and beautifully shot in China. It is based on parts of a Chinese novel. Virtually all of the people involved in the making of the film are ethnically Chinese: director Ang Lee; actors Michelle Yeoh, Chow Yun Fat, Zhang Ziyi, Cheng Pei Pei, and Chang Chen, several of them stars in the constellation of martial arts films; and musicians Yo-Yo Ma, who plays the cello solos that make up much of the soundtrack, and Coco Lee, who sings the pop anthem with which the film ends.

This argument didn't sway my students, though it altered the criticism a little. Now they agreed that the film was Chinese, but didn't reflect the real China—it was a China for the West, a case of what the late literary and music critic Edward Said called Orientalism. Ang Lee had taken the China that real Chinese knew and made it into an art object, a study in exoticism for an audience that understood little or nothing of the true China. *Crouching Tiger* was picture-postcard China. What else could one expect of a director born in Taiwan and educated in the United States?

The students' critique was accurate. Ang Lee was returning to China with this film, but with artistic and technical sensibilities effectively molded in the West. His career in filmmaking has been largely confined to the West, so it is no surprise that he has brought to this film about China exactly the kind of sensibility or bias the Chinese students detected in *Crouching Tiger*. The mainland also has only a tenuous hold on most of the other figures I have just named: among the actors, Michelle Yeoh is from Malaysia, Chow Yun Fat from Hong Kong, and Chang Chen from Taiwan. Yo-Yo Ma was born in Paris and educated in the U.S.; Coco Lee, born and raised in San Francisco, is similarly distanced from her geographical Chinese origins.

In short, my mainland students judged *Crouching Tiger* to be inauthentic because its makers did not themselves emerge from the mainland culture in its current form. What then does it mean to be Chinese, where does that cultural authenticity begin and end, and what values does it engender?

The answer lies most clearly in the students' response to one actor in the film who was indeed born and bred in China: Zhang Ziyi, whose first major film was a release by China's leading native director, Zhang Yimou, titled *The Road Home* in the U.S. In *Crouching Tiger*, Zhang Ziyi plays Jen, a young aristocrat who runs

away from home and gets involved, to everyone's eventual disadvantage, with the warriors played by Chow Yun Fat and
Michelle Yeoh. Student responses to her role bordered on the vit-
riolic: no good Chinese girl would behave the way she did; she
was wild, self-indulgent, undisciplined—in short, a Westerner.

Interestingly, the students' condemnation of Zhang Ziyi's role
in the film carried over to her behavior as a professional. She is
known—do fan magazines play a role here, or is this the official
press?—for hanging out with the Western film crowd, which the
students saw as a rejection of her roots. In this, they compared
her unfavorably with Gong Li, the female lead in such Zhang
Yimou films as *Raise the Red Lantern* and *The Story of Qiu Ju*. Gong
Li, at least according to the lore purveyed by my students, knows
that her place is at home.

When I suggested to them that Zhang Ziyi's role corre-
sponded to what one read in the press of young Chinese under
the influence of MTV and other Western influences, they agreed
that Jen, in the film, might be fairly characterized as "the new
Chinese girl." They were careful, though, to distance themselves
from her. Though they themselves are in their late 20s, in a program that demands an awareness of and alertness to global culture, and though women make up a substantial part of each class,
no one in any of the six sessions was willing to take the label of
new Chinese girl or boy. The phenomenon was playing itself out
in the next generation, they claimed, the teens of today who
might be the Westernized Chinese adults of tomorrow.

All of these exchanges occurred with laughter and good spirits. But the students' judgments on *Crouching Tiger*, and specifically
on Zhang Ziyi, were just that—assessments of value and values,
to which they brought absolute moral certainty and apparently
unflinching sociological authority. When I suggested that the

culturally ambiguous, cosmopolitan China of *Crouching Tiger* might well be the China of their future, they agreed, but that didn't make them any happier with the film or Jen, "the new Chinese girl." It took an in-depth analysis of the action in the film itself—an analysis they themselves provided with remarkable consistency in results across the six separate sessions I held—to bring them around.

Once Upon a Time in the East

Despite its foreignness in the eyes of my Chinese students, *Crouching Tiger, Hidden Dragon* works with conventions well known to Chinese audiences. Ang Lee uses a genre, the *wuxia pian* or martial arts romance, that has a firm place in Chinese literary, theatrical, and cinematic culture. The film recounts the story of a warrior, Li Mu Bai (played by Chow Yun Fat), who has decided to give up his fighting ways. He does so in a quite literal, symbolic fashion, by turning over his sword, the Green Destiny, to his life-long friend and sometime martial partner, Yu Shu Lien (Michelle Yeoh). Mu Bai asks Shu Lien to give the sword to Sir Te, a Mandarin in Beijing who seems to be something of a patron to the couple. Shu Lien is dismayed at the thought, but Mu Bai indicates that he has reasons for his request, and she agrees, suggesting that he join her in Beijing when he comes back from Wudan Mountain, where he learned his martial skills and will now go to ask forgiveness at the grave of his master for giving up his art.

Shu Lien then sets out for Beijing. She is the owner and CEO of Sun Security, a company that she has inherited from her father. When she arrives in Beijing, her client comments that Sun Security has been at its best since she took over—so Shu Lien emerges as the businessperson in the film, and a successful one at that. She next goes to find Sir Te; like Shu Lien, Sir Te is taken aback at Mu Bai's desire to give up his sword, but accepts it as a short-term gift. He also takes the opportunity to lecture Shu Lien on the folly of ignoring one's emotions, and recommends that she and Mu Bai stop pretending they don't love each other and satisfy their deep and long-standing desire for a union.

As she goes to put the Green Destiny in Sir Te's study, Shu Lien meets Jen (Zhang Ziyi), the daughter of Governor Yu, also a guest of Sir Te. The governor has just come with his family from the west to take up his office in Beijing. Jen plies Shu Lien with questions about her warrior lifestyle, and the discussion moves from the Green Destiny, which Shu Lien shows the young woman, to Jen's impending marriage to one of the great families of Beijing:

JEN
(longingly)
It must be exciting to be a fighter, to be totally free!

YU
Fighters have rules too: friendship, trust, integrity. . . . Without rules, we wouldn't survive for long.

JEN
I've read all about people like you. Roaming wild, beating up anyone who gets in your way!

YU
Writers wouldn't sell many books if they told how it really is.

JEN
But you're just like the characters in the stories.

YU

Sure. No place to bathe for days, sleeping in flea-infested beds.... They tell you all about that in those books?

JEN

You know what I mean. I'm getting married soon, but I haven't lived the life I want.

YU

So I heard. Congratulations. It's the most important step in a woman's life, isn't it?

[ANG LEE AND JAMES SCHAMUS, *CROUCHING TIGER, HIDDEN DRAGON: PORTRAIT OF THE ANG LEE FILM*, PP. 40–41]

The two women part on amicable terms, but that night, the chief steward in Sir Te's household discovers someone stealing the Green Destiny. He gives chase, and Shu Lien soon joins in. The fight that ensues between Shu Lien and the masked thief, whom we quickly recognize as Jen, is the first of the flying sequences that martial arts aficionados find exaggerated, and it ends without clear result—with the help of a hidden marksman, the masked Jen escapes from Shu Lien. But the battle gives the two women a chance to measure their strength in a relationship that will continue, sometimes in combat, sometimes in confidence, for the rest of the film.

When Mu Bai arrives, he discovers both the theft and the growing public awareness that his archenemy, Jade Fox (Cheng Pei Pei), is in town. Jade Fox killed Mu Bai's master, and the announcement that she has resurfaced makes him realize that he cannot yet give up the Green Destiny; he still has to avenge his master. He comes close to confessing to Shu Lien that he has abandoned his warrior ways for her, but is interrupted. Shu Lien assures him that she will find his sword using her own methods, and the chase is on.

At the level of plot, the rest of the film is straightforward: Jen has the sword, and Mu Bai and Shu Lien do what they need to do to get it back. The retrieval is complicated by Jade Fox, who turns out to have hidden successfully over the years by becoming Jen's governess and therefore a member of Governor Yu's household. During that time, Jade Fox has schooled Jen in the martial arts, thus becoming not only her governess but her martial arts master. At every point where Jen is in danger of losing the Green Destiny or succumbing to the influence of Mu Bai and Shu Lien, Jade Fox disrupts the influence the couple seems to gain over the young woman.

The pursuit is also complicated by the appearance of Lo (Chang Chen), known to the ethnically dominant Han Chinese as Dark Cloud, a desert warrior who becomes Jen's lover during her family's sojourn in the west of the country. Their romance starts out as a series of pitched one-on-one battles after Lo's bandits attack the governor's household convoy and Lo himself makes off with a comb Jen was holding. Her pursuit of him ends with what Western audiences might quickly define as two free spirits coming together, but their lovemaking after she tries to stab him is, so far as I could determine, the most important reason the Chinese students write Jen off as a "wild," Western-style lover.

For viewers inclined to Hollywood endings, *Crouching Tiger* does not satisfy. In a climactic battle scene, Mu Bai retrieves the Green Destiny and kills Jade Fox, but not before she has mortally wounded him with a dart dipped in the same poison that killed his master years before. Finally chastened, Jen hurries off to prepare an antidote to the poison, leaving Shu Lien to watch over her dying companion. Mu Bai confesses his love for Shu Lien, and admits that it is his love for her that persuaded him to abandon his warrior ways; he then dies, just as Jen reappears with the antidote. Shu Lien's initial impulse is to execute the younger woman with the Green Destiny, but with the sword blade at the girl's throat she relents, only admonishing her to "be true to yourself." Jen then goes to find Lo on Wudan Mountain, and after a brief reunion, throws herself into a chasm.

This is tragedy on a Shakespearean scale. Indeed, the film's combination of visual beauty and foiled human aspirations is reminiscent of Laurence Olivier's sumptuous screen rendition of *King Lear* (1984). But the similarities go beyond that film-to-film comparison: in Shakespeare, the sheer beauty of the language inflects the bleakness of the plot in much the same way that the visuals of *Crouching Tiger*, including the fight sequences, infuse with meaning the sorrow and loss that the story itself conveys.

Jiang Hu, or the World of the Warrior

If Shakespeare's *King Lear* focuses on the madness of one old man, Lee's *Crouching Tiger* depicts a world intimately familiar to the students who populated my sessions—or rather, it depicts two worlds: the world of the warrior and the world of the emperor. The relation of these two determines the course and significance of the film.

When Jen and Shu Lien first meet, the young woman is unstinting in her admiration for the life that she imagines the older woman must live. In the scene quoted above, the two of them play out a short version of mentor–protégé, mother–daughter relations, even as the talk turns to weapons and questions of freedom and social obligation. Story emerges as a key notion in their conversation, the medium of dreams in Jen's case, but a vehicle for delusion in Shu Lien's older, wiser perspective, to be deconstructed as fully and firmly as possible. The term *jiang hu*, translated in the subtitles as "underworld," surfaces only briefly in their conversation, but it is understood as the place where Shu Lien lives her life, the place where, in Jen's view, freedom and violence rule. This notion generates the tension between the two women about how one can, or ought, to live. Shu Lien sidesteps a direct confrontation about it as they end their conversation: she simply congratulates Jen on her impending marriage, when the younger woman clearly invites condolences.

That diplomatic elision on Shu Lien's part typifies all of her actions in the film; she constantly seeks to accomplish her goals with a minimum of intervention or self-assertion, and with an eye to maintaining appearances. The same approach and the same tension come up again in the scene immediately following, a meeting between Sir Te and Governor Yu, Jen's father. In fact, the two scenes form an introductory diptych to the topic of the world of the warrior—according to my students, another and more accurate way of translating the phrase *jiang hu*.

SIR TE

A sword by itself rules nothing. It comes alive only through skillful manipulation.

GOVERNOR YU

I see your point. Please continue.

SIR TE

The Imperial Court isn't the problem. With royalty and officials everywhere, the Royal Guard keeps security tight. But

Peking is not like the West. Here, you'll find all sorts of characters. Proceed with caution in your quest for law and
order. Don't depend only on the court. Contacts in the
Giang Hu underworld can ensure your position. Be strong,
yet supple. This is the way to rule. [p. 43]

The world of the warrior exists outside the realm of the power
elite, but it shores it up. In story, it is a world of freedom, where
might is right and women can live like men in defiance of social
convention; at least, that is how Jen sees it. Shu Lien's response—
that the life she has lived is deeply dependent on rules—only begins to reflect the discipline to which she has subjected herself as
both a businessperson and a fighter. She reveals later that she and
Mu Bai have never married because her fiancé, who died in battle,
was also Mu Bai's companion and Mu Bai has sworn to avenge
him; both hold themselves to the standard of loyalty beyond the
grave. Mu Bai takes the personal commitment a step further, into
a realm of mystical commitment and monkish equilibrium an-
chored by his loyalty to his master at Wudan. Shu Lien is more
pragmatic, more inclined to respond to the needs of those around
her, but she is very conscious of convention and the values implicit in it. For both characters, the world of *jiang hu* commands
personal engagement and rigorous discipline, and that makes
them reliable allies in the mandarins' search for social stability.

The tensions inherent in Shu Lien's initial conversation with
Jen—freedom and responsibility, self-expression and ethical restraint—emerge fully in the scenes among the various characters
as the chase for control of the Green Destiny takes them away
from Beijing. Theirs is a journey into the wilderness, where only
personal strength can ensure survival. That strength, however, is
both physical and spiritual: from the beginning, it is clear that a

sword fighter's prowess is tied to his or her inner clarity about the self and its place in the world, a constant awareness that transcends the merely technical and without which technical excellence is unachievable. Here, one shapes one's life through self-discipline and self-sacrifice in service of a greater good: for Shu Lien, that good is of this world, while for Mu Bai it is otherworldly; yet for both, it is a world of what we would today call professional commitment.

Like our professional sphere today, the world of the warrior depends on a fully articulated sense of ethics, a code that resides in the individual and determines his or her every action. The initiates maintain the standards of the profession, and they advance those who demonstrate unusual skills, giving them the authority that goes with performative excellence. Theirs is a deeply meritocratic world, governed by a mentoring spirit that fosters multiple local hierarchies of master and disciple. Yet despite the standards Shu Lien and Mu Bai bring to *jiang hu*, or perhaps because of the multiplicity of those standards across schools, their world is also fundamentally unstable, an environment where violence is at least selectively the norm: the world of the warrior is also the world of the gangster, or at best the warrior with a code from one of many different rival schools. No single warrior authority unites them; in political terms, theirs is a decentralized and pluralist realm where, however strict the individual's discipline, diversity rules the wider social scene. Leaving aside for the moment modern interdisciplinary professional feuds—exhausted emergency room doctors against eager malpractice lawyers, or number-crunching engineers against design-dazzled architects—*jiang hu* has all the earmarks of business as we know and practice it today, professional engagement of the extreme, frontier variety.

On Being a Professional

With that modern profile of business in mind, in 2002 a few members of the World Economic Forum's Global Leaders for Tomorrow launched an initiative to produce what quickly became known as "The Proposed 'Hippocratic Oath' for Business." The initiative took the form of a draft oath, written and posted to a Web site at the private Spanish business school Instituto de Empresa. The author was Angel Cabrera, then dean of the institute and one of the global leaders who had conceived the project. Cabrera posted the draft oath on the Web, with the idea that MBAs from a number of schools around the world would collaborate to produce a final version of it; MBA schools at large would then formally agree to have their students sign it as part of their graduation ceremonies.

The model for the business oath is the oath first articulated by the ancient Greek physician Hippocrates. Doctors in training continue to this day to take the Hippocratic oath on finishing their studies, at least in the West. Though the text now exists in multiple versions—each intended by its respective author to reflect current conditions in the medical profession—the consensus is that the spirit of the oath still satisfactorily captures a doctor's professional obligations, and that taking the oath has real value for practitioners.

Cabrera's draft "'Hippocratic Oath' for Business" captures both the aspirations and the pitfalls of such a document:

THE "HIPPOCRATIC OATH" FOR BUSINESS

As a manager of a corporation, an advisor, or an entrepreneur I pledge to fulfill, to the best of my ability and judgment, the following covenant:

I will safeguard the interests of the enterprise's shareholders and other financial claimants.

I will utilize natural resources in an efficient, sustainable way, thus ensuring the rights of future generations to enjoy a clean and resourceful planet.

I will respect the rights and dignity of the individuals working for the enterprise, as well as the people that may be affected by its activities.

I will acknowledge my commitments with my clients, suppliers, and allies, and will respect their rights.

I will remember that I remain a member of society, and that as a manager, an advisor or an entrepreneur, my ultimate goal must be to contribute to the creation of public wealth. I will assume the responsibility for my acts in the execution of my duties and will respond to society for them.

If I do not violate this oath, may I enjoy life and art, and personal success, may I be respected while I live and remembered with affection thereafter. May I always act so as to preserve the finest traditions of business and may I long experience the joy of helping improve the lives of my fellow human beings. This pledge I make freely and upon my honor.

[SEE BIBLIOGRAPHY FOR FULL CITATION]

To what does this oath commit managers in a business enterprise? The oath combines so-called shareholder and stakeholder views of the corporation and the manager's role in it. The manager has a responsibility first to shareholders, but then to non-business members of the society, as represented in the focus on the environment and sustainability. Then comes a commitment to employees, the firm's business network of suppliers, and so on, and even—one might speculate—one's competition. The language of "rights" is introduced here twice, in a way that is all-encompassing: the United Nations Universal Declaration of Human Rights supplies the unspoken context. Finally, at the same level of aspiration, the closing clauses then move beyond the list of stakeholders to address the perennial question: What is a business for? The purpose of a business is to create public wealth, Cabrera answers, an assertion that he backs with a reference to "the finest traditions of business."

This is sweeping language, of the type one associates with oaths. Still, rhetoric alone does not make an argument, and so the question also arises: Do we agree with this view of business?

The points of potential disagreement in the draft oath stand out immediately. While North American readers are generally satisfied that shareholders come first in the list of constituents professional managers must consider, many other readers are not, and even North American firms such as Johnson & Johnson abide by corporate values statements that put customers and employees and communities ahead of shareholders. In an about-face on the same argument, the notion that the firm's ultimate goal must be the creation of "public wealth" generates a tension not resolved in the oath itself: Is the goal public wealth, or is it private wealth—that of the shareholders, the managers themselves, and the employees, to the extent that the corporation considers profit sharing and other means of benefiting the internal constituents? And what are "the finest traditions of business"? In a popular list of business traditions since time immemorial, lying, cheating, and stealing figure prominently. Readers note, in this context, that the oath says nothing about businesses abiding by the law, or the role of government writ large, and it provides no means of enforcement.

As of this writing, the "'Hippocratic Oath' for Business" is still in draft form, despite discussion sessions at various business schools and an open forum about it in Germany's leading business periodical, *Handelsblatt*, in 2003. At the same time, Cabrera, now President of Thunderbird, the Garvin School of International Management in Glendale, Arizona, has enlisted the school's Honors Council in the project, and hopes to include the pledge in Thunderbird commencement ceremonies in 2005, as well as in introductory courses and other parts of the curriculum. For purposes of this argument, moreover, even in draft form the oath points us toward a key component in the professionalization of business activity. Cabrera's manager pledges to abide by three essential elements of professional practice contained to a comparable degree in the original Hippocratic oath: (1) expertise, (2) ethical standards, and (3) service to individuals in the larger society. So the document does capture the big picture of professional commitment. What the business oath lacks is a sense of guild allegiance that the original Hippocratic oath emphasizes: the devotion to one's fellow doctors, but equally to the teacher who has imparted his art and science to the oath taker. In the original Greek document (however corrupted in the early years), the notion of mastery and fealty to a master comes through as strongly as Li Mu Bai's devotion to his master at Wudan in *Crouching Tiger*.

That master–disciple relation would be one way to address the lack of control over individual performance that critics note in the draft business oath. At the same time, the absence of a statement on the matter signals a larger question about the professional oath for business: Does the substance of business management correspond to historical definitions of professional

practice, thanks to the business community's voluntary commitment to key areas of practice that we already recognize from
medicine, law, engineering, and so on? What about the question
raised earlier regarding leadership and flexibility?

Beyond Social Engineering

Kenan Sahin, the founder and CEO of TIAX, LLC, a technology,
product development, and technology-based consulting firm located in Cambridge, MA, is unambiguous on the question:
"Businesspeople are not professionals, they are leaders!" he declared in a panel discussion at Sloan in the spring of 2003. "Professionals have influence, leaders have power. A CEO decides he
wants a building here, and the professionals come in to make
that possible!"

It should have been a heady moment for the MBAs in the audience, since leadership, too, has a nice ring to it, and Sloan, like
many other business schools in the U.S. beginning in the late
1990s, had been preaching leadership as a key business concept.
What, then, was the social value of professionalism? Sahin's
statement flew in the face of MBAs' often-stated view that they
are professionals. Moreover, it was hard to disregard his views,
given his career in both academics and business: after almost
fifteen years' teaching at MIT, Harvard, and the University of
Massachusetts, Amherst, in 1982 Sahin founded a telecommuni-
cations software company, Kenan Systems, with a $1,000 invest-
ment; its success eventually earned him such accolades as Ernst
& Young's Entrepreneur of the Year award in 1998. In 1999 Sahin
sold the company to Lucent Technologies for $1.48 billion.

The appeal of being a professional is clear. The concept began, at least in the West, with the clergy in the late Middle Ages who would profess an oath to God, effectively offering the commitment of their faith in Him and to their role as representatives of His word. Once secularized, the notion of specialist commitment gradually spread to other occupations, law and medicine first, which has given those fields normative status in relation to other areas like engineering and accountancy that today also claim professional status. The economics of the professions are much debated: whether the selectivity of professional bodies is intended to keep standards high, or simply to monopolize a lucrative market. And the money involved is important: by the nineteenth century in England, the professions were a way for individuals to rise into the middle class and beyond, reaching levels of social status on a par with the upper classes and the nobility, even though that status was not certified by inherited wealth. The white-collar status of professionals today is a legacy of that shift in social relations.

The initial shift may also have been a precursor of a second, equivalent revision of the notion today: Are policemen, building contractors, nurses, and salespeople any less professional than judges, architects, radiologists, and management consultants? People wrestle with these definitions, and particularly with the way we use the adjective *professional* in contrast to the noun *profession*; that is, police officers can behave in a professional manner, which makes them good officers, but it doesn't, for many, make them professionals. The notion of expertise is central to these distinctions, but it seems evident that social status also plays a role, as does history.

Business sits uneasily astride the social divide. First, there are traditional historical bans on practices such as usury, and belittling but frequently quoted comments about people who focus on material gain, from venerable sources such as Aristotle, Confucius, and the Bible. Second, the connection of business generally to commerce keeps activities even as highly evolved as investment banking in a gray area where it might be considered a trade, even though the expertise it requires from—and the income it generates for—individual practitioners clearly place them in the company of other professionals. So perhaps business is really nothing more than commerce, still today.

At the same time, the sums earned by people at the top of the corporate ladder, particularly in the United States, place them beyond the comforts of merely professional activity. Here, Sahin's declaration that businesspeople are leaders, not professionals, becomes relevant: the influence generated by and for contemporary business leaders puts them in the company of men and women who run national governments, and puts their companies as social units on a par with those entities. So does professionalism confer on the business community a status it requires to enhance its public image, or is it an inhibitor to the scope of operations that businesses have enjoyed for some time now? Does business break the professional mold, and if so, to what end?

The World of the Emperor

The power relations articulated in *Crouching Tiger* apply again here. We have already talked at length about the world of the warrior, represented at its best by Mu Bai and Shu Lien, who operate according to a strict code of ethical conduct. But in the film and in the analyses offered by my Chinese students, the other world, the world of the imperial court in Beijing, is never far away. In the end, it determines the fate of the characters in the film just as much as they hope to control it themselves by exercising their carefully honed skills. The dynamic is one of push and pull, dependency and rebellion. A Chinese civil servant once commented to me that *jiang hu* is traditionally seen as tied to the peasantry and posing an intermittent threat to imperial authority. From Mao on down, he argued, a central theoretical and practical question for the Chinese Communist Party has been whether it could create a "sustainable" government rooted in the peasantry. In short, whatever the warriors' perceived social status as professionals, they mark a fault line between two competing modes of governance: the people from which they come and the emperor whose authority they are enlisted to serve.

The world of the emperor surfaces early in the film, most explicitly in the conversation between Governor Yu and Sir Te cited above, where the two men focus on the pragmatics of social control. If Mu Bai and Shu Lien represent the world of the warrior, Sir Te and the governor represent the world of the emperor in *Crouching Tiger*, by virtue of the official positions that they hold. The forces of law and order are omnipresent in the visuals of the film, down to the smallest details. When Shu Lien's convoy first arrives in Beijing, we see her turn over her passbook for inspection by customs guards at the city gate. With their approval, she moves into the city, but even then Lee's camera lingers on the street surface, paved in such a way as to provide what are essentially tracks for Shu Lien's cart wheels. After the convoy passes through the gates, the camera shifts first to Shu Lien's destination, where she unloads her cargo; then it follows her into the teeming streets, then moves up and back for a panoramic view of the Forbidden City, the imperial palace at the center of the community.

These early scenes define the social dynamic in the film, telling us that higher powers will play a central role in the plot. Where the world of the warrior is decentralized, pluralist, ethics-driven, and meritocratic, the world of the emperor is centralized, top-down, law-driven, class-based. Where the world of the warrior embodies instability and loyalty to one master or one school of fighting among many, the world of the emperor focuses on stability and adherence to a single convention. Where the world of the warrior depends on technical expertise honed through an otherworldly spirituality, the world of the emperor depends on pragmatic people skills; that is why Sir Te feels comfortable pressuring Shu Lien on her relations with Mu Bai, and she in turn becomes a hinge figure in the latter's attempted retirement—he is trying with all his might to go over to the other side, a conversion for which she provides both the motive and the means.

The ethical life as practiced by the professional makes demands that any ordinary mortal might want on occasion to escape; the world of the emperor, though characterized by laws that channel individual action, also allows more individual discretion than the codes of *jiang hu*, once appearances have been satisfied. The world of the emperor has a forgiveness factor—or perhaps it is simply a matter of benign neglect—that the internally motivated world of the warrior does not. For in the end, the difference between the two worlds, between a world of law and a world of ethics, comes down to the source of the control. In the world of law, the rules are imposed from outside, and they are imperfectly enforced as a result. The system is impersonal in its all-encompassing reach, an indifference to particular circumstances that informs both its punishments and its moments of grace. In the world of ethics, by contrast, the rules introduced by the master are internalized and then imposed from within, and the only possibility for a reprieve from one's self-discipline lies in death—or, possibly, in the slide from one side of the social divide to the other, as Li Mu Bai attempts to do. Small wonder that, for all its corruption, its lack of moral fiber, the world of the emperor persists.

Crossing the Line

And yet there is a third possibility, at least in today's postimperial world. The above analysis emerged from all six of the sessions I conducted with my Chinese students. With little or no coaxing on my part, they laid out the two worlds that we have examined here, and cheerfully walked me through the intricacies of *jiang hu*, with which they are all deeply familiar from other films and lore. But the interpretation of the world of *Crouching Tiger* as a two-tier phenomenon I have also heard outside of China, in seminars at Harvard and MIT and Aspen. And so, the notion that we live in a world that balances law and ethics, authoritarian command and pluralist diversity, class networks and meritocracy—perhaps that notion applies to all of us, whatever our national, ethnic, or temporal provenance. And for all of us, perhaps, the professional sits astride the dividing line between authority and freedom, responsibility and rights.

My Chinese students suggested as much before our sessions ended. When one of them mentioned Robin Hood as a Western analogue, I began in scholarly fashion to explain that, in at least one modern-day interpretation of the legend, Robin was a Saxon aristocrat who had been unseated by the Norman invaders. Then I realized that, in my chosen reading, Robin had lost his place in the world of the emperor and indeed fallen into the late medieval British equivalent of *jiang hu*. As other students in these sessions pointed out, though with fewer filmographic specifics, the same might be said of many of the protagonists in modern American Westerns—the Gary Cooper character in *High Noon*, many of the figures in John Ford's films, and Clint Eastwood's hard-bitten loners. These figures on the fringes of American society are more conscious of the principles their society claims to uphold than the good citizens themselves; they are skilled at their craft, which is often martial in nature, and they don't suffer fools gladly. In these respects, they replicate the principled stand that Shu Lien and Mu Bai adopt in an apparently very different setting, and like them, they try to make lives that keep them integrated with the society on which they do, after all, depend for a sense of who they are. They do not generally throw themselves off mountains, as Jen does at the end of *Crouching Tiger*, which is probably a good thing for both them and us, but they do finish the job and ride away into the sunset.

So the pervasiveness of this social configuration suggests that we can talk about universal—which is to say, nonsituational—ethical standards, not just in this book, but in daily life as well, and we can deliver on our responsibilities in accordance with them. To do so, however, we need to see how the big picture painted by my students in response to *Crouching Tiger* captures the American scene. How do we do so?

In the United States, businesspeople can be found in both the world of the warrior and the world of the emperor. The location only depends on who you are, your chosen industry, and the time in your career. We start in an apprentice system that sets professionalism as its highest value. We become practitioners, and we end in a certain number of cases by becoming the heads of multinational corporations. In short, a few of us have the potential to reincarnate the emperor, with all the trappings of power and authority that that implies. Though my Chinese students seem to be more aware of this possibility than their American counterparts, the conception that they advance transcends "Asian values," or the realities of communism with Chinese characteristics, to capture the realities of business practice in the global arena and in the United States as a trend-maker for it.

When Kenan Sahin dismissed the professional phase in the business trajectory—"Businesspeople are leaders!"—he simultaneously recognized a problem with American business management and offered a solution for it. Whether consciously or unconsciously, he was commenting on a failure of the current MBA experience: it represents the apprenticeship years that should give students a code of professional practice, but seem to have done so with only indifferent success. The firms that hire the younger generations both before and after the MBA experience seem not to be supplying the principles that the MBA education has also let slide.

Sahin correctly recognizes that leadership takes business management into a different arena, and supplies the engagement that business needs with the rest of the world. In the language that we have articulated here, the businessperson who leads crosses the line between the world of the warrior and the world of the emperor, making his technique a part of the larger system and enhancing it. The real battle over ethical practice, and the real contribution it can make, occurs in the realm where ethics seems secondary to law and the established order, not the coin of the realm.

That said, the professional only delivers on this potential if the apprenticeship years have done their work, or rather, if we have seen to it that the apprentice does his or her work; that is, if he or she learns the basics of a professional's relation to the rest of the world—expertise, standards, accountability, and service—before entering the arena solo. Armed with that preparation, the core of the world of the warrior, the professional can engage with the larger society and make a difference. Indeed, if Mu Bai and Shu Lien are any indication, the professional needs to make that move, not so much because he or she needs to retire, but because crossing the line gives scope to the talents developed in the process of acquiring mastery.

The fact that Mu Bai and Shu Lien were not able to do so, that he was maneuvering to retire rather than engage his world on a

new level, and that her role as CEO of Sun Security still had her
following the tracks laid down in the cobblestones of Beijing, suggests the danger of the two-tier system: neither side will acknowledge the possibility of movement across the line. The barrier
arises for many reasons, wealth being one of them. It is no accident that the emperor is invisible in *Crouching Tiger*. His wealth
puts him outside the pale of daily existence for the vast majority
of his followers, and it is no different with the wealthy players in
today's global economy. Our MBAs dream of being professionals in part because they can't imagine, even with models like Mi-
crosoft's Bill Gates and financier George Soros before them, what
it might be like to live those other lives. But the system works only
if the fledgling management consultant can imagine his or her
ethical practice upward into the stratosphere of global technology and finance, and if the figures at the top remember that they,
too, once had to learn the ropes, and that those ropes are partly
responsible for holding the empire together.

That imagination and recollection is leadership. It can manifest
itself at all levels of the hierarchy, across the two worlds, but we see
it most readily at the point where we have to call upon the standards
we have acquired from a master to negotiate the vastly more complex commitments that await us across the line, where our skills are
simply the basis for action in a complex environment. At that stage,
the self articulated through speaking up and speaking out becomes
all-important, as the unraveling of *Crouching Tiger* proves.

Master, Master, Who Is My Master?

We have talked at length about Mu Bai and Shu Lien as professionals, and they are key figures in the film. Much of the strength

and drama of *Crouching Tiger* derives from the script's insistence on positioning them so that they are under maximum pressure at all times, whether social pressure from the central administration or professional pressure in *jiang hu*. In that stressful state, they and we are constantly aware of them as social beings, selves by virtue of their place in the world. The same can be said of the other, secondary characters—the governor, the mandarin, the police, the servants.

The exception to this rule is Jen, the governor's daughter who engages with Shu Lien early in the film. An aristocrat by birth and habit, a warrior and outlaw by inclination and gesture and capability, her career drives the action in the film. More than any other factor in the communities that make up the world of *Crouching Tiger*, it is her personality and will power that keep people on edge, defining and redefining their allegiances, and she alone of the many characters who populate the film actually sees the big picture, from the top of the society to its bottom. While pursuit of the Green Destiny forms the plot backbone to the film, Jen's theft of the sword and subsequent escape with it are the real source of the dramatic tension here. She has deliberately taken herself out of the world of the emperor, focusing as she does on escaping her marriage and the lack of freedom that it implies. With equal deliberation, she enters the world of the warrior, believing the stories about it to be true, despite Shu Lien's warnings to the contrary.

Jen's commitment to the story of *jiang hu* represents an idealism that those in the world of the warrior themselves don't fully possess or, perhaps better, can't afford to possess. Where Mu Bai, for all his self-discipline and martial skill, still wants quietly to withdraw from one world and find refuge in the other, Jen succeeds in mounting the most public of renunciations, stepping out of the world of the emperor at what Shu Lien says should be the culmination of her career as a woman—her wedding day. Having exited her birth world, she enters the world of the warrior with equal fanfare: as one North American small-business owner, a woman in her early forties, recently commented to me, *Crouching Tiger* is "all about girl power."

Yet Jen's story transcends gender; where the other characters cluster around the border between the worlds of the emperor and the warrior, trying steadily to keep both in view, Jen blazes across their horizon, following a dream in which no one else believes, and which she apparently has the intelligence, the competence, and the means to make real. Small wonder that she fascinates everyone she encounters; she is a visionary leader in the making. But what is her vision?

Jen's fascination for the other characters expresses itself first and foremost through the battle that Mu Bai, Jade Fox, and Shu Lien wage for the young woman's soul. While we aren't told how Jade Fox joined the Yu household, it is clear that, in her time with the family, she has devoted herself to training Jen in the martial arts, and that they have, at least in appearance, the close ties that go with a master–disciple relation. At the same time, their master–disciple relation is anything but traditional: Fox's failings and Jen's unusual intelligence and ability skew the authority that binds them, so that Jen feels she has to hide her skill.

For Mu Bai, the secrecy in the two women's relationship is an evil that will affect both the girl's long-term being and her impact on the larger society. He regards it as his duty to correct her course, and starts by giving her a proper lesson in fighting, which is simultaneously a lesson in what true mastery might mean for her. He has the advanced skills that she still lacks, and he has the inner, moral focus that he judges she needs. Jen responds to Mu

Bai's advances with a steady ambivalence, though, just as she keeps her distance from Jade Fox. If she feels contempt for the latter's inadequate skills, she questions the purity of Mu Bai's motives, an instinct that Shu Lien shares, as her jealousy over his interest in the younger woman reveals.

In the end, it is Shu Lien who comes closest to a true master's relation to the younger woman. As I noted earlier, after Mu Bai dies Shu Lien has the opportunity simply to execute Jen; instead, she sends her off to find her lover, Lo, with the admonition only to "be true to yourself." With that farewell, Shu Lien turns Jen over to her own literal-mindedness about the world of fantasy, and brings her to the grand gesture, a declaration of faith in legend that is itself the stuff of legend. During her time in the desert with her bandit lover, Lo, he tells her the story of a boy who threw himself off a mountain to save his ailing parents; legend had it that doing so would make one's wishes come true. After a brief reunion with Lo, Jen throws herself from the bridge at Wudan; in so doing, she is honoring the legend, living out the ethical practice in the story, and finding what is perhaps the only plausible response to Shu Lien's contradictory command to obey no one other than herself.

That one enduring act is perhaps the best example of leadership the film has to offer, after all the examples of mastery and the brooding, invisible presence of the emperor. Jen submits to no one, accepts no one else's version of reality. Her career in *Crouching Tiger* speaks to the tension that we feel in every culture around people who insist on doing things their way, regardless of what we feel are our best intentions. In Jen's case, the possible explanations for her behavior seem polar opposites: she could be a spoiled brat—an aristocrat, as Shu Lien points out, and not one of us—who has always had everything she wanted, when she wanted it. In this view, she has all the arrogance of her place in society, flouts the norms of her milieu, and simply wrecks the lives of others in a world she understands only from bedtime stories. The alternative explanation of her character derives from her manifest abilities and the sheer intensity of her behavior: Jen displays a sense of self that has nothing to do with the world of the emperor, or the world of the warrior, or submission either to Jade Fox or Li Mu Bai or even Shu Lien. She has moments in the film, concentrated around her encounters with Lo in the desert, when she seems little more than an animal, acting out of passions that she cannot control. She is indeed no one other than herself.

But who is that self? Is it the animal, the aristocrat, the would-be warrior? She is none of those things and all of those things, and in that she expresses best what it means to be a leader. For all the fury, the apparent selfishness—or perhaps thanks to those qualities—she generates a strong attraction in everyone she encounters; they seem, in fact, unable to leave her alone, which perhaps best defines leadership. As Shu Lien's initial response to her indicates, her vision seems to others nothing more than a childish commitment to the world of make-believe; yet that vision is in fact an idealized version of each of the characters and what they do, and that is a hard vision to resist, even for the most modest of persons.

As with everything Jen has done in the course of the film, the moment when she jumps from the bridge at Wudan is an expression at once of extreme selfishness and total selflessness. It is a selfish gesture because it puts an end to everyone's attempts to bring her into their world, even Shu Lien's when she admonishes Jen to be true to herself. It is selfless because she sacrifices herself for Lo and Lo's wish, and probably does enact Shu Lien's admonition. Our inability to say whether she is selfish or selfless embeds her gesture in our memories and keeps us returning to it, trying to decipher what it really means. In that sense, whatever her true motives, Jen becomes the ethical benchmark for the characters in the film, and for us. She can be seen as totally lacking in ethics—a sense of the community and of her place in it—or the most ethical in a group that runs the spectrum from Jade Fox's persistent criminal intent, to Sir Te's live-and-let-live benevolence, to Mu Bai's priestly demeanor, to Shu Lien's long-suffering discretion. She puts herself beyond the pale of daily decisions by making the gesture that seems to respond to everyone's need for them: this is the all-meaning purity of the leader.

She is a leader also because she bridges two worlds and sees the big picture, combining spiritually driven technical excellence and a knowledge of the system that confers identity by rank. The fact that her reach seems more than she can live with does not diminish her impact. It only suggests that the right kind of mastery must be a very good thing, for her and for us who may learn from her example. Grounding the mastery of story in the specifics of professional responsibility might have kept her from spinning out of control and taking her world with her. It isn't a small charge, and few of us fully rise to it when it presents itself in the form of a young hire with great promise. But story takes us a good distance in that direction, if we are willing to remember it.

Applications: Mastering the Organization

What, then, would successful mastery look like today? The notions that successful organizations should give their people opportunities to improve themselves, that the knowledge those people bring to the organization is in fact its greatest asset, that a viable organization learns from its own experience—all of these principles drive successful management practice today. Peter Senge and others have codified them under the title "the learning organization." In his best-selling book *The Fifth Discipline* (1990), Senge uses the term *personal mastery* for one of the four disciplines that leads into systems thinking, the fifth discipline—Senge's way of seeing the big picture: "People with high levels of personal mastery are continually expanding their ability to create the results in life they truly seek. From their quest for continual learning comes the spirit of the learning organization" (p. 141).

The notion of mastery supplied by my Chinese students takes the learning organization a step further, or perhaps—for Western purposes—a step back, to forms of apprenticeship that we seem to have lost, at least in the United States, and that would make it a teaching organization. Senge touches on this notion, too: "'Leader as teacher' is not about 'teaching' people how to achieve their vision. It is about fostering learning, for everyone" (p. 356), a democratizing impulse in business that has been elaborated more recently by human resources expert Noel Tichy and others working in leadership studies. I have seen it on occasion, in the managing director of a highly successful financial services company who keeps his operation small enough that the entire staff can sit in one room, and he can then explicitly and physically model behavior for those he has hired; in the CEO of a Fortune 500 company who comes to executive education seminars with his senior staff, so that they can talk with one another and with others from outside the company about what it means to be inside the company; in the flat organizational structures favored by companies in the new economy, whose young leaders have the political idealism to believe they can maintain the model once they've grown beyond the start-up mode.

The instructional element is key here, and goes beyond mentoring as we discussed it in the previous chapter, or the kind of short-term training that many Wall Street firms give their new hires. Mastery is about day-in, day-out interaction with the apprentice, in spite of the pressure to specialize and compartmentalize decision-making processes in the name of efficiency. In terms appropriate to American life today, it is more like coaching, with the depth of exposure and the team element that that implies. Mastery thus applies to two different, though related figures: the first is the learner, from the teacher's perspective a work perpetually in progress toward excellence; the second—drawing on the terms offered us by *Crouching Tiger* and by my Chinese students—is the teacher, the one who knows how to model and inculcate excellence, trains the disciple and, in so doing, continually pursues excellence in him- or herself through the perfection of others.

Senge's "personal mastery" encompasses both, but the cultural conditions that we have explored in the preceding pages emphatically propel the notion beyond the person and the organization into the realm of governance. Again, this is true both East and West. In a *New York Times Magazine* article reviewing the after-effects of the merger of the German firm Daimler with the Chrysler Corporation in 1998, the German writer, Peter Schneider, puts a finger on the failure of American firms either to realize or to acknowledge this potential. "Scenes from a Marriage" describes the cultural differences that emerged as the two companies became one. Schneider has spent extended periods of time in the United States, and writes affectionately of U.S. forces liberating the area of Germany where he and his family were waiting out the end of World War II. So he is even-handed in his treatment of the two parties, and ultimately demolishes national stereotypes on both sides, with a good sense of humor and concrete suggestions about the way in which we do business across cultures.

That said, Schneider found in DaimlerChrysler a different kind of America from the "populist" image with which he approached the assignment. If Daimler executives ate in the same cafeteria as their rank-and-file workers, Chrysler had a carefully segregated set of eating facilities at their Auburn Hills, Michigan, headquarters, designed to insulate management from its people, and Schneider notes in passing that management also had its own parking garage. He focuses most, though, on the massive pay differential between the Chrysler and the Daimler executive teams.

Schneider writes:

> *Compared with their American counterparts, German managers were collecting pocket change. The year before the merger, the combined salaries of the top ten executives at Daimler-Benz came to about $11 million, compared with $16 million for Chrysler's top 5 managers. In that same year, [Chrysler CEO Bob] Eaton earned $6.1 million, plus options that brought his total compensation to $11.3 million. And these earnings were far surpassed in the wake of the merger, when Chrysler managers exercised their stock options. Eaton himself is said to have raked in $70 million. That same year, [the CEO of Mercedes-Benz, Jürgen] Schrempp made do with about $2 million.*
>
> *When asked about this discrepancy, Schrempp is said to have replied quite casually that he wasn't exactly living below the poverty line. [p. 47]*

American populism, or the imperiousness of American business? By now, the information on salary differentials between the U.S. and the rest of the world is nothing new to readers of the business press and the academy concerned with management.

But addressing the issue becomes more urgent in light of my Chinese students' dreams of adopting Western values. They are coming to the global marketplace from a background where government policies of the past half century and aspects of Chinese historical tradition have sharply limited individual options and individual initiative. The fact that the government itself is gradually and selectively relaxing those controls doesn't alter the fact of the change itself, and experts in China and abroad are already voicing concern over a new local corporate elite rising against a backdrop of increasing unemployment, social instability, and poverty. And the pattern is not limited to China alone among the developing nations.

In the U.S., by contrast, we seem gradually to be moving toward acceptance of more concentrated social control, even as we continue to utter the mantra of freedom. Data on the shrinking middle class and the increasing share of national wealth in the hands of a very few are there for all to see. The militarization of American culture has continued apace, in part because of our foreign policies, in part because of the politics of fear on the home front. The threat to personal freedoms isn't simply a result of the current Bush administration's war on terror, though it seems increasingly a cost of doing business in America. In *Roger and Me* (1989), Michael Moore documents his unsuccessful pursuit of an interview with then-GM Chairman of the Board and CEO Roger Smith, to confront Smith with the ruin of Flint, Michigan, Moore's hometown and a GM company town straitened by a plant closing. In his election-year release of *Fahrenheit 9/11* (2004) on the two Bush presidencies, Moore sets out the imperial inclination in American business for all to see, accept, or dismiss out of hand (as many did at the time). In part because of their controversial nature, Moore's films have made him our modern version of Ang Lee's Jen, drawing a spectacular, filmic trajectory from top to bottom of American society that challenges us to know and be true to our principles.

One might argue that the phenomena Moore describes are limited to a single company or industry or period in American history. The truth is, of course, that we have dealt before with monied or business elites. Consider just three high-level historical examples that trace an evolution on the subject: it was James Madison who observed with apparent neutrality in "Federalist X" that men were by nature unequal in their faculties, and therefore likely to be propertied to unequal degrees, and that those inequalities would be the source of faction as the new republic got underway. Alexis de Tocqueville, writing in the 1830s on *Democracy in America*, admired Americans for their eagerness to form associations, but worried that over time these might give rise to a new manufacturing aristocracy, which would outdo the old-time European nobility in its abuse of power. Finally, many of America's presidents during the first half of the twentieth century ran on platforms designed to curb the documented reach of corporations, from Teddy Roosevelt to Woodrow Wilson to Franklin Delano Roosevelt to Dwight Eisenhower, the Republican president and former career military officer who gave us the cautionary phrase *military-industrial complex*.

Today, despite the flurry of the past several years over corporate malfeasance, Americans seem to have decided as a culture that business models can and should apply to many other aspects of our lives, from volunteer organizations to schools to government itself. It's an interesting notion, because even the enlightened managers who design and run the flat-structured dot-com and Internet-related companies will tell you that corporations are not democracies; they couldn't run them if they were.

The prospect of business models gradually becoming dominant in a society that prides itself on its democratic traditions bodes ill, therefore, unless we find a means of reconciling the two. But no one so far has stepped convincingly into the breach, whether politician, filmmaker, or even businessperson. George Soros has begun to unfurl a plausible and very public critique of modern capitalism, even as his Open Society programs aim to bring the benefits of the system to countries that previously operated under communism. It remains to be seen whether he can articulate and implement corrections to a system and its failings that he himself has mined very successfully for decades.

These tensions compose the big picture, American-style. Again, we have choices: about the degree of freedom we believe our society really can tolerate, before it and its individual parts exceed individual managers' abilities to manage them successfully; about the amount of control we need to impose, and in whose interests, before we begin to stifle the spirit that sets America apart in much of the world's eyes. Ethical practice has a role to play here, too, once we recognize the interconnectedness of professional standards, leadership, and authority, and the importance of mastery as an institutional arrangement for maintaining those ties.

Again, we have many ways of running our organizations, including the MBA programs that send young men and women to work in them; we have already seen examples of how real people do so. However differently we manage them, the principle of mastery stands out as a means of ensuring that professional standards will filter up through the organization, even as long-range executive goals and perspectives filter down to inform the standards themselves. Despite historical and cultural associations to the contrary, the notion does not of itself bring with it a soul-stifling authority. It puts a human face on the organization and its larger purposes for everyone, ensuring that those at the top of the hierarchy actually work with those just beginning to climb the ladder, and demonstrating to those starting out that no decision is as simple as a lack of information makes it seem. Mastery makes it possible for individuals to see the big picture and influence it in their own way; that freedom is the overarching benefit of the teaching organization, and seems well worth having, whatever our cultural origins.

CHAPTER 4

Break the Rules, Make the Rules, Absorb the Costs

The Ethics of Entrepreneurship

Reading Through Success

It is not easy to find stories of successful businesspeople in classic Western fiction. Something about business success sets writers' teeth on edge, at least those on whom we have conferred the status of classics: witness Sinclair Lewis's *Babbitt*, Emile Zola's *Germinal*, Thomas Mann's *Buddenbrooks*, F. Scott Fitzgerald's *The Great Gatsby*, or Tom Wolfe's *The Bonfire of the Vanities*. The list is long, and the message consistent: the pursuit of wealth, while an understandable vocation, generates unhappiness in all whom it touches. Wealth works in fairy tales and romance novels, though even there, retribution is always just around the corner; but fiction that pretends to reflect reality as we know it takes little pity on the tycoon.

So I was delighted when Sanford Lottor, Principal of Literature and the Professions, invited me to facilitate a discussion of Liam O'Flaherty's short story "Two Lovely Beasts." The story's protagonist, Colm Derrane, has some problems, which we will discuss below, but as I read the story for the first time, I was amazed that, in this well-

crafted piece of prose, the subsistence farmer who turns successful entrepreneur actually does succeed. The ending of the story
leaves no doubt that Colm triumphs in his ambition to "rise in
the world."

In fact, after reading the story two or three times, I became a
little anxious. After all, I had an hour-and-a-half to fill with the
discussion of a story that led unambiguously from poverty to
riches, from anonymity to fame/notoriety, and stopped there—
no decline and fall. After my participants had cataloged the
means to and components of this upward trajectory, what would
we have to say? Was that why writers avoided business success,
or perhaps any success—was it just too boring?

In rising desperation, I reread "Two Lovely Beasts," looking for
the complicating factor that would make Colm's story a subject
for reflection rather than simple self-affirmation. Who doesn't like
to think of him- or herself as successful? My participants were to
be a group of twenty silver-haired entrepreneurs, all men who
wanted the time now to reflect on their lives and their work. I had
enjoyed working with this group the previous year. The Smaller
Business Association of New England sponsored the gatherings
under the rubric "Leadership and the Nature of Power." By the
time I joined the moderator team led by Lottor, the sessions had
the feeling of a reunion: good conversation, good materials, great
rapport among the seminar participants. In the story of Colm Derrane, the participants would see the rise of a man of strategic gifts
and perseverance, very much like the men they themselves had
been at an earlier age, and they had every right to that satisfaction.

By the morning of the seminar I'd found my secret weapon.
Emphatic though obscure clues had emerged from the text, pointing to an agenda behind the author's neat depiction of entrepreneurial success: as Colm launches his enterprise, he does so in the

shadow of a single phrase—"the law of God and of the people"—
that colors both his actions and his consciousness of them. "The
law of God and of the people" is shorthand for the ethical param-
eters of existence in Colm's village, the norms by which he and his
fellows govern their lives. But what might that law be?

I leaned on this phrase, and finally realized that, for such a
business-wise, contemporary story, the language of "Two Lovely
Beasts" has an archaic quality that goes back well before its publication in 1948. At first reading, the anachronism of the language
and the world it portrays has a certain charm; but if O'Flaherty is
trying to illustrate the advent of a new economic era and new
business practices, the charm would seem a poor strategic choice
to enhance the story's efficacy. In mostly Catholic Ireland, moreover, wouldn't "the law of God" likely be Catholicism? If that was
so, I reasoned, O'Flaherty must be telling us something about the
spiritual quality of Colm's rise. Wasn't the archaic language he
used reminiscent of the Bible? By Biblical standards, what were
we to make of Colm's rise in the world? It was a place to start, and
it would give the participants something to ponder. Thus armed,
I was ready to discuss Colm's rise and to hear my entrepreneurs
apply O'Flaherty's lessons to their own lives and careers.

We came to "Two Lovely Beasts" after sessions on Herman
Melville's *Billy Budd* and another short story, John Updike's "Made
in Heaven." That put me and O'Flaherty in the post-lunch slot, a
precarious position in a day-long seminar, because people have
often expended their best efforts and begun to think about the
end of the day. Still, this group had energy to spare, and the session started pretty much as expected. In the apparent absence of
any acquaintance with the tradition that good fiction destroys
good businesspeople, my entrepreneurs didn't reflect on the rar-
ity of Colm's persevering against all odds to the end of "Two

Lovely Beasts." With great efficiency, they used Colm's story to summarize the traits of a successful entrepreneur:

1. Colm is a visionary: he articulates a business strategy, complete with historical precedents and a long-range plan.

2. He is persistent: overcoming many obstacles, he reaches his goal of business success.

3. He is flexible and imaginative, characteristics blended under the misapplied and mildly pejorative term *opportunistic*: when he sees an opportunity, he adapts to the circumstances, and makes the most of a situation he hadn't previously anticipated.

4. Colm is utterly focused: nothing exists for him beyond his game plan.

5. He is a motivator: in the face of resistance from his family, he finds the means to bring them on board as collaborators in his enterprise.

6. He is self-confident: when the rest of the inhabitants of the seaside village in which he lives doubt and even ostracize him, he continues on the path he has set for himself.

7. And yet, he is not a risk-taker: when I suggested that entrepreneurs were commonly known for taking risks, the group assured me that entrepreneurs were the most risk-averse people in the world. They plan everything out in advance, so that they encounter no surprises. They can then take with confidence what everyone else regards as a risk.

8. Finally, Colm is lucky, with difficult situations resolving themselves to his benefit at crucial moments. While good luck may not indicate any particular merit on the lucky person's part, one can read the difficult situations from which Colm extricates himself as proof that he has earned his luck—he himself suggests as much.

The participants spent forty-five minutes enumerating Colm's entrepreneurial skills. It was a lively discussion: these men enjoyed sparring with one another, introducing war stories to illustrate the challenges and successes they shared with Colm. They were the owners, the presidents, the executive vice presidents, the executive directors, the chief operating officers of companies that provided engineering services, published business directories, manufactured airflow sensing devices and shrink packaging machines and forged iron products and office products; they distributed janitorial supplies, did contract research in optical physics, and consulted on a host of corporate issues. They had a wealth of experience, and they had come to share that experience and talk about how it might best be applied to business situations still ahead of them or their staffs. They were having a good time.

Still, the tension of exploration and the give-and-take of ideas gradually waned. The waters of the river that had been a healthy discussion dropped and eddied. In short order, we would be in a classroom swamp of shifting limbs, side comments to neighbors, low laughter at inappropriate moments, the occasional drooping eyelid that lets a moderator know he has successfully bored a roomful of people. The participants had found in Colm's story exactly what I had initially found in it: a not terribly thought-provoking lesson on strategic competence, with—for this audience—a feel-good result. Along the way, I had asked several times whether the group agreed that Colm was an ideal entrepreneur; each time, with a few qualifications but mostly nods and smiles, they agreed that Colm represented the best qualities in someone who wishes to start his own business. No contest—end of story.

But it wasn't the end of the story. If Colm was such a good entrepreneur, I asked, what did people in the room make of the fact that he appeared to have earned his business success by violating every one of the Ten Commandments?

The consternation engendered by that question was instantaneous and loud. The river of discussion that had been slowly drying up suddenly turned into a flash flood of roiling reassessment and self-appraisal that my colleagues and I didn't have the time to contain and channel—we had a wrap-up still to go. But the degree of the participants' dismay spoke to the fact that, when confronted with the shadowy code that I had finally brought into the light for myself, the participants, too, saw the contradictory connection of the Good Book to Colm's entrepreneurial spirit. It distressed them, and distressed them so much the more because of the investment they had collectively made in affirming Colm and his rise from a hardscrabble background. What nerve had he touched in these men who had made good, and why had they and I not noticed, or chosen not to notice, the ambiguous foundation on which Colm might be accused of having built his success?

This chapter explores the business template that my entrepreneurs eagerly applied to Colm's success, and the ways in which his experience deviates from our ready and idealized application of it at the outset. As with our previous texts, *The Country Bunny and the Little Gold Shoes, Cheaper by the Dozen,* and *Crouching Tiger, Hidden Dragon,* personal experience played a major role in the participants' reading of "Two Lovely Beasts." Anecdotes during the session indicated as much. They read themselves into Colm's experience, but the superposition of one story on the other led to a blurring of differences and motives. Moreover, given that most of those around the seminar table shared both start-up business experience and a long-term acquaintance, it was natural that they should in session have evolved a relatively homogeneous reading of the business dimensions of the story. They had their story, too, and their consensus was perhaps as much about their communal history as it was about Colm's.

Beyond the participants' initially favorable assessment of Colm's rise, their response to the gradually revealed but fundamental tension in his career also tells us a great deal about how we craft both a successful business and a business success story. To what extent do we read Colm's rise through the lens of his success? Would failure produce a different evaluation? To what extent do we retrospectively use his success to validate our own, and did the entrepreneurs' consternation stem finally from the realization that, if they identified with him in his strengths, they might also have to embrace his apparent violation of nonbusiness norms, norms that many of them might hold dear? When they were building their careers, how did they negotiate the joining, overlap, or conflict of personal and professional values? None of the war stories they shared in session sounded a note of sorrow or regret. How had they managed to avoid Colm's missteps, or had they made the same moves and simply put away the memory?

As we work through various aspects of "Two Lovely Beasts," the central question becomes: To what extent do we succeed by virtue of the single-minded story we tell about our success, and can we live in peace with that exclusive and often exclusionary self-explanation? If not, the corollary question becomes: Can we tell a story that includes many voices and multiple commitments, and still succeed? If so, on what or whose terms?

The Temptation of Colm

"Two Lovely Beasts" begins with Kate, a neighbor, bursting into Colm Derrane's house, hysterical at the loss of her cow. Each of the families in the village, an unnamed location on the Irish coast, has one cow and twenty acres. To lose one's cow is to lose the source of milk for one's children, and Kate has a lot of them. The misfortune is not hers alone, though: in the village, all are supposed to contribute to one another's support. So Kate's loss will in fact take milk out of the mouths of Colm's children, as they immediately and sullenly realize.

But Kate hasn't come to beg for milk. She probably knows that she will get it by virtue of the village system, and can let it lie for the moment. She has something else on her mind: she wants to sell her now-orphaned calf, and thinks Colm is just the person to buy it; his cow, she reasons, is already feeding one new calf. Mindful of the village system, Colm rejects Kate's request, but temporizes by agreeing to let her put her calf to nurse on his cow for a few days. Kate accepts this limited offer with apparent grace; but she has gotten her foot in the door now, and in the days that follow she gives Colm no rest—once the calf is in his possession, she insists that he must buy it. He balks, citing his poverty and the hard conditions in which they all live; but Kate overrides his objections, praising his energy, ability, and initiative, and taking a look at the big picture:

> "The English have started fighting the Germans a second time," Kate Higgins whispered. "They won't stop until they have dragged the whole world again into the war with them. The fight will last for years and years, same as it did before. There will be a big price for every-thing fit to eat." [p. 7]

This is the only moment in the story that gives us a temporal context for the events described in it. World War II has just begun, and Kate invokes the memory of World War I in order to persuade Colm that she has a winning strategy. And so, for reasons that even he can't entirely articulate, he finally gives in to her: when Kate brings him to the sticking point, he gives her her asking price without bargaining.

Kate's wily seduction of Colm occupies more than a third of the story. In that sense, Colm's interaction with her does more than originate the sequence of events that leads to his business success: it is itself a major focus of the story. Yet their negotiations illustrate a surprising aspect of the way in which we judge success: for all the time and attention O'Flaherty lavishes on Kate's role in Colm's story, for all the clarity with which Kate herself lays out the plan for one man's role on the world stage, everyone to whom I have taught this story asserts emphatically that Colm is a visionary. Like my successful entrepreneurs, every group assigns Colm the glory of a winning formula, as well as the skill and perseverance to make it a reality. I usually need only to ask a follow-up question or two before someone says, "Well, it was really Kate's idea...."; but their initial reading of the story elides her input, and awards Colm the glory of having thought up the means of his own triumph.

Some of this communal blindness can be ascribed to the story's outcome. After Kate sells Colm her calf, Colm applies her strategy and succeeds, for Kate's argument about the two world wars is in fact a prescient recognition of his and her place on the world economic stage; in the one paragraph quoted above, Kate encapsulates the principle of war profiteering, and Colm has the wit to act upon it. However successful Kate's business plan for Colm, though, her other idea—that the price of the calf will allow her to buy a cow on loan—does not work. Impoverished, she squanders what little cash she has, neglects her children even as she tries to care for them, reviles Colm for having bought her calf, and—after two of her children die of malnutrition and pneumonia—finally loses her wits and is confined to an asylum. We then read these different outcomes back into Colm's and Kate's beginnings, and reassign the early evidence of their relative business competence and incompetence.

A different, subconscious desire is probably at work here, too, not just to round out but to sanitize what might qualify as an archetypal business story. To view Colm as a successful entrepreneur, the reader has to give him ownership of Kate's idea; but we have also, if we want to preserve the purity of his business model, to ignore the sexual politics of the opening pages in "Two Lovely Beasts." Why does Kate approach Colm, after all, and not some other villager— his own newborn calf aside, why does she target Colm, and how much leverage does she really have in the Derrane household?

Here, a third player in these early moments of the story becomes relevant. When Colm finally makes up his mind to buy Kate's calf, the last obstacle he must overcome is his wife. O'Flaherty makes clear that Colm's wife dominates her husband, in spite of his various qualities, and that his purchase of the calf is his first successful household rebellion. As their neighbor, Kate would know the politics of the Derrane household. When she comes to Colm, she has just lost her cow, but we are told that she has also quite recently lost her husband. In her negotiations with Colm, Kate spends as much time telling him what a man he is as she does telling him how he can make his fortune by helping her out. In short, Kate's economic and business acumen may simply represent a cunning turn in her focus on reinventing her own life, including a replacement husband.

We don't like to think of start-ups originating with a woman who needs a man, or a man who needs a woman to praise him because his own wife won't, but the business reality of "Two Lovely Beasts" suggests that our entrepreneurial motives can be quite mixed. That's a hard message to convey: it certainly isn't one that faculty would want to offer in an MBA classroom. A group's impulse, then, is to decide that Kate's motives and behavior disqualify her as a satisfactory role model, and simply eliminate her from the start-up picture painted in "Two Lovely Beasts."

Interestingly, we could in principle eliminate Colm on the same grounds: when O'Flaherty writes of the "anticipation of venery" (p. 12) Colm felt in choosing to buy the calf, one can easily read Kate into that initially obscure phrase, and the power over his own life that her admiration—whether feigned for the occasion or real—puts within his reach. In this sense, one can fairly say that Colm has been tempted into his entrepreneurial career, rather than making the informed business decision we would like to see in these early pages, and that we believe we ourselves would make. So why exempt him from the same imputation of mixed, and finally low, motives? The short answer to the question of why we protect Colm is that breaking and then making the rules, effectively recasting the world in our own image, has benefits beyond the enterprise itself, in that it allows us to reinvent ourselves, and that, too, is part of Colm's undertaking.

Colm and the Village: Defiance, Leadership, and Abdication

With his wife at least temporarily humbled and the purchase behind him, Colm has now to face the disapproval of the villagers, and more specifically of Andy Gorum, the wise man and informal leader of the community. When Colm joins the other men at their regular gathering place on the evening after the purchase, Gorum reminds Colm that the village has a social safety net:

> "You know you are breaking the law," Gorum interrupted. "It's no use trying to talk yourself out of it."
>
> "How could it be against the law to help a widow?" Colm shouted.
>
> "Indeed, it isn't," Gorum said. "We'll all help her, please God, as much as we can. That's how we live here in our village, by helping one another. Our land is poor and the sea is wild. It's hard to live. We only manage to live by sticking together. Otherwise we'd all die. It's too wild and barren here for any one man to stand alone. Whoever tries to stand alone and work only for his own profit becomes an enemy of all." [pp. 14–15]

The technical point at issue here is simple. By choosing to buy Kate's calf, Colm has opted to give it milk from his own cow that would otherwise go into the mouths of his and Kate's children, as well as other needy souls in the village. As Gorum points out, Colm has chosen a path that may redound to his exclusive profit, not—as the law would have it—to everyone's benefit.

In response, Colm finds useful the rhetoric that Kate has previously applied to him: he proclaims his courage in resisting the law, and walks out on the gathering. Colm and his family are then ostracized by the villagers, and so begins a time of considerable suffering for them. Even in midsummer, the season of plenty in the village, the family survives on potatoes and salt in order to ensure that the calves have enough to eat. The rest of the community feasts on an abundance of fish, poultry, dairy products, and vegetables; though Gorum earlier argued that communal need binds the villagers together, they clearly have very good moments, too, and are appropriately grateful for them.

The season of abundance in the village exposes the nature of the difference that Colm has created between himself and the villagers. It is first and foremost a matter of control: in buying Kate's calf, Colm has chosen to break with village tradition, but also with the cycle of the seasons that determines feast or famine for the community. Colm aims to raise his two beasts, regardless of the give-and-take that characterizes the relation of the village to its natural surroundings. He aims to wrest permanent and consistent plenty from the ground around him even if, as a short-term result, he and his family are constantly in need.

And yet, after that initial, stark season of contrast between the Derranes and the villagers, nature comes to Colm's rescue. In September, two of Kate's children die of pneumonia, and Kate goes mad and is committed to an asylum. Thus Colm has the opportunity to rent her pasture land, which gives him the grass he needs to keep feeding his calves. The villagers, impressed by both his perseverance and the luck that seems to be running his way, abandon Gorum and turn to Colm as the new wise man of the village. Having been shunned for setting himself apart, he now becomes a leader because he has successfully defied the law at least "of the people."

Having reestablished himself and his family with the community, Colm perseveres in raising his calves. They become yearlings, but still he waits to sell them. He tells his wife that the proceeds from the sale will allow them to open a shop. His combination of daring and apparent good luck proves irresistible to the villagers:

When Colm went around with his horse and cart, accompanied by one or other of the children, everybody was eager to do business with him. The people sold him whatever they had available and they forbore to drive a hard bargain. He soon had to take the house and barn that belonged to Kate Higgins, in order to store the great mass of his goods. Within a few months he was making trips to the town twice a week and getting high prices for all he had to sell. [p. 30]

In the end, Colm sells his bullocks at a tidy profit. The moment brings him to tears, and he apparently has the modesty, encouraged by his wife, to recognize luck and his God for the success that he and his family have experienced. As his wife points out, though, the villagers' attitude toward them has changed again: envy has replaced admiration, and Colm's formula no longer sits comfortably with the people, for whom his success has become simply too great.

So Colm and his family move into town, leaving behind them a village that, by the villagers' own account, has been devastated in the process of helping Colm to rise. When Gorum drunkenly curses Colm in parting, his invective conveniently elides the fact that the community has cooperated in its own destruction, but neither he nor we can ignore the reality that Colm's enterprise has gutted a viable subsistence economy to feed the distant but far-reaching war machine. Nothing in the story suggests that Colm recognizes the loss, except as a renewed ostracism for him and his family. He does not look back as he moves on to the next phase of his career, a man in pursuit of perpetual growth.

O'Flaherty doesn't label this action for what it is, the evident clash between the collectivist structure of village society and Colm's emphatically capitalist inclinations. As one of the founders of the Irish Communist Party, though, O'Flaherty must have had something of the political struggle in mind when he wrote this story. If one takes seriously the notion that Kate Higgins has tempted Colm into his war-profiteering, mercantile ways, then she is the capitalist serpent in the collectivist, subsistence-economy garden, and Colm, after wrestling at length with his knowledge of the "law of the people," bites the apple of individual profit, and makes good. Unlike his Biblical models, Adam and Eve, he leaves Eden without a backward glance.

The (Im-)Balance of Work and Family Life

The larger social and economic implications of Colm's rise to fortune don't readily register with many readers. The consensus seems to be that he should take care of himself, and that the villagers can then follow his lead or suffer for their lack of initiative; for all the glory of those midsummer months, poverty reigns during the other ten months of the year in the village. On occasion, a participant will invoke Adam Smith's "invisible hand" from *The Wealth of Nations* (1776), in which Smith argues that self-interest will do more to foster a healthy society than good intentions and high moral ambitions. It is a view that social commentators have echoed ever since in defense of Anglo-American–style capitalism.

And yet, for all their approval of his behavior toward the village and the values on which it is based, most readers also believe that Colm has taxed his conscience with other, more personal sins. We have already seen that, at the beginning of Colm's enterprise, his wife protests his insistence that the family stick with their subsistence diet so the calves have enough milk. In the face of his indifference to her complaint, she moves to a rebellion more typical of their relationship in earlier days—she takes the fireplace tongs and tries to brain him. He quickly disarms her, but then apparently decides that he needs to go a step further:

> Colm took down a dried sally rod that lay stretched on wooden pegs along the chimney place.

"You'll be obedient in future, my good woman," he said. "On my solemn oath you will."

He began to flog her. She tried to bite his legs. Then he put her flat on the ground and laid his foot to her back.

"I'll kill you when I get a chance," she cried. "I'll have your life while you are asleep."

Then she folded her arms beneath her face, gritted her teeth and received his blows in silence. He had to go on beating her for a long time before the sturdy creature surrendered and begged for mercy.

"All right, then," Colm said calmly when she had done so. "Do you promise to be obedient from now on and to make no more trouble about the calf?"

"I promise," his wife said. [p. 21]

Reader response to this scene ranges from the amused, to the indifferent, to the horrified. In an effort to minimize the problem, someone will usually introduce situational ethics: in 1940s Ireland, Colm might have considered it perfectly all right to beat his wife as he does here, especially since he apparently believes he is teaching her a lesson, rather than simply taking out his frustration on her. The diverse audiences with which I have had the pleasure of working over the years, though, produce local expertise when one most needs it: in a midcareer executive education program at the MIT Sloan School of Management, a technical manager in his thirties from the west of Ireland spoke emphatically to the mores, even half a century earlier, of his birthplace; where he came from, he assured us, whipping your wife into submission had never been considered good form.

Moreover, the story itself makes clear that, sexual politics and family romance aside, by village standards Colm's behavior can only be considered extreme. At the beginning of the beating, his wife screams for the children to fetch the neighbors, who do then cluster at the gate, uncertain whether the ban on consorting with the Derranes extends to letting Colm "murder" his wife. Once free, she dismisses them with a sneer for their gossipy interest, but both her and their instinctive responses suggest that Colm has broken with the norms of civilized behavior.

All the more puzzling then, particularly for those who find Colm's behavior unacceptable, that his wife should submit to his project in the wake of the beating; and she does so, not just at the time of the beating but again later, when she tearfully and penitently promises to work with him. One can read into this surrender a twisted identification of the victim with her torturer, or simply a wifely confirmation that might is right. Whatever the case, this moment marks a turning point for Colm, at least as it affects the internal organization of his enterprise. With the moment of family trauma successfully resolved, even the children pitch in to help Colm in his project. O'Flaherty notes that this internal harmony plays a role in bringing the village back to Colm, along with his remarkable luck.

As in any organization, though, Colm's family needs steady reminders of the reasons they live and work as they do. In a moment that rang true with my entrepreneurs, O'Flaherty highlights a salient difference in the life and business stories of Kate and Colm. After Kate loses two children, goes mad, and is committed to an asylum, the Derranes suffer, too; but the outcome is very different:

> *Everybody in the house got terribly thin and weak. Yet Colm's iron will buoyed them up to such an extent that there was no illness. . . . He himself looked like a skeleton, for he practically went without food in order that the children might have as much as possible.* [p. 26]

The business phrases that describe this scene are "self-discipline," "self-sacrifice," and "commitment to a vision." Faced with Colm's behavior here, one might almost forget that the family is suffering not so much from natural hardship as the father's monomaniacal pursuit of his goals; indeed, Colm's commitment is so visceral it seems a force of nature. The argument in Colm's favor—and many participants have made it—is that he suffers as much as his family does; perhaps he suffers more, because he has their suffering on his conscience. Yet he is clearly practicing a double standard: he insists that the calves eat their fill, because only then will they grow up healthy and by implication salable. This is a good husbandman's perspective—but what about the husband who is starving his family, and more specifically, the calf-equivalents that are his own children?

Here, we can return to the debate in Chapter 2 on *The Country Bunny and the Little Gold Shoes* and *Cheaper by the Dozen*. In the elaboration of Colm, Inc., the family plays the role of employees, committed to doing his bidding. Here, too, the employees really are the CEO-figure's offspring, as they were in both those books, though Colm also subjugates his wife. Yet the "workers" don't have the advantage of parliamentary process, as did the children in the Gilbreths' book, and if the bunnies were just bunnies in Heyward's story, the Mother Cottontail's autocratic managerial practice still seems not to have allowed for the outright starvation that Colm imposes on his family.

Readers inclined in Colm's favor will often make the argument, when confronted with the stark evidence of his abusive behavior, that he has trouble communicating, and that he improves his skills in this area over time. As a form of communication, the beating that Colm administers to his wife early on certainly might warrant "rephrasing," but it clearly communicates his new and absolute intent to rule the family, and his wife gets the message. In this reading, "Two Lovely Beasts" tells the story of a man who lacks people skills, to the point where he willingly violates the "law of the people"; in the process, though, he discovers that people matter, that he can't succeed without them, and that some means of handling people work better than others. Colm succeeds in part because of his business acumen, but also in part because he redeems himself by learning to give people—at least his family—their due.

This interpretation of Colm's entrepreneurial debut works for many. Readers do generally feel that, by the end of the story, he has redeemed himself for most of his harshness toward his family. Again, because his business success will fuel family wealth, delayed gratification becomes a part of good family management. But what if Colm hadn't succeeded—what redemption would he have then? The village mantra, "the law of God and of the people," works both ways: it restrains individual initiative, which is why Colm breaks with it; but it also guarantees a safety net in cases of distress. Yet Colm walks away from it, confident that he has a better solution.

Coming Down from the Mountain

In situating Colm's governing ethos, one can easily invoke what sociologist and political theorist Max Weber called the Protestant ethic. Colm does so himself, though without the label. Although the putative Catholicism of the village suggests a denominational twist to this view, one could argue that Colm is indeed protesting not just the economic but the religious arrangements in the village, creating both anew. Colm's managerial style depends on self-sacrifice, deferred gratification, accumulation of capital, and faith that such suffering will be rewarded, and the formula works. But who does it work for?

It certainly works for Colm. Colm's God is not the wrathful God of the Old Testament: He rewards His servant even though, in Biblical terms, Colm commits a pretty long list of offenses. As I mentioned earlier, one can make a comprehensive case for Colm's having violated every one of the Bible's Ten Commandments (Exodus 20: 1–14) in his determination to "rise in the world." His worship of the calves defies the admonition to hold no other gods before the God of Moses, or to make a graven image of the invisible, or take the Lord's name in vain (Commandments 1 to 3). The work schedule on which Colm has placed both himself and his family violates the admonition to rest on the seventh day, and his abuse of his children instigates a violation on their part of the admonition to honor their father and their mother (Commandments 4 to 5). The villagers accuse Colm of having killed Kate's children; the underlying psychodynamics of his purchase of her calf suggests he lusts after Kate, and the villagers again would argue that he has stolen Kate's property from her and her offspring, violating her memory in the process (Commandments 6 to 10). Finally, Colm is effectively living out his own version of the Golden Calf story (Exodus 32), in which his "two lovely beasts" serve him much as the other calf served the idolatrous Israelites.

How does he get away with it? At first blush, the answer would seem to be that Colm so closely identifies with his purpose that he becomes like God, is in fact his own god. In that sense, he does observe the law of God, because that law is Colm's law. The autonomy implicit in this formula goes far to explain my entrepreneurs' enthusiasm for Colm: even as they face the risks inherent in starting up their own business, many entrepreneurs do what they do for the pleasure of having to report to no one. The rush of starting a business includes the kind of total dedication that Colm's experience depicts, and entails the all-engulfing expectation that everyone else who has a hand in the project will commit to it as the entrepreneur him- or herself does—or else. Witness Colm's children, at the best and worst of moments.

Dedication to the project can become an excuse for the leader to shrug off human decency as a managerial principle. It depersonalizes what otherwise might look like insistence merely on having one's own way. The entrepreneur will argue that it's all about survival of the firm, that without the firm, there would be no sphere in which to do the right or ethical thing. This view certainly applies to Colm's story: by the time he sells his bullocks, Colm has internalized Kate Higgins's business plan for him, and the villagers follow his lead in making it a success; at some level, everyone succeeds because Colm succeeds.

His way would appear then to be a formula for general success, and that prospect drives his expansion for a time. It doesn't stop at the gates to the village, though. After a certain point, the complexity of his operations takes Colm beyond his birthplace and into an arena apparently governed by rules other than those of the village. Tensions inevitably follow. We don't see Colm in the town to which he and his wife are headed in the closing lines of "Two Lovely Beasts," but it seems safe to say that their success has given them a network very different from the one by which they have previously lived. As both Kate and Colm realize early on, the calves are his means of escaping the strictures of village life and plugging into a set of connections that, during World War II, suddenly give him global reach. For a subsistence farmer from the west of Ireland, the shift is almost inconceivable, but nonetheless real: before he has even sold the bullocks, Colm's business of collecting comestibles from his fellow villagers makes him a part of that larger network, opening up prospects that have little or nothing to do with the local, seasonal rhythms that previously formed the horizon of his expectations.

One could argue that Colm never anticipated the effect his rise would have on the village—the destruction of its cohesiveness, its leadership structure, and its relative harmony with nature, which we would now describe as a form of sustainable development. By the time he gets that far, of course, he apparently doesn't care. But one could argue in his defense that he would have been hard-put to anticipate something he has never experienced. In this scenario, he is less smart than he himself would like to believe, but very good at exploiting the small advantages that surface as he plays out his role as the end node of a very long and complex supply system, designed to feed warring armies. In other words, Colm's entrepreneurial behavior merely responds to economic forces and historical circumstance, rather than driving them. He is indeed, as I suggested earlier, an instrument of Adam Smith's "invisible hand," contributing to large-scale economic change while seeing only his own self-interest. Colm personifies economic man; while his own ambition may have become his God, the power that moves him comes from less tangible, but much more powerful, sources.

So, is Colm a self-declared god or a capitalist tool? The answer depends on who is telling the story. From Colm's limited perspective, he has broken free of a world of narrow horizons, and entered one of limitless possibilities. He has allied himself with the power that emanates from the center, and has found a way of making himself useful to it. He abandons the social values by which he has grown to maturity and embraces a set that recognizes strengths that he has always had, but that seemed of relatively slight importance under the constraints of village life.

Armed with that recognition, he doesn't worry that he has bought his new freedom at the cost of other values, at least in the short to medium term. He has opted for wealth, and the system will reward him by giving him the material gain and influence that he wants, and a new identity into the bargain.

This reincarnation of Colm brings with it the condition that he avoid asking himself too many probing questions, though: his comments to his wife as we reach the end of his story make clear that he believes he has earned his success, even earned his luck. Having broken the law of God to reach his goal, he invokes it again once he has arrived, without reflecting on what he might really owe to it and the community in which it gave him his start. We really do enter here into a world where the end justifies the means. Colm can write off the unethical behavior in which he has indulged from beginning to end of his story, because his end gives him what appears to him a viable, new, God-sanctioned ethic. He has become a player, and so long as he obeys the laws governing the larger sphere into which he has entered, he will only enhance his status.

On the surface, he appears to have completed the first two steps of entrepreneurial ethical practice, breaking and making the rules. Colm then does what many successful people have done when confronted with the third step, absorbing the costs—they reinvent themselves with the leverage provided by abundant resources, reading their end success back into their beginning and thus denying that there were any costs. In shifting his sphere of action to the town, Colm effectively puts behind him any concrete reminder of the world from which he sprang, and that can no longer hold or satisfy him. He will spend the rest of his life dealing with the dissonances, though, unless he can distance himself ever further from the voices of his past; in short, if he runs fast enough, he will maintain the fiction of blessedness. The word we some-times apply to this formula for prolonged self-evasion is *progress*.

That failure to register costs at the end plays back into Colm's initial engagement, too. If the evidence shows him clearly and confidently breaking the law of God and of the people, it also sug-gests that he does not make new laws to replace them. Rather, he appropriates—we might more accurately say submits to—a new set of rules that is already codified and that he conveniently misidentifies as God's in order to maintain the fiction of entrepre-neurial, divinely sanctioned autonomy. He posits continuity with his old life and values, but he now lives by Adam Smith's "invisi-ble hand." Colm could claim independently to have discovered the notion, but his poor communication skills dog him to the end. He seems not to consider himself anyone's messenger. There is a dour quality to his triumph that suggests he feels he has no story to deliver. With his family a postscript, his story is his alone, illustrating an exclusivity that severely constrains his ethical prac-tice as an entrepreneur, no matter how quickly we approve his business strategy and even some of his managerial tactics. Colm's story is about spirit as much as it is about execution, finally, and the spirit comes down to the last word in the last sentence of "Two Lovely Beasts"—"ruthless," which is to say, indifferent to anyone else's welfare. If no one else is on the playing field with you, you don't need a story, and you don't need any rules at all.

"Every Child a Winner"

Did Colm have a choice? Could he have told the story differently, fulfilling both parts of the injunction to break and make the rules? My experience with the Smaller Business Association of

New England (SBANE) and the group we assembled there suggests that he did. The various entrepreneurs' individual insights moved us in that direction. But even more, the life of the group's unspoken leader, John C. "Jack" Rennie, made it clear that entrepreneurs can and do make major contributions to the social welfare, without violating the basic behavioral patterns that the group laid out in our discussion of Colm's virtues.

Jack had the aura of a man used to making things happen. He spoke rarely, but when he did, my co-moderator, Sandy Lottor, noted, "he spoke straight from the shoulder." He was the sometime president of the association and a major force behind our seminars. He was also the chairman and CEO of Pacer Systems, Inc., a Billerica, Massachusetts, company of about 275 employees specializing in systems engineering and design for the manufacture of aviation products. Further back, he was a Naval Academy graduate and had been a naval aviator and test pilot. After a stint with Raytheon, Jack had gotten his start in business in 1967, trading on his knowledge of the computer programming language FORTRAN to develop general-purpose digital computers for airborne operations. Jack and his cofounders were ahead of the defense technology curve, and they stayed there, expanding into ship- and land-based systems. Much of their work was classified.

By the mid-1990s, Jack had already made a name for himself in the world of American small business. Once Pacer was firmly on track, he began advocating for small business interests, helping to found National Small Business United, the local chapter of which was SBANE, where we met for our seminars in leadership and power. He later chaired the larger organization, a role that took him to Washington to advance the cause of small business. At various points, he was president of the Research Institute for Small and Emerging Businesses, chair of the Small Business

Foundation of America, and served a term on the board of the U.S. Chamber of Commerce.

At the same time, he began actively promoting educational reform in Massachusetts. The oldest of nine children and the father of five, he was committed to quality public education for the sake of both the children and the companies that would one day employ them. Jack's firm originally partnered with K-12 schools in Burlington, Massachusetts, the town where Pacer was then located. The success of that initiative led to his involvement in a state-sponsored effort to develop small business and education partnerships across the commonwealth, resulting over time in 6,000 such arrangements.

In 1988 Jack helped found the Massachusetts Business Alliance for Education (MBAE), which he also chaired. The MBAE became a major force in the push to reform public education in Massachusetts, producing a study, "Every Child a Winner," that served as the basis for the Education Reform Act of 1993. The Massachusetts Comprehensive Assessment System (MCAS), was a direct result of the act. The system, a series of tests, is designed to ensure competency as students move toward graduation from high school, so that they have a demonstrated mastery of basic skills on leaving school. There is an element in this concept of the discipline that Jack himself applied to his work, a focus on teaching and the responsibility for teaching that we have already explored in our discussion of *Crouching Tiger, Hidden Dragon*. The system monitors for competency during the apprenticeship years, with an eye to equal opportunity on graduation.

As one might suppose, the implication that the K-12 experience is at some level vocational has made MCAS controversial since its inception. Resistance arose in part from results: when the first round of tests was administered to eighth graders in 1998, fourteen percent failed the English portion, forty-two percent failed the math, and forty-one percent failed the science. The number of passes has come up substantially since then, thanks to a system of retests and other steps, but MCAS has highlighted the ills of the public education system, as it was designed to do, and made concrete the specter of an unprepared, unemployable work force. From the beginning, too, educators and other interested parties have maintained that the system forces teachers to teach "to the test," thereby limiting both their initiative and the breadth of the curriculum that they might otherwise be tempted to offer. A liberal arts response to a mechanistic template, this criticism offers instead a progressive focus on each child developing at his or her own pace. Where the business community sees a need for educated workers, the liberal critics see a need for educated citizens.

Jack himself recognized the potential for harm in the system. Having pushed for rigor and accountability, Jack and the MBAE argued in a follow-up proposal in 1999 that a graduated set of diplomas might be in order. In the end, Jack favored a gradualist approach even as he persisted in believing that something had to be done to ensure student preparedness. Lottor commented: "On the surface, Jack was not a bleeding heart kind of guy. He believed in business. But he understood there were also other values." That view informed his support and active promotion of the literature seminars at SBANE. He was outspoken about the value of the liberal arts in a professional setting, but he clearly felt the need for a solid foundation on which to build those later, more complex skills. This, too, is a form of mastery, an approach to social development that borrows much from Jack's own educational and military background.

Jack died in 2001, so he didn't see the much more positive numbers being reported by MCAS as the first class reached

graduation. Still, his influence is still felt and routinely acknowledged in the education and small business arenas. The Massachusetts Board of Education dedicated its 2000 Annual Report
(released in March 2001) to Jack's memory, citing him as "the
father of educational reform in Massachusetts." In September
2003 the U.S. Small Business Administration awarded Thomas
Menino, the mayor of Boston, the John "Jack" Rennie Award for
outstanding leadership. In his acceptance speech, Mayor Menino
recognized Jack's devotion to the cause of small businesses, both
locally and at a national level. Jack's contribution is the stuff of
which leaders are made and by which they are measured.

One could argue that Jack's devotion to the cause of small
business and education was essentially self-seeking, that he was
advancing his interests on a slightly higher and more abstract
plane than most individuals would be inclined to do. What was
good for small business generally was good for Pacer, and for the
larger companies that it became through merger and acquisition.
Educational reform would also serve Jack's business interests, as
well as his own kids coming up through the grades. In this view,
his activism was only a particularly developed form of enlightened self-interest. He was only a better educated, somewhat
more worldly version of Colm Derrane.

It is very hard to sustain this argument, though, in the face of
the depth and breadth of Jack's involvement in the community.
The invitation to a testimonial dinner in his honor in 1995 listed
two dozen roles he had played or was then filling with various
organizations and initiatives. It is hard to imagine any one individual so involved, so committed, primarily for his own narrow
benefit. This is especially true as Jack had already assured his own
material success, and must have recognized that he would not directly benefit from the bigger, long-range endeavors in which he

was engaged. Jack's career speaks to an entirely different concept of what it means to do business, to be an entrepreneur, from what we see in Colm and "Two Lovely Beasts." His success did not involve breaking with the community, though he built his business on technical breakthroughs. He maintained continuity around those innovations, and pursued social change designed to enhance rather than simply to replace structures he had previously known.

In Colm's support, one could argue that Jack was a part of the system from the very beginning, in a way that Colm was not. With a degree from the Naval Academy, years of military service, and an initial job at Raytheon, Jack was well positioned to launch Pacer on the trajectory that it then followed. He had the know-how, he had the connections, he had the good will of his target clientele; he didn't need to put anything behind him. Colm, by contrast, was working in what felt to him like the void, coming from nothing to success. At first glance, his story appears closer to that staple of American mythology, Horatio Alger's fictions for boys about boys rising from rags to riches. Colm has no support network, not even his family or the village in any consistent way. So we can forgive him, the argument runs, a few errors in judgment; he was facing almost insuperable odds. The support for him among the professionally like-minded entrepreneurs of the SBANE seminar suggests the plausibility of this view.

Other factors contribute to this assessment of Colm. The pained surprise that many audiences have felt on discovering the underlying structure to Colm's career tells us a great deal about the power of story to shape, but also thereby to limit, our perception of our own personal and professional practice. For reasons of limited resources, and out of sheer efficiency, we like to compartmentalize our experience: here lies the personal, here the professional. Do the two have anything in common, either in practice or at the level of values? Especially if the two occupy different physical spaces, and involve different faces and emotional cross-currents, it makes sense to keep them separate: here is how I live, here is how and where I work. These are my separate codes for dealing with my separate worlds.

We also love success, even when it seems a little flawed. As I indicated earlier, readers who possess "the whole story" display an eagerness equal to Colm's own in reading his ultimate triumph back into his initial behavior. Once we see him successful, we want to believe that his means did justify the end, or that they can be dismissed as insignificant, or reinterpreted in light of the results. He had to beat his wife, because she wouldn't have let him succeed; or, he was a poor communicator, and he did the only thing that occurred to him would be effective—and in any case, his wife saw the light as a result. He had to starve his kids, because otherwise they wouldn't have had "bacon for breakfast" (p. 29) later in life; children have no concept of delayed gratification, and he played his role as a good father by imposing the concept and its practice on them.

Finally, we believe in our need for leaders, and accept the possibility that leaders may in turn need a little more latitude in their behavior, in their ethical practice. Most of us believe that leadership requires the sort of sacrifice from followers and self-sacrifice from leaders that Colm's story records. I have taught "Two Lovely Beasts" in China, where the story's portrayal of the transition from a collectivist to a capitalist mode of economic activity directly reflects conditions on the ground. The Chinese students appreciate the historic, macroeconomic parallels, but they also place historic value on the leadership Colm displays in managing his family. It is easier to see Colm as a leader when he puts his kids on a starvation diet if you learned in grammar school about the conditions during Mao's Long March of 1934–35: thousands of Mao's supporters died during that extended military maneuver, but 15 years later Communist forces triumphed over the Kuomintang and liberated China. Were the deaths worth it? Even President Kennedy's "Ask not what your country can do for you; ask what you can do for your country"—apparently so much less lethal—speaks to the same leaderly use of sacrifice, and self-sacrifice, to assert the right to rule.

The constraint of story lies in our inclination to make the narrative build, and to read the result back into the logic that leads us to it. Colm succeeds through hard work and luck, elements we recognize and appreciate. Purifying the story—crafting it—requires eliding the poor communication, the self-absorption, the indifference to the immediate community, in both the initial phase of Colm's enterprise and later, when the villagers make him their leader and he then abandons them for the town. In short, we make the best of Colm, because he makes the system work, indeed becomes the system.

And yet, there is that nagging sense that he might have done things differently. The wife beating keeps surfacing for women participants, sometimes to the point that they categorically deny Colm any legitimacy as a person or a businessman—there are some things you simply have no right to do. My Chinese students believe that, whatever the promise of global capitalism, the collectivist spirit had and still has much to recommend it. At the very least, the natural and economic conditions described at the beginning of the story make collectivism a viable solution until further economic and spiritual development occurs. And even Colm's most ardent supporters generally concede that, at the very least, he ought to offer a role model to those he leaves behind, or that, in line with current models of corporate philanthropy, he might reinvest some of his profits in the community. Participants occasionally joke about a Colm Derrane Foundation.

The ethical challenge in "Two Lovely Beasts" lies in deciding how much we can afford to overlook as we assert the value of the success Colm achieves. We are always to some extent prisoners of our conclusions or endings: Kate Higgins went to an asylum, so Kate Higgins couldn't have come up with Colm's business strategy; Colm made a go of his enterprise, so he must have thought up the business strategy of buying Kate's calf and raising two lovely beasts. In real life, though, the conclusion may be infinitely deferred. Jack Rennie clearly saw a future for the Commonwealth and the nation that exceeded his own life span, and he acted to achieve it. There is no indication that his pursuit of better opportunities for the children of Massachusetts or the small-business owners of America cost him his own business success; quite the contrary. At the same time, that pursuit was by definition one he could not complete on his own: his vision had to involve colleagues, friends, legislators—in short, the whole of the society in which his business took its place.

The objections, hesitations, amendments to Colm's career have one thing in common: they all focus on "the other," those people who are not Colm himself. Colm makes no bones, after his initial resistance to Kate's blandishments, about taking care of number one, with an extension of concern to his family—as long as they do exactly what he tells them. The "making rules" piece of this entrepreneurial step toward ethical business practice inescapably involves other people, though. The story that we build here is at some fundamental level the story of the collectivity; without it, there really is no future for the vision that the entrepreneur articulates, or the rules that underpin it.

Does this limit the autonomy entrepreneurs love? It certainly does, if autonomy means doing whatever you want, whenever you want to do it. For most entrepreneurs, though, the enterprise is a very specific undertaking: their firms provide a particular product, or a particular service, or a range of products and services for a particular clientele. You may elaborate on that line, or start a new business for a new product or service, but the specificity never disappears. Jack Rennie's enterprise was no different, but his vision for the role of the businessperson went well beyond the walls of Pacer. His was and still is an unusually broad and generous interpretation of what it means to run a business. Not everyone has his energy; not everyone has the opportunities from which he was working. But the future of any business enterprise is conditioned by the circumstances that Jack sought to address. For him and for all of us, breaking and making the rules means coming up with the stories that capture both the concreteness of the here and now and an open-ended faith in the future. For those who do so, absorbing the costs evolves into reaping the benefits.

CHAPTER 5

Tell Good Stories
Living and Leading the Revolution

A Day at the Temple

"The U.S. is our big enemy; Japan is our forever enemy."

It is December 2001. I am standing with two of my Chinese International MBA students in the courtyard of Beijing's largest Buddhist temple, Yonghe Gong—the Palace of Peace and Harmony. Our breath frosts in the air, mingling with the smoke from joss sticks that worshipers have placed in the bowls in front of the largest Buddha in the temple. It is bitterly cold, hardly the weather for sight-seeing; but having come halfway around the world to teach, I can't go home having spent my entire visit in the classroom or my appropriately named luxury hotel, the Shangri-La.

My companions are part of the International MBA program at Tsinghua University, the MIT of the People's Republic. Yichao—for me, "Richard"—is the quintessential student intellectual, widely read and well-spoken. In his late twenties, he is already going bald; steel wire-rims adorn a face that I know from scrolls of great antiquity. Yanling, or "Serena," has stuck in my memory from a visit the previous spring, first because "Serena" bears no evident relation to her real, Chinese name, but also because she seemed seven months earlier to embody the clean, eager virtues of a good child of the revolution. She was focused then, purposeful, not very worldly, not terribly aware of her own impulses, yet courteous and very cheery. In her own way, she lived up to the serenity of her adopted name.

I am surprised to see so many visitors at the temple, given more than fifty years of Communist rule in the People's Republic. Richard and Serena assure me that many of the worshipers at the temple are not Buddhists, but are simply hedging their spiritual bets. Buddhism is nice, Serena comments, in that it allows such flexibility. This is a veiled allusion to our discussion over lunch, when another of their classmates, Willa, said with a smile that nevertheless bordered on a challenge, "Christianity is a missionary religion. They want always to make converts." It takes no prompting for me to remember the American missionary tradition in China, especially since I have on occasion taught stories by Pearl Buck, the daughter of American missionaries who was born and grew up in China, and wrote at length and to great acclaim about her birthplace. Yes, this assertion feels true.

Willa didn't stop there, though, adding that U.S. policy—the U.S. was by then already in Afghanistan—resembled Christianity in its aggressiveness. China, by contrast, was "not aggressive. Asians are patient: we will wait, not force." The truth is, she says, that the Chinese are surrounded by enemies: the Indians to the south and west, along with Indo-Pakistani tensions and first the Taliban and now the U.S. beyond; the Russians to the west and north; Korea, Japan, and Taiwan to the east. The world is fraught with danger, and the Chinese have no one to turn to in case of need. They are on their own. I have heard this assessment of

China's place in the world from others, but only now is it beginning to sound like a theme.

During the nonaggression argument about Chinese national character at lunch, I had refrained from bringing up the Cultural Revolution of the 1960s and 1970s. In fact, one hardly meets a soul in the People's Republic who doesn't regard those years as at best a mistake on Chairman Mao's part, and at worst a catastrophe for the country. The students at lunch were equally blunt about other aspects of their culture, asserting that Chinese firms are plagued by corruption and that the country would know no relief until the government tightened accounting practices. Since we are already well into the Enron scandal in the U.S., I don't feel in a position to comment either way.

I have always thought of China as a self-confident giant with a long history and venerable culture, iron-willed leaders, and a huge percentage of the world's population—a giant now very efficiently getting to its feet in the global economy. China is growing faster than any other part of the world. True, the Western powers flexed their muscle in China during the nineteenth century, but today? Is this notion of vulnerability perhaps the work of a very persuasive public disinformation effort by the government, the lingering aftermath of the Cold War? Or have I missed something in my reliance on film, fable, and a hasty preparation for these trips?

Serena, however, is engaged in a fully revisionist version of our lunch conversation. I begin to recognize what a Sinologist I know has described as "the new muscular nationalism"—I just didn't expect to encounter it in Serena. "Chinese are aggressive inside," she says, "not outside." And then, without prompting, she adds, "I can trust Chinese. Not all of them are dishonest." This feels like at best a modest gain over the earlier consensus about rampant corruption. So how does one know whom to trust and whom not? And what are the rules governing such trust? She begins to answer, but the conversation bogs down as we try to sort through the difference between laws, on the one hand, and on the other, the ethical standards that govern the gray market and legislate daily interactions of all kinds.

We have by now wandered out the main gate to the temple, and are strolling down a neighboring street in the direction of Beijing's Confucius Temple, Yanhuang Art Museum. The municipality has preserved the street as an example of the old city architecture. Lined with trees, it forms an axis between two rows of the one-story, gray-brick and tile-roofed houses that once were standard urban construction in China. From the air, the blocks look like mazes, but inside they have the feel of a carefully protected space.

I know the look, because at Tsinghua University the president's office has just been installed in a similar, restored complex. There, the austerity of the gray stone is relieved by Chinese-red trim and other colors, and the windows allow one to see through the buildings, never more than one room deep, to trees planted in courtyards on the far side, as though there were no distinction between inside and outside. The regularity of the construction, the austerity of the base color range, the balance of sight lines around buildings and plantings, are a world away from the giant figures, the flags, the ritual, and the bright yellows, reds, and greens of the Buddhist temple. The harmony is one I had always associated with Japan; yet this, too, is China.

"We are a Confucian culture," Richard says as we step over the high threshold into the museum grounds. "Not Communist?" I respond. Pointless to speculate what Confucian Communism might look like, even with the "Chinese features" that one keeps hearing cited in these discussions of modern ideology; but the evidence for the straight Confucian link is scant, too. As we walk into the first courtyard of the museum, I realize we are the only visitors. Statues of the sage litter the first courtyard, and a courtyard or two further along a temple-like structure contains more figures, watched over by women in traditional dress behind a counter laden with brochures. The space feels neglected, as though it were more a repository than a living memorial to the Master.

The emptiness only emphasizes the cold that I felt earlier, before the Buddha. By now, Richard has recognized my discomfort, or perhaps he, too, without hat and gloves, is finally feeling the cold. As an example of China's continuing Confucian character, he notes that the sixty members of Tsinghua's Chinese Traditional Culture Club are reading Confucius' *Analects* together, and Lao Tze, too. Professors come occasionally to give guest lectures. In the wake of the Cultural Revolution, Confucius is gradually being rehabilitated, but slowly, in fits and starts. It hasn't generated much attendance at the Yanhuang Art Museum.

Do modern Chinese feel they can practice the Confucian virtues? I ask. Richard hesitates, but Serena steps in again. Her outspokenness makes me feel I must have missed something on our first encounter, seven months earlier, or that she has had a conversion experience—to what, I can't say. She has shagged her long, straight black hair, applied makeup, and raised her speaking voice: "Confucius is outdated," she says, "but he is in our hearts. What he wants—rule by moral force—is instrumentally out of date."

Is rule by moral force ever out of date? And if it were, on what basis does she propose to rule? Instead I ask, "So how do Chinese businesspeople trust one another?" The answer, I know, is not likely to be Confucian virtue, as Confucius himself had little use for trade or commerce. He was, like Thomas Jefferson long after him, committed to agriculture as a way of keeping men honest.

But then, what else? Obviously, someone has articulated a code that allows people, in the midst of apparently pervasive corruption, to get along and make business happen.

Richard has fallen conspicuously silent. Is Serena, with her slightly flawed English, expressing a wish rather than an actuality when she says she trusts her fellows? To what values does she adhere, and how does Richard hope to yoke two apparently irreconcilable philosophical positions: an international MBA program that talks, as most MBA programs do, to the bottom line, and a traditional culture club, one of whose idols is a sage who believes in the "gentleman"? I have seen people like him in American MBA programs, students who want the methods of a straight business degree, but feel most at home working in nonprofits or the social sector broadly defined. They have only gradually begun to feel accepted and acceptable in the business school environment, as we expand the range of areas in which managerial skills are appropriate. Social enterprise beckons to them, suggesting that they might meld the bottom line with new visions of ethical practice for themselves and the rest of us.

Still, it's difficult. Here in China, with a culture that dates back millennia, perhaps thinking about the intersection of culture and market-oriented business skills is less of a stretch. I would certainly like to think so, capitalizing on the fact that formal business education is a relatively new endeavor in China. Sometimes, late entry means competitive advantage. But if China is a Confucian culture, where are all of the Master's adherents? Why are we the only ones in this courtyard, surrounded by statues of him under a cold Beijing sky, when the temple down the block was so busy? Is "rule by moral force," as Serena put it, less appealing than the color and ceremony of other, more materially ordered social systems? What about ethics, my sole reason for being in Beijing?

Revolution, or Change Management?

This is, I decide, a riddle for which I have some obligation to provide an answer—if not for Serena and Richard, then for myself
and, conceivably, for their successors in their own and the other
MIT-China programs. I am puzzled by the implications for an
ethical worldview of what they and their classmates have said
about business in China. I am equally puzzled, after putting aside
what feels like their wounded anti-Americanism—"Why must
you convert us?"—by Serena's comment on the Japanese. Not
that I blame her. I have heard the same from other Chinese of her
generation, none of whom experienced World War II and the
Rape of Nanjing—the whole history of Japan in China during the
1930s and 1940s. At the very least, the Chinese wanted an apol-
ogy—shades of the U.S. spy plane interned on Hainan Island in
the spring of that year—and they didn't get it.

And yet, in part in the name of reconciliation, the previous
April I assigned the students the Masayuki Suo film *Shall We
Dance?* (1997). Set in today's Japan, the film had worked well for
me on a number of occasions with Western audiences. It was
remade in an American version starring Richard Gere, Susan
Sarandon, and Jennifer Lopez in 2004. I had concerns about taking the Japanese original to China, but hoped the film's message
and appeal would overcome long-standing cultural antipathies.

Happily, I was right. The film recounts a moment in the life of a
Japanese middle manager, who dutifully rides the train to and from
his job in the city until the day he sees a beautiful woman standing
in the window of a ballroom dance studio overlooking the train
tracks. Suddenly, he is struggling to master dance steps every week
with people who, in his office world, would only qualify as losers in
the race of life. All six Chinese IMBA classes loved the film: in

Guangzhou, groups of students stood up in order to be able to see the screen better when I showed a clip. They laughed uproariously at all the right moments and all the appropriate characters, and quickly produced the points I hoped to elicit from them as we discussed the film, and that Western audiences had also identified.

So, what made the story work? In the pages that follow, we will look at *Shall We Dance?* as a microcosm of the process by which stories bridge social divides and make it possible for us to talk across cultures, East and West, North and South, ancient and modern, business and nonbusiness. We take our stories for granted, but we might equally take for granted the fact that the best ones are the ones that we all share, no matter how culturally and temporally specific they seem to be. Finding those stories is crucial to ethical practice because they guarantee a constant freshness in the way we see the world.

We will also look at *Shall We Dance?* as an exploration of what could become a sea change in the relation of business to society at large. Despite the global rhetoric around ideologies and political positions that permeated my visit with the Tsinghua students, and despite the fact that, as they correctly observed, ideology colors much supposedly analytic rhetoric about the triumph of Western-style business, this is neither the permanent revolution advocated by Marx, Engels, and Trotsky, nor the episodic one implied by our assertion of our "unalienable Rights." Rather, it is a steady, quiet, truly cosmopolitan revolution, composed of the decisions we make daily around the globe to achieve our own and others' well-being, and that works with the bottom line as a significant component of the whole. We intuitively recognize these small-scale changes when we hear of or see them, and we know them for their large-scale social ramifications. Sometimes, as in *Shall We Dance?*, we even spot the people who can catalyze change for whole communities—ethical leaders for communities that have lost, or never been granted, "moral force." The protagonist of *Shall We Dance?* is one such figure, but one among several of equal talent or aspiration: as a group, they offer a different model of leadership, one perhaps better suited for our cross-culturally knowing and politically attuned times.

Mr. Sugiyama Learns to Dance

Shall We Dance? tells the story of Shohei Sugiyama, a dutiful, somewhat reserved white-collar worker who appears ready to abandon his sense of decorum and his society's norms in pursuit of the woman he has glimpsed on his evening commute home from work. She turns out to be an instructor at the dance studio: Mai-*san* has performed on the pro circuit, but has been grounded by her father, the owner of the studio, for initially unspecified reasons. Tormented by the recurrent sight of her standing in the studio window gazing at a horizon he can only imagine, one night Sugiyama finally bolts from the train and enters the studio, on the pretext of wanting ballroom dance lessons.

The result is not, as one might suppose, a Hollywood romance just waiting to happen. Sugiyama balks at the price of private lessons with Mai, and in disappointment joins a group class under the direction of Tamako-*sensei*, who is the older, ranking member of the teaching staff in the studio. She is also the studio's manager. With Sugiyama in the class are two other men, one there at his wife's behest, the other a diabetic whose doctor has prescribed dance for fitness. None of the men has any apparent natural talent, and so become the willing recipients of Tamako's patient instruction.

The cast of characters at the studio also includes Toyoko-*san*, instructor and competitor on the amateur dance circuit, who works a day job cleaning houses. For my Chinese students, she was the "fat woman," and the source of much of their amusement, as she is for my Western students—some humor translates easily. There are also the various customers, mostly male, who come for lessons. Toyoko makes clear to Sugiyama that many of them have come to the studio for the same reason as he, with no success at getting to know Mai. And then, shortly after Sugiyama begins his lessons, a colleague from work appears. Like the house-cleaning Toyoko, Aoki-*san* is an amateur dance circuit competitor. His appearance at the dance studio in a wig and outfit cloned from a well-known Latin dancer causes both him and Sugiyama considerable embarrassment.

In fact, embarrassment colors much of the interaction in the studio during the early phases of this story. With the exception of the older woman teacher, Tamako, everyone in *Shall We Dance?* would rather see their lives differently than they appear: Mai would much rather be competing at Blackpool, the English hub of the ballroom dance world; Toyoko and Aoki long to be successful performers on the amateur circuit and free of day jobs that poison their lives; and Sugiyama wants desperately to be with Mai, when he isn't ducking his head to avoid being seen as he climbs the stairs to the studio.

Meanwhile, back at home, Sugiyama's wife begins to suspect that her husband is having an affair. She tells their teenaged daughter that she has always wanted to see him have more fun. He has always seemed, she says, so serious. He doesn't even want her to get up in the morning to prepare his breakfast, and we know from home scenes that they sleep in separate beds. Now, she hires a detective to find out why he comes home late on certain nights, where he goes for parts of the weekend, why she smells perfume on his shirts when she does the laundry, and why he seems more energetic and upbeat than he once did. In short, while Sugiyama doggedly follows Tamako-*sensei's* "quick-quick, slow-slow" lead at the studio, his family life, never intimate, moves toward confrontation and even further embarrassment.

Even Salarymen Get the Blues

"What is wrong with Sugiyama-*san?*" I ask the obvious lead question, and the answers come quickly, and in numbers. That he has a boring life is clear: those who know something about Japanese culture will identify him as a *salaryman*, a popular term for the Japanese business cadre that constitutes the managerial mainstream—solid workers with moderate expectations for their career future, good consumers who keep the economy turning. The train on which Sugiyama rides every morning and evening is full of men just like him, in gray and dark blue business suits, briefcases in hand.

Moreover, he himself comments late in the film that he has had certain goals:

> "I married at age 28. Had a child by 30. At 40, I bought the home I longed for. I've worked so hard for these things. I thought it was a happy life, but after I bought the house—something changed. It's no reflection on my wife or on my love for my daughter. But something was different. I need to work to pay the mortgage. I accepted that— but something was still missing."

With both Asian and Western audiences, this confession usually elicits relatively high-flying commentary on the importance of goals in a person's life and new horizons. Sugiyama has

reached the goals he set himself. Now what? Others comment
that the goals he achieved were not his, but society's. Small wonder, then, that he is unhappy to have reached them—he should
have set his own. Depending on the age of the audience, or its inclination to do the arithmetic, someone will then suggest that
Sugiyama is suffering from a midlife crisis. It seems that men
everywhere suffer midlife crises, and there is a cross-cultural
consensus that women suffer them, too, though earlier and because the children are grown, not because of work.

From that realization, it is a short leap to the question: Why is
Sugiyama interested in Mai? Any good-sized seminar will have
half a dozen answers in short order. They start with the view, almost invariably voiced—roguishly—by men in the group, that
Sugiyama wants an affair: Mai is a beauty, a willowy, graceful
young woman with presence and a sense of style. Sugiyama's
wife doesn't even see him out the door in the morning. Who
wouldn't want an affair with Mai?

But then, alternative explanations surface. Sugiyama is unhappy with his life. When he looks at Mai, he sees someone else
who is unhappy with life. He feels a common bond with her, and
wants to get to know her, not necessarily to have an affair. A variant on this explanation has it that he wants novelty. Mai, with the
dance studio behind her, represents that novelty. Even if
Sugiyama isn't specifically chasing after Mai, he is doing what
many conformist men in crisis do at this stage: they seek to dis-
tract themselves—a new hobby, golf, a new woman.

Americans sometimes suggest that men at this stage want
control, want to be their own boss. A midlife crisis can trigger the
inclination to leave a secure job and start a business. Sugiyama
doesn't have that option, though, at least to those who profess
knowledge of Japanese culture, and those who have a strong sense

of this particular man's character. In *Shall We Dance?*, it is hard to tell whether Sugiyama is depressed because he has achieved his goals, discovered that they were hollow all along, realized that they didn't take him as far as he hoped, or simply wants a new set. One senses that he has reached his potential in his current job. He isn't likely to move up in the ranks, and he won't leave, because his company holds the mortgage on his house and he has job security. He really is stuck, in and out of the workplace.

As the midlife crisis argument fills out, the plot of *Shall We Dance?* takes on a certain grim predictability, and its implications for an audience who might identify with Sugiyama's suited character are discouraging at best.

Not All Professionals Wear Suits

And yet, escape beckons exactly where Sugiyama has located it, just not in the form he anticipates. Whether or not you buy the "misery loves company" argument for Sugiyama's interest in Mai, the question arises at this point: Who is Mai? Is she really unhappy, and if so, why?

Comments that she and others make at various points in the film suggest that she has had a significant career in dance. She was a semifinalist at Blackpool, before an accident removed her from the competition. She knows all the players on the Japanese scene well enough to meet with a top male dancer to explore a partnership. She is proud of her place in the pantheon of ballroom dancers, and dismissive of those who don't excel as she has done. She will not dance in a room full of "lounge lizards and show girls," the amateurs before her who dance simply because they enjoy it. She also has a highly developed sense of professional standards: when Sugiyama intercepts her on the street one night after work, she declines his invitation to dinner on the grounds that she doesn't meet privately with her students.

That refusal is the key to understanding her, or at least to understanding her view of herself. She sees herself as a real professional: she lives for and by dance. She has great expertise (despite her competitive failure, she is very good at what she does), she knows her peers, and she has a keen sense of standards. And yet, few viewers of *Shall We Dance?* see past Sugiyama to Mai as she sees herself: a model of professional behavior. We have a pretty fixed notion of the professions, more often than not tied to a uniform: gray suit, white coat, judge's robes, and so on. And yet, Mai believes she stands in their company.

Once presented as such, Mai's self-identification as a professional generates one further explanation for Sugiyama's interest in her, one usually advanced by the women in the group. He is, they say, drawn to her by the longing he sees in her when she stands at the window. By the time the entire story of the film is told, it isn't hard to imagine that she is looking out the window toward Blackpool, to a place and a moment when she was at the peak of her practice. Late in the film, she tells Sugiyama that she and her partner fell at Blackpool, and that she now realizes she fell because she was dancing for herself rather than with her partner. Like Sugiyama, Mai has not lived up to her potential: her accident is, in fact, the result of her failure to live up to her own professional ideal. She does not dance for and with others; in professional terms, she fails to see that she must serve.

As a result of her failure, Mai's father bans her from the competitive circuit, returning her to the beginning of her art/business in the studio. There, she learns to serve her students, but grudgingly, as Sugiyama discovers; and yet, for all her failing in this regard, her aspirations and achievement turn Sugiyama's pursuit of her into a mutual learning experience, one that redounds to the credit of both. It offers the beginning of a counterargument to the thesis of a routine midlife crisis for him. In this view, he is not looking for an easy conquest; after all, at the beginning of the film we first meet him after work, sober, with a drunken and mildly aggressive female colleague; and at the studio, Toyoko is obviously enchanted by him—the man has options. Recognizing the meeting of Mai and Sugiyama as a meeting of two professionals with similar aspirations in different arenas casts Mai as Sugiyama's role model rather than a catch, someone who has been to a place he himself would like to reach. She in turn longs to dwell in an excellence and achievement that seems to have eluded her grasp until he arrives. Each reaches with and through the other for something better.

A Lesson in Team-Building and Distributed Leadership

A good bit of *Shall We Dance?* needs to play itself out before Mai and Sugiyama's shared aspirations become evident to most of us. At the outset, in a narrowly organizational view, it becomes clear that Mai and Sugiyama both suffer from motivational problems. Certainly Tamako, the manager of the studio, sees them that way, and responds as a good manager would. Students consistently recognize the older woman as the benevolent maestro of the studio, working the group in order to help the individual members discover themselves and their potential, and to create a new community. Her managerial style goes well beyond hand-holding: in the end, she manufactures a situation that changes this film from a meditation on midlife crisis, professional failure, and social exclusion to a powerful lesson in team-building, distributed leadership, and successful social dynamics.

Unlike Mai, who admits she danced for herself only at Blackpool, Tamako places her employees' and customers' needs at the forefront of her efforts. Like any business, the studio has a bottom line, and one has the sense that Tamako needs to address it. Yet her vision encompasses a wide range of factors in calculating the yield she wants from her operation. As she carefully brokers relations among the various characters, she reveals a very sure sense of each person's foibles, and the organizational means of tilting each in favor of his or her strengths. When she invites the various participants in the life of the studio to enter the Eastern Japan Amateur Dance competition, she finds a project that will bring them all together as a team.

The stages by which she does so are subtle and many, and become visible only over time. Like Toyoko, Tamako quickly assesses Sugiyama's interest in Mai, apologizes for being less attractive than her younger subordinate, and then proceeds to teach him the steps he needs at least to be able to dance with Mai. She also recognizes Toyoko's interest in Sugiyama, and puts the two of them together as the core team. But then, it becomes apparent that Aoki, on the skids because of a failed partnership with a younger woman, would serve better as Toyoko's partner for the Latin portion of the competition, and that, in turn, means that Mai needs to tutor Sugiyama. After all of these criss-crossing arrangements, Tamako has stitched together the team that will go to the competition.

The scene that marks the culmination of her planning occurs about two thirds of the way through the film, and unfolds over five or six minutes to the tune of The Drifters' 1960 hit song "Save the Last Dance for Me." It builds around strategy sessions, largely led by Mai, involving that icon of corporate planning—the whiteboard. Together, the studio members work through their dance numbers, crafting moves to help them draw and hold the judges' attention; they work on their skills together, in varying constellations, and they invest time and energy well beyond the routine dance lessons in which we have previously seen them engage.

I said earlier that the characters in the studio labor under a persistent feeling of embarrassment, at least at the outset. The strategy planning scene stands out for the degree to which that atmosphere has vanished: everyone now seems consistently happy, with the happiness of people engaged in what they regard as a meaningful communal project. Each contributes what he or she does best: Mai has the technical expertise; Aoki and Toyoko have the passion; Sugiyama has the commitment, despite inexperience; and Tamako contributes managerial or organizational know-how, together with an ability to size up her human material and the needs it engenders. Each person in the studio leads from his or her strength, and this diffused but coordinated responsibility results in a textbook case of successful group dynamics.

Effective business applications emerge from this scene, once one gets past the clowning, the music, and the culturally marginal setting. The people skills Tamako subtly deploys here are skills that matter in any organization, and the deep personal satisfaction that previously unhappy, unmotivated, unfocused people derive from their collaboration is—or should be—any organization's persistent goal. It doesn't matter that the lessons are learned on the dance floor; the motivational techniques are the same, and so are the rewards. It only takes imagination to make connections across the disciplines, which is in itself an important managerial skill.

Ethics Matters, Too

The human resources message of *Shall We Dance?* should by now be clear. But the film doesn't stop there: as our characters craft the world of the dance studio, professional ethics also comes very visibly into play.

I have already referred to the point at which Mai refuses Sugiyama's dinner invitation, citing her relation to him as teacher to student. Although viewers gloss that scene as an example of her haughtiness, it can also be interpreted as a statement of ethical practice; Mai herself remembers regretfully, in the continuing euphoria of preparations for the competition, that she was very rude to Sugiyama at that point. Yet she also offers him the story of how she became involved in dance: when she first went to Blackpool with her parents at the age of five, everyone admired one competing couple. They were disqualified when another team ran into them, and the male partner ended up in the hospital; yet their failure became the source of Mai's professional aspirations. She comments to Sugiyama, "My parents were very impressed. I asked why. Father explained that, to the end, he tried to protect his partner. . . . Since that first day in Blackpool, dance has become my entire world."

When confronted with this quiet but all-encompassing moment, viewers take two broadly opposed views. Those who find Mai cold and difficult read the moment as a psychological clue to her style: she doesn't trust other people, and doesn't trust her partner, which is why, years later, she herself fails at Blackpool. What she sees as a child exemplifies the importance of trust in her life, the need for the perfect partner; but the emphasis on perfection, of course, means that she is fated for disappointment.

The other perspective detects in Mai a very high set of standards, developed in direct response to her parents' approval of the male partner's behavior in a crisis. This view brings out the coincidence, in Mai, of personal and professional views: her deep personal response to her parents and her belief in the importance of trust overlap with a professional assessment of what one can and must expect of a good dancer. In her story, Mai quickly conveys the glamour of the scene at Blackpool, one that the film itself amply documents. Yet her story is clear: she commits to dance not because of the bright lights and pretty dresses, but because of a moment that expresses the essence of professional commitment. The male partner at Blackpool protected his partner from harm, even though he caused himself suffering in the process. In this moment of self-sacrifice and service, Mai finds a motive for her own profession.

Mai's reminiscence about Blackpool and her profession of faith in dance trigger a similar life narrative and profession of faith from Sugiyama, in which we learn his history—"I married at age 28. Had a child at 30. At 40, I bought the home I longed for"—and his sense that he has missed something very important along the way to fulfilling these goals. He is brave enough to admit to his fascination with Mai, and to recognize that his motives were hardly pure. But he also reveals that her rebuffing him over dinner set him straight and, by his own admission, taught him to love dance:

> "I really felt like giving up. But if I had, I would have been everything you accused me of. Of course, it's true that affection for you was what brought me to the class. But to be confronted with it," he pauses, smiles self-deprecatingly, "was a shock. I thought, 'she didn't have to be like that.' I wanted to prove to you that it wasn't because of you.

I'd said I was here to dance. But—" and here he hesitates until she prompts him to go on, *"no sooner did I decide to continue, than I really began to like it."*

Sugiyama can now admit to his inappropriate ambitions because he hasn't lost her. For those who see him looking to fulfill his ambition for excellence with and through her, he has in fact captured, or learned how to share, the spirit in her that matters most to him. The project of competing has brought them together over dance, and this exchange reveals that it was again an ethical moment that made the project possible. Both recognize the unpleasantness in Mai's refusal to dine with Sugiyama, because he is her student; but by his own admission, this moment of principled rigor made him a true convert to dance. In effect, Mai's sense of professional standards, her code of ethics, confronted Sugiyama with a painful moment of truth, a discouragement that could have ended his search for fulfillment through unconventional means. Yet it also supplied him with the means of a positive commitment, and he took it.

There is an intimacy to their exchange here that suggests many possibilities for the future. In a series of intricately though perhaps unconsciously calibrated steps, they have bared their souls to each other, and come out whole. Mai seems to have learned what she needed to free herself from the perceived dullness of the instructional routine at the dance studio, and one can imagine that Blackpool is once again a possibility for her, as indeed the ending of the film confirms. For Sugiyama, though, the challenge remains how to integrate his secret into his daily life. That, too, is a matter of ethics, but more broadly about character, for in the end, it is character that made Tamako choose him as the core male around whom to build her team for the competition.

Testing for Character

Sugiyama's detractors—and they are many—invariably come back to his treatment of his wife to prove that he is unethical and, at the end of the film, fundamentally unredeemed. A Japanese woman student of mine comments that, once he has been found out and embraces his wife near the end of the film, "he apologizes in exactly the way your ideal Japanese husband would. But it's just a cliché."

So, is it a cliché? The answer to that question hinges on another, equally complicated question: Why do the characters in the dance studio bother to include Sugiyama? Whatever his targeted interest in Mai, she doesn't reciprocate his attention—at least at the outset. From the beginning, we see any number of male dancers passing through the studio. Several of them become involved in the project to enter the competition, but none figures at the center of it. So, why Sugiyama?

One theory has it that, in the world of the studio, Sugiyama best represents the establishment. He wears the suit in this crowd; he has a good job at a reputable firm; he has, in fact, all the accoutrements of the Japanese establishment—he enumerates them himself. From the perspective of a group of marginalized characters in a marginal profession, including him means conferring a degree of respectability on their operation that they have no other means of obtaining. Some viewers have gone so far as to suggest that Mai stands in the window with the deliberate intent of luring someone like Sugiyama to the studio; she is a living advertisement for the place and its product, and Sugiyama falls for it.

And yet, for all his straitlaced behavior—indeed, because of it—Sugiyama winds up looking not quite like the stereotypical salaryman. The opening scene shows him on the town with two of his employees, the drunken female mentioned earlier, and a younger male, who is also drunk. The two of them are eager to do what custom sanctions in this case: to spend the night drinking among colleagues. But Sugiyama, who is sober, wants only to go home, and does so. Once home, he turns down his wife's offer to make him comfortable and goes to bed, having indicated that she need not attend him in the morning, either.

Is Sugiyama clinically depressed? Probably—his behavior at the outset suggests that in various ways. Is he stand-offish in the same way that Mai is? Perhaps—though he gives no indication of feeling as different from the rest of the world as she does. So, if he brings the same reserve to his interactions with others, for what reason does he do so?

Given Sugiyama's situation at the end of *Shall We Dance?* it seems safe to say that he has been reserved because he has not seen, or has not had the insight to see, opportunities for developing himself in society. He has done what he thinks he was expected to do, and done it well. Yet he himself knows, having done it, that his achievements aren't enough. In this self-awareness, Sugiyama departs from the salaryman stereotype: he has the clarity of vision to see that he hasn't looked hard enough previously, and when he starts looking, he sees Mai. But what is it that takes him there?

If Sugiyama takes forty years to find himself, the members of the dance studio see this unfulfilled potential in him from the start. Tamako in particular wishes to bring out his—to her—not-so-hidden qualities. Once she has made the necessary arrangements to put him in Mai's arms, the process begins in earnest. Early in the sequence that leads the studio into the amateur dance competition, the younger woman spends an entire scene trying to get Sugiyama to understand what it means to "lead." Needless to say, she is focused on having him fulfill his role as the male dancer in the couple, but behind that immediate, technical requirement lies a spiritual revision that she and the rest of the studio need him to undertake. And if he is a place-holder for salarymen as a class, behind the studio lies the whole of Japanese society, with substantially the same needs.

When Sugiyama's wife and daughter are tipped off by the detective and attend the dance competition, thereby revealing that they know his secret, they shock him into disqualifying himself and his team. He declares that night that he has stopped dancing, that it isn't right for him; his face suggests nostalgia but also relief as he says this. Yet both his wife and his daughter insist that he keep dancing. In a move that Asian audiences find mildly shocking, the daughter takes both parents by the hand one evening, in the midst of a fight between the two adults over her father's palpably renewed depression; she leads them out onto the lawn by their house, and insists that her father teach her mother how to dance.

At the beginning of the film, the narrator has enumerated a set of taboos that governs this and many of the other scenes in the film. Even Japanese married couples don't consider it appropriate to touch in public, we are told, so that Western-style ballroom dancing is suspect, not just because it's foreign, but because it involves public, physical contact; it is "beyond embarrassing." Nor is it appropriate for couples directly to express their love for each other. Japanese viewers say, as the Chinese said of Jen's behavior in *Crouching Tiger, Hidden Dragon* (see Chapter 3), that times are changing, and that the younger generation has a freedom that the older generation did not and still does not—a freedom born in large part from the pervasive influence of the Western media. In that sense, it is sociologically plausible that Sugiyama's daughter would take her parents literally in hand and make them move beyond their culturally determined reticence.

Yet again, one asks the question: Why bother? Why not allow family relations to return to their old status? The couple and their daughter seem to have found a way to coexist; it isn't terribly satisfying, but it works. And yet, it clearly doesn't work.

Two interpretations play out around the end of this film: the first, suggested by my Japanese student's comments above, insists that the family will return to its old habits; Sugiyama has had his fling, his wife appears to have forgiven him, and his routine is intact. The second says that, as indicated in scenes dating back to the competition itself, Sugiyama has discovered in himself unsuspected sources of strength for both his work and his family. After the competition, after he has quit dancing, he defends Aoki when their mutual colleagues mock the would-be Latin dancer, and he not only apologizes to his wife, he then follows her orders and goes to dance with Mai, one last time. His secret wish having been made public, he accepts a social, and specifically marital, framing of the wish as a condition of having it fulfilled. In effect, he submits to having his desire for renewal vetted by the society that had previously blocked the desire, and in so doing, he transmits the renewal through himself into the society as a whole.

Does Sugiyama cheat on his wife? In the literal sense, he doesn't, but as his wife suspects and he himself admits after the fact, he was "seriously involved." Does he then have the stuff of professional excellence, this bored, adulterously inclined middle manager? Can he rise to the role of leader that the team requires him to play?

As with all of the stories in this book, personal inclination will set our reading of the evidence. No amount of argument will convince some viewers that Sugiyama is a textbook case of someone who did the right thing for reasons that were at best mixed, or inarticulate and therefore poorly implemented. And yet, the case can be made; the film makes it, or tolerates our making it. Our salaryman knew he had done something wrong in doing all the right things society expected of him; he knew that something had to change, and he chose the first plausible opportunity that presented itself. The word *plausible* is key here, because Sugiyama himself decided what it means. If one accepts Mai's behavior as motivated by deep-seated ethical principles, then Sugiyama chose a solution to his problems that in fact led him to flawlessly correct professional behavior, serving him, his immediate community, and the larger society. The question is, how could he know to do that?

A Confucian in the Global Marketplace

Western notions of the self, and self-improvement, can go a long way toward explaining what Sugiyama accomplishes. In a way that Western individualism would applaud, Sugiyama wakes up from his socially induced moral slumber, realizes that he has been obediently doing what he was told all his life, and decides it's time to take control of his life. If one were inclined to be culturally imperialist about him and this film, one could argue that Western ballroom dancing itself has set him free, and certainly the film lends itself at least to the reading that it required the non-Japanese attitudes expressed in ballroom dancing to begin Sugiyama's redemption.

At the same time, my Chinese students' enthusiasm for this film and its lead characters suggests that it isn't ballroom dancing that sets Sugiyama free. Remember that this group also hated Jen, in *Crouching Tiger, Hidden Dragon*, for exhibiting what they deemed her Western-style selfishness, and specifically her Western-style romantic self-indulgence with the bandit Lo, aka Dark Cloud (see Chapter 3). It also feels at best improbable that this thoroughly Japanese man should suddenly succumb to Western influence, even in a country known for borrowing freely and productively from other cultures. At the outset, does Sugiyama have enough of what we would in the West call a "self" even to realize that he has stunted his? If one takes a universalist perspective—people are people, wherever they are, and they all have selves—it doesn't require much more argument to conclude that he does. Coupled with his midlife crisis, Sugiyama's search for meaning and purpose resembles behavior in his peers the world over.

Chinese and Japanese participants in discussions around ethical practice routinely assert that our self lies in our being human, in our humanity, but that humanity clearly brings with it the notion of reciprocity and social commitment. The concepts come straight from Confucius: humanity inheres in the Confucian gentleman, or *junzi*, the Master's ideal person. In fact, *The Analects* sets forth a series of standards for life at large very much like what we have covered in this chapter under the word *professional*: self-discipline, decorum, loyalty, and service appear at the top of the list. As in Confucius's view, moreover, so in the Anglo-Saxon world the professions, or a professional attitude, are means of acceding to the status of the gentleman. That is why earning power tops the list of a professional's characteristics for many of us; it is also why we lay so much emphasis on the gentleman-professional working beyond material concerns.

So, is Sugiyama the professional clinically depressed, or is he simply living out an inclination that my Chinese students repeatedly listed as a Confucian virtue—moderation? In *The Analects* (1.14), Confucius offers a gloss on the gentleman that suits Sugiyama equally well:

> *The Master said: "A gentleman eats without stuffing his belly; chooses a dwelling without demanding comfort; is diligent in his of-*

fice and prudent in his speech; seeks the company of the virtuous in order to straighten his own ways. Of such a man, one may truly say that he is fond of learning." [Leys, p. 5]

And what better way to explain the role Sugiyama acquires at the dance studio, in spite of his relative ineptitude at the quick step, than Analect 12.16?

The Master said: "A gentleman brings out the good that is in people, he does not bring out the bad. A vulgar man does the opposite." [Leys, p. 58]

The studio needs Sugiyama because he helps the others to be their best. He may not do so consciously; indeed, one needn't force a choice between a diagnosis of depression and adherence to Confucianism to explain Sugiyama. It isn't easy adhering to Confucian standards in a consumer society, and it seems fair to him to suppose that his behavior is a manifestation of powerful cross-currents in his culture.

Decorum or civility plays a major role in the articulation of Confucian society. The lingering view of Confucius in China today suggests that the Master approved, or has at least been used to approve, repressive social regimes. Yet the "gentleman" as defined by Confucius demonstrates the same ethical alertness that we seek in the West when we use such phrases as "Know thyself," "Dare to be true," and so on. In taking ballroom dance lessons, Sugiyama finds his way to a union of virtuous standards, East and West. He could have gone the other way, using alien culture to free himself from his own cultural constraints. He could have had a Hollywood-style romance with Mai, assuming she was willing. As we've seen, though, forces conspire to keep him honest. His team at the studio helps him to deliver on his promise because it is in fact their promise, too—the potential for humanity, in the best Confucian sense of the word.

One could argue that Mai provides the counterexample that proves Sugiyama's motivation. While she is sufficiently dutiful to accept her father's dictate that she leave the professional dance circuit, she is also sufficiently Western to resent doing so. The flashbacks of her dancing before her accident at Blackpool make her cultural heterogeneity clear. She is radiant, but radiantly Western, in garb and demeanor. She plays the competitive game to the hilt, the game of individual excellence. In the end, she learns from Sugiyama the lesson of her origins, in both technique and national/cultural disposition. As her father wishes, she comes back to her beginnings in both areas. In effect, she discovers her self, just as Sugiyama discovers his, but she finds that she can only perfect it within the collectivity, while he confronts the necessity of perfecting himself through it, in his own name.

Grounding Sugiyama's behavior in Confucian values resolves the apparent contradiction between Serena's comment that "Japan is our [China's] forever enemy" and the delight that she and her classmates took in the film. Having said that, I would argue that the fulfillment Sugiyama finds is one we can share beyond the Confucian commonality of Chinese and Japanese cultures. In the productive interaction of self and society, Sugiyama's story demonstrates the possibility of ethical leadership in the global marketplace, East and West. That, I think, would make a very good story, if we were willing to tell it. But to do that, to be leaders in such an endeavor, we need to return one more time to Confucianism, *Shall We Dance?*, and the Western tradition of professionalism, in order to review a concept already introduced in our discussions: the concept of mastery.

Educating for Leadership, Learning for Life

What do I mean by mastery, and how does it relate to living and leading the revolution?

When I put together the China seminar described in these pages, I intended to create an environment in which my students could look at the balance of self and society. As the discussion of *Shall We Dance?* indicates, that balance is a central question in the film as a whole, and can be seen as such from both a Western and an Eastern perspective. The initial bonus in lining up *The Analects* and *Shall We Dance?* lay in my realizing that Sugiyama's behavior was strongly conditioned by Confucian values; but the sequence has a meaning beyond that initial realization.

In both assignments, teaching plays a dominant role. The environments couldn't be more different: in Confucius, an ancient China only dimly visible through the conversations of the Master with his disciples, and in Suo's *Shall We Dance?*, modern, urban Japan. Yet in both cases, the key characters engage in teaching; they pass concrete knowledge and practical wisdom from one generation to the next. In fact, that seems to be their primary role, both in the story and in their lives.

Confucius has his disciples. *The Analects* are his story, in which he talks about the importance of teaching and learning, even as he engages in both; his "gentleman" seeks constantly to educate himself, and to help others in the same way. In *Shall We Dance?* the dance team models the teaching and learning implicit in such group interactions. Everyone has something to teach, and the success of the team stems precisely from a system that allows these contributions and appropriations. Tamako-*sensei* is the master of the studio, and Mai-*san*, the dancer with the greatest technical skill and the experience of competing at the highest levels. Sugiyama-*san* unwittingly teaches Mai the wonder of dance; but, at his daughter's behest, he also teaches his wife how to dance, thereby healing a rift in their relations, his values, and the fabric of society as a whole.

In short, mastery means not just the ability to do something, to perform a particular act or craft with skill. As Confucius makes clear, it means seeing that performance in a larger personal and social context, and being able to convey the big picture, the principle that inheres in the act, through the specifics of the skill that is the ostensible lesson at hand. In doing so, the master effaces the distinction between "how-to" and "how-to-be." While this process may seem inefficient because insufficiently targeted, it is the only means of successfully imparting values while communicating requisite skills.

When Sugiyama and Mai trade their life stories, they establish the context for the exercise in dance instruction that initially defines their relationship. Mastery, then, involves a skill or skills, the ability to listen to the voices in the environment where that skill might be exercised, and a willingness to establish a broad framework for that exercise, the guiding principle, without distracting an audience or clientele from it. The Master of masters, in our discussion, teaches teaching. Confucius sets the principles by which one can communicate technical skill and wisdom of any description. In his "gentleman," he creates a figure who embodies the virtues of a teacher, even as he goes about the routine of daily life.

It is hard to write or talk about mastery in a society, like today's United States, which places a premium on novelty or innovation and improvisation. Yet even in the United States, which plays a dominant role in the global marketplace where Sugiyama works and my Chinese students are trying to insert themselves, education matters. No one holds to education more fiercely than the immigrants who have populated the U.S. in successive waves over several centuries. Americans may fret over the uneven quality of public education for their children, but adult education has an ever-growing place in the society, reaching people who had previously thought they were done learning, albeit badly.

This theme may feel radically disguised to some viewers, but mastery in today's world is at the top of the list of ideas explored in *Shall We Dance?* The film is whimsical in places, and focuses on a subculture of very specific types and engagements, but it presents the truth of many people in today's workplace, not just in Japan but around the world. Work matters, but family matters, too. Survival matters, but it can take many different forms, most of them not closely related to the bottom line. Excellence matters, but so does understanding the roots from which it springs. The future matters, but so does understanding the past from which it derives, and dwelling in the present long enough to come to a consensus on both.

Mastery as exemplified in *Shall We Dance?* is about understanding and managing group discipline and individual initiative, individual competence, and group creativity. In the conflicting currents generated by these forces, the guiding light remains a faith in people's potential to do good, without dismissing the possibility of evil. It is the belief that one does well in the long term only by doing the right thing right now. It is the conviction that one can make a difference to others by imparting one's experience through story. If you have a story to tell, or an audience that needs a story, *Shall We Dance?* provides a masterly template for communicating the possibility of ethical leadership in our global society.

I have no clear explanation for the change in Serena's tone from the first to the second of our seminars together, in May and December 2001. I like to think that our stories took her, Richard, their classmates, and me beyond the level of polite conversation. In that new place, defined by mastery, we could now discuss the comparative virtues of Buddhism, Christianity, communism, and capitalism—and the practical business opportunities to which they give rise. That said, Serena's shifting stance may also have reflected what many Chinese were feeling by the end of 2001: with the success of Beijing's bid for the 2008 Olympics that July and its accession to the World Trade Organization in November, one could believe fully in China's assumption—or resumption—of a significant place on the world stage, with all the potential for good and ill that attaches to such a role. This explanation for Serena's militancy is far less philosophical, and Richard's comparative silence during those moments in our conversation implies a split that will color Chinese public discourse and government policy, both domestic and international, for years to come.

Under such circumstances, people doing business East to West and West to East will need to tell stories that help us cross borders, even as the telling reveals our differences. It may be that ideology comes first, the deal later; but human nature seems naturally to incline us to do business. Harnessing that inclination for purposes of cross-cultural progress is also a form of corporate social responsibility, and promises to generate the good stories that will define managers' ethical practice in the coming years.

CHAPTER 6

Test for Truth
Faith, Work, and the Good Society

Believing in Business

Where do we get the values that we seek to apply when we argue for business ethics? Organized religion and faith provide the background for many of us in our professional practice. Some practitioners willingly acknowledge it: Aaron Feuerstein, the CEO of Malden Mills, explained his policy of paying employees while he rebuilt their burned-out plant as a function of his faith. In moderated discussions around professional ethics, participants often speak of a moral compass, a mechanical image for an otherwise intangible set of principles. Most people who believe we have a moral compass see it as built into us, part of our substance, the true north of which is God. These faithful believe that our values, our sense of right and wrong, our conscience derive from our connection to God. They make up the little bit of divinity that each of us carries inside him- or herself, and profoundly shape our relation to our fellow man and the society in which we live.

Aaron Feuerstein aside, though, in my experience few people volunteer to a group of strangers that their faith

181

has influenced their professional behavior, even when discussing how they conceive the role of values in their organizations. A business group that meets to talk about ethical practice is likely to include a significant number of practitioners of one faith or another. One need only ask about religious affiliation to discover how commonly the two circles overlap, and to realize that an interest in one frequently implies an interest in the other. And yet, until invited to speak out, religiously committed participants usually keep silent while other members of the group articulate a notion of ethics and the self that is completely secular: "We are our experiences," a participant will say. "Our values derive from the way we were brought up, from the influences that came to bear on us as children—school, church, family, friends, events." Even the church is seen here as an empirical rather than a divine phenomenon. The environmental influence emanates from the institution, not the divinity it represents.

With prompting, the group usually enlarges its view of the sources of ethical practice. It countenances the possibility that our values are also shaped by biology, that is, by our genetic makeup. Science seems a plausibly modern ground on which to expand our definition. Yet participants tread gingerly here, fearing the first step down the slippery slope toward racism, sexism, and a belief in inherent inequality, all of which contravene modern workplace values. These values, in turn, can be traced to the secular side of American culture, and specifically to the Founding Fathers and the Declaration of Independence—"We hold these truths to be self-evident, that all men are created equal." Despite the faith-based initiatives that have characterized North American public life in recent years, many of us still do believe in the separation of church and state, not just in our legislative but also in our social arrangements.

When participants invoke the Declaration, a conversation always ensues around the question of how Jefferson could write these lines, even as he kept his own slaves and recognized that the practice would continue among his peers. We talk about the fact that only white men had a political voice at the time, and we agree that we do a better job today than we did then of fulfilling the values published in the Declaration. Yet the document as phrased seems a plausible source of workplace values, because it appeals to standards high enough, in language inspired enough, to let us make it live up to its own potential.

Secular tradition notwithstanding, this is faith of a kind, too: we call it patriotism, which functions in much the same way as other, divinely inspired commitments. Businesspeople are appropriately leery of it, as are people who think about the relation of business to politics. The economist and Nobel Prize laureate, Milton Friedman, argued in *Capitalism and Freedom* (1962) that markets are blind to political and other demographic differences, that in the ideal market we don't know whether the food we buy was harvested, packaged, and distributed by whites, blacks, Communists, or Republicans—an impersonality that elevates the market above the partisanship of nation-states and the discrimination that mars democratic process.

There is truth in this assertion, of course: at the consumer level, we may in fact often not know the skin color, creed, national origin, or gender of the person growing and picking our oranges or slaughtering our beef. Yet the market as we experience it is hardly impersonal. What about our networks? What about the whole complex of human relations that equally characterizes life in the personal and the business arenas? What about the fact that, as we noted in our discussion of *Crouching Tiger, Hidden Dragon* (see Chapter 3), few corporations in this country or elsewhere are run as democracies, and so rely heavily on some individuals for the protection of the rights of others? We can't escape the play of values, because business is about people as much as it is about Adam Smith's "invisible hand," and people gravitate toward some people rather than others for a range of reasons: ethnic identity, aspiration, physical proximity, values, and so on.

Faith—whether divinely ordained or fuzzily secular—makes such distinctions particularly clear, in that it codifies and declares the values by which the faithful believe we should live our lives. That clarity may be the source of our inclination not to introduce faith into business discussions at all: whatever light it sheds on our personal practices, it appears to cloud business issues on which we need to gain equal clarity. We may call our faith "assumptions," "opinions," or "views," but it represents a set of standards that directly qualifies our responses to our environment, adding apparently nonbusiness factors to our decision making. In short, it seems inevitable that faith (or values or ethics) and business practices should clash. Small wonder, then, that hard-headed businesspeople and sharp-witted observers like Friedman should be wary of those who preach business ethics and corporate social responsibility. Friedman put it succinctly in the title to a famous 1970 article for the *New York Times*: "The Social Responsibility of Business Is to Increase Its Profits."

We can avoid the clash by taking our values for granted, not defining them, or relegating them to another, personal sphere. From a business practitioner's perspective, that vagueness or distance may be a blessing, in that unspoken principles impede our business freedom less; we can know we have them, but still focus on goals of the moment, and adapt as circumstances dictate. Yet we have seen the risks to this approach in our discussion of *The Country Bunny and the Little Gold Shoes*, where we established the importance of speaking up and speaking out to discover our competencies and guiding principles. The stakes are high: a sense of identity and clarity in our business dealings that comes with our knowledge of what we can and will do, and what we can't and won't. Vagueness is, on balance, not a good option.

Once we accede to clarity, though, we become vulnerable to a second temptation, this one threatening from the community side of our business practice. Sometimes a clearly articulated faith brings with it the notion that we would be better off if everyone shared our values, especially if practicing those values were routinely and abundantly rewarded, and everyone else would be better off if they shared our values, because our values work for us. Why wouldn't they work for everyone else? Once armed with a set of articulated standards, many of us succumb to the urge to convert, with the aim of creating a society to our liking and the liking of others like us.

We call it the "good society." We dream of it; we believe that it will make us happy, and believe it will make others happy as well, which in turn will make us—the engineers of the good society—that much happier. Most large-scale social movements, whether of the right or of the left, take root in such dreams. Many of them are driven not by megalomania but by the justified perception that things as they are aren't what they might be for many or even most people. Social justice is a concept we can embrace in its frequent, flagrant absence; but how to get it?

Leadership is an answer of first resort. We tend to choose our leaders among those who point us in a plausibly inviting direction. The scope of their vision can, in the best of circumstances, encompass a great number of people, and that helps make them worth following. Yet experience also suggests that, the bigger our dreams, the more likely they are to produce a good society, or a journey toward the good society, that justifies itself at the expense of the people for whom it was originally imagined. This is in fact a managerial challenge: how to grow a social enterprise so that it remains true to its original intent, even as we invoke our beliefs, seek to institutionalize our solutions, and create the organizational structure that will sustain them.

The good societies for which we actually have records show a predictable pattern of rise, decline, and fall. They are neither permanent nor infinite, and sooner or later their leadership fades away. That may help to explain why, even when our faith is a secular faith, we tend not to declare it in discussions of business and business ethics, but fall back on the impersonal diversity or unpredictability of the market and the experiences we derive from it; the product, the service—those are real and can be provided here and now. Yet the stories need to be told, too, because they focus our energies on what we could conceivably become; in that sense, they represent the more down-to-earth managerial challenge of growing and envisioning growth. The managers who tell these stories go beyond practice to codification, often acquiring or being accorded, first, a leadership role and then, over time, the authority or rank that streamlines a leader's actions. Their trajectory tells us a great deal about the relation of our beliefs and the stories we tell about them to organizational success.

This chapter discusses several such attempts at the good society, with particular attention to the role of faith in the process. Our stories include Robert Duvall's film *The Apostle*, about a fictional preacher in the American deep South; Martin Luther King, Jr.'s "Letter from Birmingham Jail," about his imprisonment for stepping into the civil rights struggle in Birmingham, Alabama, in the early 1960s; and Robert Bolt's *A Man for All Seasons*, a fictionalized, dramatic re-creation of the historical sixteenth-century confrontation between Sir Thomas More and King Henry VIII of England. Conflict is central to all of these stories, and that, too, is a part of the relation of belief to business practice—the tension around values created by cultural, political, religious, and organizational difference. We will end with the story of a contemporary American businessman, Richard Ross, whose life is a testimony to the better possibilities for the good society.

Though we have moved back and forth between history and fiction in other chapters, our discussion here draws the line separating the two a little differently. In articulating a vision of the good society, we inevitably and explicitly combine elements of social awareness and faith, an assertion of how things are and how they might be. The social critique of race in America leveled by Martin Luther King, Jr., for example, is historically verifiable, though the vision of a better America that he articulated is fiction until we make it real. That is King's intent: story, here, asks to become reality.

Opportunities for deceit or simple human error abound in this process, in part because of the suffering that characterizes so much human history. Under those circumstances, we are eager to accept the first plausible vision that comes along. As we have already said, though, the effects of building these social systems are potentially as huge as the vision itself, for good and ill. That is why we have to test for truth: ethical practice demands vigilance and a willingness to resist our own and others' stories, if they promise more than they can deliver, and stories of the good society always keep us watching the far horizon of hope. Testing for truth takes us the fifth and last step on our journey, challenging us to steer a course between the Scylla of self-doubt and the Charybdis of moral certitude. As we will see, the good society lies in the story that makes us most aware of that course.

How Sonny Dewey Became the Apostle E. F.

Robert Duvall had difficulty placing *The Apostle* with Hollywood studios, despite his track record as an actor. In the end, he produced the film himself, taking the lead role of Euliss F. Dewey, a Pentecostal Texas preacher known as "Sonny." Sonny is a big man with a talent for "shouting," a white man in shades and a white suit who borrows most of his moves from the black preachers to whom he listened as a child in small Texas churches of the 1930s. The opening scene shows us one such morning service, at which the young Sonny seems a reluctant participant. Somewhere along the line, though, he catches fire, because the next scene shows us a slightly older boy holding forth from the front of the church in the same manner as the older, black preacher: "I've been a minister of the Lord ever since I was 12 years old, back when God called me."

How he was called, Sonny doesn't tell us, but by the time of the action in the film, he has parlayed his skills into a big church and a large and devoted following. The only exception seems to be his wife, Jessie (played by Farrah Fawcett). Jessie has taken a lover, the youth minister in the church. Sonny suspects her of infidelity, but hasn't identified with whom. He is also at something of a disadvantage, because he himself has been less than monogamous. When he goes to find Jessie at the church and asks her to pray with him to restore their marriage, she makes clear that she knows about his philandering ways, and tells him to leave her alone. Then she takes Sonny's church from him, relying on legal arrangements he made when he established it. Bereft of both his wife and his church and congregation, and having discovered the identity of his wife's lover, Sonny finds the couple and his children at a baseball game. When the younger man tries to keep Sonny from dragging away his family, Sonny hits him with a baseball bat, putting him into a coma from which he will not recover.

The infliction of physical harm shakes Sonny out of what had up to this point seemed mostly a world built of words—Sonny alternately preaching, praying, posturing, and persuading himself and others that he has access to a better place. The blow he administers brings down his world in a way that neither Jessie's adultery nor her usurpation of his church could. Now he flees, abandoning his car, his wallet, and his identity along the way. At a remote fishing camp he stops to rest, re-baptizes himself "the apostle E. F.," and, taking a tip from a solitary fisherman he encounters there, travels to a remote Louisiana town, convinced that God has given him a sign.

In Bayou Boutté, Sonny puts together a new life and a new church with the help of local residents and a retired black preacher. He cannot escape the past, though: ultimately, the radio advertising for his One Way Road to Heaven church reaches Jessie's ears; she informs on him, and he is arrested during an evening service. The youth minister has died of the blow Sonny gave him. Sonny's mother, with whom he is very close, has died as well. He is a bit like the Biblical figure of Job, suffering a series of injuries that test his faith; and yet, when Sonny looks on his new church in the midst of all of his woes, he finds it in himself to quote Elihu, who reproaches Job for inveighing against his Lord: "'Stand still, and consider the wondrous works of God.' Job 37:14."

Leading Against the System

Whose creation is the church—God's or Sonny's? Are the two separable? Sonny ultimately goes to jail, but as the closing credits roll, we see him working on a chain gang, leading his fellow inmates in chants of "Jesus." He is irrepressibly inclined to lead. He gravitates naturally to the role, and people seem inclined under even the most trying circumstances to follow him. Yet, as the hint of divine arrogance might suggest, he is first and foremost a leader against the system, an opposition figure despite his faith.

This opposition plays itself out at two levels—one organizational and one personal. For those used to thinking of the Church with a capital "C," the place of organized religion in *The Apostle* will surprise, because it is emphatically outside the establishment pale. Again, the early scenes in the film effectively set the stage. The adult Sonny is driving down the highway with his mother (played by June Carter Cash), when they come upon a car accident. People have been hurt, and the State Police are already on the scene. No one pays much attention to the victims—in fact, the troopers are much more interested in a dog that seems to have escaped from one of the wrecked cars.

Sonny pulls over, takes his Bible in hand, and makes his way across a field beside the road to the car furthest from the scene of the accident. Inside, he finds a young couple, the boy immobilized, the girl unconscious. Sonny places his Bible on the roof of the car and begins proselytizing, speaking for the injured boy and walking him into accepting Jesus. Though mute, the boy is clearly grateful to have the attention, and after Sonny has left the scene we see the girl's hand flex on her companion's arm, in a suggestion that she, too, has been revived by Sonny's ministrations.

During the conversion, the police suddenly take an interest in Sonny's activities. One of the troopers approaches the car, telling Sonny to leave the victims alone. He keeps the trooper at arm's length while talking to the boy, so that the scene quickly becomes a stand-off between the law of the state and God's law. Sonny's body language tells us that he knows he is infringing on someone else's turf. Throughout the scene, he moves furtively, hunched over and looking around to make sure that the police don't notice him. A man of mercy, he seems to have something on his conscience.

After the fact, he clearly expected the police to stop him from preaching his message to the injured couple. Sonny has personal faith on his side, but secular authority gives it no credence. When he finally pulls his head and hands out of the wrecked car, having "saved" the wounded driver, the trooper says sardonically, "I guess you think you accomplished something in there." The ambulance arrives to minister to needs that the police can identify, but only we know about the moving hand of the girlfriend, a response to something that the uniformed police and emergency medical technicians cannot provide, and that Sonny intuits.

In this world of small miracles and small churches scattered across the countryside, each with its own preacher, each with his own flock, we have an American portrait of a system beneath the system, ruled by individuals with a skill—the ability to preach—and a sense of the fabric of their local communities. Their power outstrips the official network for speed and accuracy of information, and governs behavior through peer pressure and public opinion—ethical norms—that have little to do with the law. Sonny is at home here, and demonstrates abundantly his ability to organize and minister to his fellow men. He is a man on a mission, with the strength to make it happen, and the community responds to that conviction.

The network of the faithful in Sonny's good society is pluralist and very diverse: by the end of the film, the church—now co-pastored by the Reverend and the Apostle—has Caucasian, Asian, and African-American congregants. In the spirit of inclusion, Sonny welcomes them all, forging a cohesive group from apparently disparate individuals. In many ways, his mission corresponds more closely to the secular ideology we traced to Jefferson and the U.S. Declaration of Independence than the actual practice in that lay environment. That may explain in part why Sonny finds himself leading this congregation that embraces him first in small numbers, and then with growing fervor and adherents.

Still, a position outside the system imposes severe constraints on the authority that might accrue to a leader. Sonny's furtive conversion of the couple in the car signals that fact; he is a subversive rather than a revolutionary in his social arrangements. On the personal level, moreover, he seems incapable of either systematically leading or including himself in the community he leads, a fatal impediment to each of his experiments in social construction. He is, as the earlier conflation of God and self suggests, a man divided against himself.

Black Like Me: Part I

Much as it epitomizes the best features of America's commitment to pluralism, The Apostle unfolds in the world of the nation's problematic attitudes toward race. The Apostle reproduces a pattern that viewers of American film and readers of American novels will recognize from many other stories: the white leader figure, virtuous or sinful, who surrounds himself with followers most often of another race, the "natives" who, white supremacists argue, need the benefit of the white man's greater wisdom. It is hard to argue convincingly that Duvall's Sonny breaks this mold. He is the dominant figure in the film, and he has the energy, the good health, and the smarts. The fact that he also has a history— a criminal one—doesn't alter the power dynamic in the film.

At the same time, Sonny is engaged in a lifelong project that can only be described as reverse "passing": unlike light-skinned blacks, some of whom did their best to hide their racial identity—a theme in both American film and fiction during the early part of the twentieth century—Sonny has cast himself in the mold of the black preachers to whom he was exposed as a child.

The strategy of appropriating black mannerisms worked for Elvis Presley and other white blues rockers who rose to fame and fortune by adapting black performance to a white audience. For Sonny, the racial crossover is more complicated. On the morning of his first sermon in the One Way Road to Heaven church, he and the Rev. Blackwell look at the congregation that they have assembled: a skinny woman and a fat woman and her two little boys, all black. Blackwell comments with a smile that whites won't come because they think from Sonny's radio spots that he is black; the blacks, by contrast, know he is white, but they don't mind because they like his preaching style. Sonny gladly preaches to them. Unlike the white musicians, he does not attempt to bring the vitality of the black religious community to whites; in his passion for preaching, he goes where he is needed.

Whatever the craving for power that drives him, he also feels most at home with those few early parishioners, and with the Rev. Blackwell and his wife. Sister Johnson and Sister Delilah provide the face and set the mood for the congregation. Blackwell becomes a father figure to Sonny, who ultimately confesses his crime to the older man. The black characters' roles in these scenes suggest an ethic that runs counter to Sonny's own manic brand of Christianity, but one that he eagerly seeks out. His black congregation lives the inclusiveness that he preaches, even as they respond to his focus on ecstatic worship.

And yet, for all their acceptance of him, Sonny can't settle down. Faith for him is less about mutual appreciation than the act of conversion, an assault on the unenlightened and on God Himself, and so he shuts himself out of the comfort of his own creed. He fails at passing, a figure neither black nor white, a figure on the margins even as he leads his flock to discover the wonders of community to which he believes he has access. This disjunction brings us before the larger cultural particularities of his faith, best expressed in a comment made by a participant the one time I taught the film.

A Little Commercialism Goes a Long Way

In the wake of the events of September 11, 2001, I was looking for material that would allow me to explore with a group the relation between faith and leadership. I was concerned about the role of faith and values in Osama bin Laden's mission, and the faith response that it elicited from the Bush administration. I chose *The Apostle* because it blended the elements of faith and leadership that we have already discussed, and positioned it so that the seminar would feed into it as a culminating assignment. Yet the film generated only a good, not a great, discussion, after faith-related conversations of much greater intensity to which we will return shortly.

I commented to one of the participants afterward on the relatively muted response from the group to Sonny's story. He responded that *The Apostle* was perhaps "too American" to work well for our group. It was a novel view: although the students drawn to the course that semester were as international a group as any I had had, in or out of Sloan, we were still operating in an American environment, which the group had accepted and saw almost universally as a benefit rather than a cost to their careers. Moreover, the notion that a film could be "too American" (or too much from any national perspective) worked against the premise of the course that recognizing such differences conferred strategic business advantage.

While I didn't challenge the student at the time, I did later wonder about his response. Did he mean that *The Apostle* was too regional? Was this really a complaint about Southern accents? What to make then of the scene when Sonny witnesses priests blessing Louisiana fishing boats in French? That seemed cross-cultural. What to make of the Pentecostal frenzy that characterizes much of the film, and that represents the global growth element in all major religions today, including Christianity?

The American quality of the story lies in the nature of Sonny's leaderly qualities, as expressed through his faith. Specifically, he demonstrates a surprising knack for blending the religious and the commercial, as his interactions with the "establishment" in Bayou Boutté demonstrate. Somewhere between the unofficial network of the faithful and the official system of the state, the local radio station keeps the community informed of daily happenings. The owner, Elmo, is a white man who knows his community and knows his listeners. He also knows the kind of person who wants to use his station, and for what ends. He and Sonny exchange pleasantries when Sonny arrives in Bayou Boutté, and Sonny then turns to him after he has persuaded the Rev. Blackwell to help him launch a new church. Sonny wants to advertise over the radio, but Elmo wants to hear his credentials first, and to set guidelines:

SONNY

I've got a holiness background.

ELMO

It's got to be a pay-before-you-pray deal...no fancy stuff...
no speaking in tongues over these airwaves...so what kind
of preacher are you, anyway?

SONNY

Oh, well, I can preach on the Holy Trinity, Old and New
Testament, Hell, Resurrection—you name it, I can do it. I
can preach on the Devil backwards and forwards. I can do
about anything you want to hear, but—no tongues.

This exchange speaks volumes about the cultural expectations for what Sonny has to offer. He is nothing less than a religious entrepreneur, selling his skills and his wares to whoever
will buy them. Nothing in his delivery suggests that he feels duty-
bound to any religious authority, and we know that he is running
from the authority of the state. What remains is a kind of in-
grained hucksterism. Sonny is a salesman for whom the Bible is
his stock in trade.

When my student expressed concern that *The Apostle* was "too
American" for use in a multicultural ethics seminar, I suspect he
meant this quality in Sonny. In a global business community that
recognizes the United States for its positive bias toward entrepreneurs, Sonny has taken a dominant cultural trait from the world
of American commerce and applied it to salvation. He is peddling
faith, and seeking a faith market for his brand of redemption. The
problem isn't so much, then, that the film portrays American cultural peculiarities that no one other than an American could understand; rather, the problem lies in the possibility that an alert
audience, and particularly an alert international audience, will
understand the film as a commentary on American ways and

mores. They will see that the film accurately represents aspects of
global American hegemony, rewritten into a religious format,
and puts a very specific spin, through this peculiarly American
brand of engagement, on the notion of faith writ large.

Can one simply book a ticket for the One Way Road to
Heaven? A short scene during the church renovation suggests
that Sonny believes it possible. Here, as throughout the film, he is
surrounded by kids, whom he uses as props for the nicer moments in his evangelizing. At one point, he eases them into a
chant of "Revelation, Revelation, Revelation!" Chanting and
laughing, they pour out the door of the church and look up to the
steeple, where one of Sonny's adult followers, on cue, opens a
bag that Sonny has handed him and releases a cloud of dollar
bills that floats down to the children.

There is, then, enough ideological content in this film to make
many a world-conscious viewer uneasy, amused, or angry. *The
Apostle* mounts a critique of American entrepreneurship, in both
business and the business of religious conversion. And yet, Duvall
seems to say, there is power in this connection. Even as Sonny regularly reveals his huckster side, he demonstrates genuine insight
and an understanding of how best to use it for his community's
welfare. When he finally confesses his crime to the Rev. Blackwell,
the Reverend tells him, "We love you. You've helped many *many*
people in the town!" And that, of course, is the essence of Sonny's
presence in Bayou Boutté, from the food boxes he leaves anony-
mously at impoverished residents' doors to the understanding he
brings to people who don't fully understand themselves.

He is in every sense a leader—God's salesman, the Apostle.
He is also a murderer. In his own mind, Sonny is at once the servant of God and God's equal, the creator of worlds. The conflation of roles makes for an impossible situation: Sonny is both

aggressor and victim, servant and master, and his vision falters
as a result. Despite his rhetoric, he knows no humility. We can
punish him, but the punishment neither stops his fundamental
drive to lead nor makes it possible for us to salvage the many
qualities of his leadership, either for his flock or for the society as
a whole. In this scenario, where faith and violence go hand in
hand, everyone loses.

Black Like Me: Part II

As a model for leadership, then, Sonny falls far short of the level
one would want to establish in a class on business ethics. By the
spring of 2002, when this seminar was in progress, we had had
more than enough examples of leaders who turned out to have
feet of clay—the executives at Enron, Global Crossing, and Im-
Clone, to name just three scandals then evolving in the public
arena. That, as much as Sonny's "American-ness," may explain
the relatively tepid response the students in the class displayed
toward the film. The economy of his misdeeds was too familiar
to be encouraging, and in the spring of 2002, in the larger economy of imploding firms and scarce job offers, my students were
looking for encouragement wherever they could.

Fortunately, they found more viable versions of the good society at other points in the semester. In a course dominated by
fiction, Martin Luther King, Jr.'s "Letter from Birmingham Jail"
(1963) stands out as a work of social criticism and an exhortation;
and yet it is, in a very real sense, the story of King's and other
black Americans' resistance to discrimination, segregation, and
disempowerment. In a class concerned with leadership, moreover, it distinguishes itself as an exercise in leadership rather than

a tract about it. The "Letter" is a call to action, or further action, a sermon, and a persuasive argument targeting white Americans particularly, but all Americans, as King attempts to explain his movement and the beliefs on which it rests.

In the "Letter," King was responding to a public statement made by eight Alabama clergymen in April 1963, urging blacks in Birmingham to desist from social unrest. The American civil rights movement of the 1960s was already well underway, and with it came violent clashes. Implying that King was an "outsider" and therefore an inappropriate figure to lead the black community in Birmingham, the eight signatories urged restraint and adherence to local laws, leaders, and resources. In his response, King passionately defended the nonviolent resistance he widely advocated and personally practiced in those years as a means of achieving equal rights. He also directly accused the Church and the civil authorities of preventing blacks from exercising their civil rights.

Like Sonny in *The Apostle*, King is a preacher; like Sonny, he is also a salesman—the "Letter" makes these similarities evident. And yet the differences are instructive. Sonny includes the children of his congregants in every aspect of his work, and he is a good father, but his conversation with his kids consists, so far as we can tell, of quizzing them on the books of the Old Testament, and he reaches the pinnacle of his youth ministry in the cloud of dollar bills he rains on his young followers during the church renovation at Bayou Boutté. King takes another tack:

> When you suddenly find your tongue twisted and your speech stammering as you seek to explain to your six-year-old daughter why she can't go to the public amusement park that has just been advertised on television . . . and see her beginning to distort her personality by developing an unconscious bitterness toward white people; when you

have to concoct an answer for a five-year-old son who is asking:
"Daddy, why do white people treat colored people so mean?"... then
you will understand why we find it difficult to wait. [p. 69–70]

The children here represent the fundamental humanity of both King himself and the audience to which he appeals. His daughter assumes that children are children, regardless of color; discrimination assumes otherwise. His daughter and son ask only to be themselves, and so, by implication, does their father. For King, everyone has a self; that is why he refers to his daughter's "personality." Discrimination assumes that some people, "colored people," have a lesser self.

For King, that instruction quickly perverts the self that is God's gift to everyone. Whereas Sonny seems convinced that he has a self in need of recognition, but also of redefinition and redemption, King holds to the initial validity of that self and asks for conditions that will preserve it. As a preacher, he reaches beyond the confines of his profession and his church to appeal to the whole community. Indeed, if one of the students in the seminar found *The Apostle* "too American," nothing could be more American than King's appeal for social justice based on America's founding values:

We will reach the goal of freedom in Birmingham and all over the
nation, because the goal of America is freedom. Abused and scorned
though we may be, our destiny is tied up with America's destiny. Be-
fore the pilgrims landed at Plymouth, we were here. Before the pen of
Jefferson etched the majestic words of the Declaration of Indepen-
dence across the pages of history, we were here.... We will win our
freedom because the sacred heritage of our nation and the eternal will
of God are embodied in our echoing demands. [pp. 81–82]

So, wherein lies the difference between King's faith-based leadership and that offered by the Apostle E. F.? "Letter from Birmingham Jail" has as visible an affiliation to religious observance and to faith as any moment in *The Apostle*, and it is permeated, like the preaching in the film, by the style of generations of black preachers. Part of the story quality of King's "Letter" stems precisely from his rhetorical skills, including the repetition that marks Sonny's "shouting." And yet, where Sonny becomes intoxicated with his own voice, King weaves elements of social criticism, activism, ideology, and religious commitment into a comprehensive statement on what America might be, as articulated in others' voices. King's "Letter" builds the good society on the values and virtues of his predecessors, contemporaries, and putative descendants. He cites Jefferson and the Declaration, and trusts to our common better nature to sort out the true meaning of those words for our times.

The result is a document that inspires, and that routinely hits home with readers, both American and foreign. The "Letter" inspires faith because it defines the good society in terms to which we have all committed, and that as a result includes all of us instead of excluding any of us. Its rhetoric reveals an author who expects the best of people, rather than fearing the worst, who trusts that we, too, want an order that ensures our rights against all challenge, and imposes on each of us the responsibility to protect them. He preaches and practices nonviolent direct action, whereas Sonny Dewey practiced direct violence and preached in substantially the same spirit. No one ever argues that King's "Letter" is too American, or that his words should be doubted for any other reason of ideology or style.

Readers who know modern American history might question King's leadership because of his alleged infidelity to his wife

or the questionable scholarly honesty of his Ph.D. dissertation or
the politics of the civil rights movement. These are battles that
we have fought around most prominent American figures, from
presidents to actors to corporate executives. We cannot separate
the person from the performance, it seems, and that is probably
a good thing because it reminds us and them of their humanity.
At the same time, the standard would, if strictly applied, disqualify many leaders. As with Jefferson and the Declaration, then, we
are forced back on the story of King's "Letter," if we are to come
up with lasting values.

When tested for truth, it still stands: King turns a mirror to
us, asking whether we wish to tolerate the wrong that we do ourselves, or instead live up to the good that he sees and hears us
proclaiming. His authority is our authority made explicit again, a
collaboration on the good society that we cannot let pass us by.

Going to Jail, and Going to Heaven

Robert Bolt's *A Man for All Seasons* (1960) triggered impulses in
the class similar to those they displayed in response to King's
"Letter." In the play, Bolt tells the true story of the clash between
Henry VIII, King of England and founder of the Church of England, and his Lord Chancellor, Sir Thomas More (1478–1535). The
subject of the conflict is well documented, as Bolt reports in his
preface to the play: Henry got a papal dispensation to marry his
brother's widow, Catherine of Aragon. When he later realized
that Catherine would probably never give him a male heir, and,
moreover, when he fell in love with Anne Boleyn, Henry asked
for a papal reversal of the original dispensation, arguing that his
marriage to his brother's widow had put him in a state of sin.

When the Pope refused to annul the marriage to Catherine, Henry broke with the Church and appointed a bishop who would grant him his wish. In the process, he had Parliament pass an Oath of Supremacy, asserting his authority as head of the Church of England, and required all of his subjects to take it. Thomas More, an able statesman and for a time Henry's Lord Chancellor, but also a good Catholic, refused to take the pledge. After much pressure from the king and his supporters, and after a period of imprisonment, More was found guilty of high treason and beheaded. For this, the Catholic Church made More a saint in 1935.

The play generates intense emotions both for and against More's position. Audience responses tend to divide into realist and idealist camps. The realists believe that More simply threw his life away, and hurt his family in the process. The idealists argue that, given his religious convictions, More had no choice but to do what he did. His role as a professional comes into the discussion, too, since he also stands by his faith in the law to extricate himself from a difficult political situation. As with King's "Letter," it is difficult to resolve the question of the man and his morals. What remains is the story, and the breadth of vision that it compels us to apply to our own leadership skills.

The play sets two different kinds of leadership at odds: the unquestioned authority of Henry, who *is* England, and the more administrative talents of Thomas More, deeply influenced by his religious beliefs, who aspires to *serve* England. Whereas Henry leads by virtue of his rank, Thomas leads by example, which costs him his life. By that standard, some readers find it difficult to speak of him as a leader at all. He also appeals to a higher authority, his God, and that, too, is difficult for a secular audience to factor into a discussion colored by a focus on the art of the possible.

In these classroom discussions, the elusive but essential element proves to be the number of people who share More's commitment to a faith, though not necessarily More's faith. Bolt has More directly address the problem of the self, recognizing the possible divergence of secular and religious views. In a conversation with the Duke of Norfolk, who is a friend to More but caves in to the demands of the king, More supplies the connection between God and self. Norfolk has asked More to go along with the Supremacy Act:

> **NORFOLK**
> *(With deep appeal)*
>
> Give in.

> **MORE**
> *(Gently)*
>
> I can't give in, Howard— *(A smile)* You might as well advise a man to change the color of his eyes. I can't. Our friendship's more mutable than *that.*

> **NORFOLK**
>
> Oh, that's immutable, is it? The one fixed point in a world of changing friendships is that Thomas More will not give in!

> **MORE**
> *(Urgent to explain)*
>
> To me it *has* to be, for that's myself! Affection goes as deep in me as you think, but only God is love right through, Howard; and *that's* my *self.* [pp. 121–122]

More's insistence on the role of the self in his meditations and the actions to which they lead generally has the realists arguing that he is neither high-minded nor principled, but selfish. The idealists' counterargument recognizes the value of his example, and sees in his focus on the self a measure of More's selflessness—the self he defends is, as he says in the passage just quoted, the spark of the divine in him. After a lifetime in the public eye, he resolutely refuses to lead either the forces allied with the king or the forces waiting to resist him. In both cases, he knows, his actions as a leader will cause extensive harm, and thus dim or extinguish that divine spark.

Such self-assurance would probably have done much to ease the pain of being oneself that Robert Duvall's Sonny experiences in *The Apostle*. As with Martin Luther King, Jr., history suggests that Sir Thomas More did things that tarnish his saintly image. And yet, More routinely draws fervent support from lay readers, just as he drew the support of the Catholic Church, for taking a stand on the value of the individual and individual belief. If readers are less unanimously supportive of his steadfastness than they are of King's, he nevertheless crystallizes debate around issues of faith in a way that no other figure does, including King, whose strategy in "Letter from Birmingham Jail" takes his argument beyond the realm of faith.

In the seminar that included King and Bolt and ended with *The Apostle*, I remember the heat of the debate around More in our first class on the play. I was puzzled, two sessions later, that seminar participants couldn't or wouldn't put him away. We were moving on to other texts, and yet More seemed to be on the students' minds. In response to a comment from me on the persistence of More in our conversation, one participant finally confessed: "Well, I'm actually quite devout." Her apparently impromptu admission opened spiritual floodgates for the group. By the end of the session, it had become apparent that roughly a quarter of the students regarded themselves as committed Catholics. For them, More was Saint Thomas More, and the dilemma of his life, as portrayed by Robert Bolt, raised a host of questions about the way in which they would reconcile their own personal beliefs and professional lives. The moral compass suddenly had a source, and the importance of faith and of the divine in defining oneself emerged for all to see.

The professions of faith made by my students in the spring of 2002 may represent a statistical aberration. I think, though, that they were typical of classes I have had at Sloan and elsewhere. People who have religious commitments rarely put them aside, even if they choose not to talk about them. The difference with this seminar lay in the timing, in these participants feeling the pressure of and need for faith in unusually stressful times. The economy was souring, the professional interests that my students represented were under significant public scrutiny, and a symbol of the activities they expected to practice, the World Trade Center, had been targeted and destroyed by forces that claimed to see a larger, spiritual violation in the work that they, my students, were training to do.

Here again, we test for truth: though we may not agree on the message of A Man for All Seasons, we do agree that the debate is fundamental, as demonstrated by the heat that we bring to it. Like King, More went to jail believing that he had no alternative but to do so, if he wished ultimately to go to heaven; in Bolt's rendition of his story, he is willing to suffer for his beliefs, indeed believes that he must do so if others are to have the freedom of theirs. For Sonny, a man like most people composed of visible elements of good and evil, going to jail was the alternative to going to heaven, and he went to jail knowing he had earned it. For my students in the spring of 2002, King and More represented the crucible that they, too, might have to face someday, a challenge that no one rises to easily, including, by their own testimony, both More and King. And yet, in rising to it, the students would make themselves leaders. History had certified it as the truth, and more recent history offered ready examples to bolster the case. Here is one of them.

In Memory of Richard Ross

On the morning of September 11, 2001, Richard Ross boarded American Airlines flight 11 out of Boston. I had met Richard in the mid-1990s. I was flattered then by his open enthusiasm for what I did. He liked to chat about business ethics. What started as a brief exchange about the subject at a sunny summer picnic on Cape Cod, though, gradually became a firmer relationship in gritty, often gloomy Boston. Richard ran a management consulting firm, the Ross Group, which placed programmatic emphasis on caring for the people in its client organizations. He was also involved in many philanthropic enterprises in the area, and would call me to attend the fund-raisers he himself attended or, in some cases, hosted. He seemed convinced that, given my professional interest in ethical behavior, I would share his passion for good—and invariably nonprofit—causes. In the summer of 1998, we drove together to Lenox, Massachusetts, to confer with Tina Packer, the artistic director of the theater troupe Shakespeare & Co. Richard was on Tina's board of directors, and she was looking for ways to raise more money. They had developed an idea that would bring Tina's artistry, Richard's business acumen, and my classroom skills together for week-long, tuition-generating trips to London.

The day of our visit, I picked up Richard at the Newton Marriott, a suburban hub just off the Massachusetts Turnpike. I felt that Richard had asked me to drive as his discreet way of making me part of the project—tapping in the thin, you-too-can-contribute edge of the wedge. He was, as always, nattily dressed, in a blue blazer, an open shirt, and light pants, a short, square man with a jaunty walk and a big smile—a man on a mission. As it turned out, he was also a man with laryngitis, so that he spoke barely above a whisper for our two-hour trip to Lenox. Richard being Richard, though, physical ailments didn't deter him. He talked with hardly a break for those two hours, moving from one topic to another in a husky voice, but with unflagging enthusiasm for both his subject and the very act of communicating it. All I had to do was drive.

In Lenox, Tina started our meeting by putting Richard through some deep-breathing exercises, which mostly embarrassed him but did actually give him more volume. He and Tina were a good match: she is a big-hearted, assertive woman who knows where she is going, and he was equally, evidently sure of the importance of getting her there. We reached no conclusions on that day, but agreed that we had a scheme. After lunch with staff and a tour of the theater company's then-home—Edith Wharton's estate, "The Mount"—Richard and I headed back to Boston. Now the conversation focused mostly on family—his wife, Judi, and his two daughters and one son, of whom he was infinitely proud. I remember most from the ride to and from Lenox Richard's consistent optimism, even buoyancy. He had nothing but good things to say about anyone. Everyone in Richard's world had redeeming qualities because they could all contribute to the greater good. He emanated the comfort of a man who has had extraordinary good luck, recognizes it as such, and wants to do everything he can to share it with others.

In the spring of 2001, Richard invited me to speak on business ethics to a group of his long-time friends and business associates. We met over lunch in the Ross Group seminar room, talked a bit about why I use story to teach ethics, and discussed *The Country Bunny and the Little Gold Shoes*. From Richard's point of view, I knew, it was one more, small stroke in the crusade for good business behavior, another attempt to link business to the rest of the world, where what businesspeople did had real but not always positive results. Richard, our wives, and I met for dinner about a month later, a thank you for the session I had done with his friends. Typically for Richard, the evening was a vigorous exercise in Socratic dialogue, a thorough exchange of ideas in a thoroughly personal setting. Three months later, he was dead.

For his memorial service a week later, the city of Boston closed off one lane of the River Way, a major drive through the city, to provide adequate parking. Hundreds of people came to the service at Temple Israel, in the Longwood area of Boston. I'm sure that some came as a way of bearing witness to all of the 3,000 people who had died on September 11, and that fact heightened the poignancy of paying homage to this one man. Richard's two daughters and one son paid moving tribute to their father, as did others. What I remember most, though, were not the speeches, but the sobbing of Richard's eldest child, Abigail, as the service ended. She had given a thoughtful, articulate, loving homage to her father earlier in the service. Now there was only this: the sound of unadulterated grief filling the big, gray-gold space of the temple above an utterly silent crowd.

What kind of a man could elicit that feeling? And more: take a man who believed so much good of so many people—what would he have been thinking as his plane flew over Manhattan on its way toward the World Trade Center? Could he have found goodness in the hijackers, or in his and his fellow passengers' by then clearly dire situation? What would a man like Richard have thought at that point about ethical behavior, and the means of making people happy? And where would he draw the strength to think at all, rather than to wish simply and devoutly for a solution, cost what it might to others?

In the summer of 2004, I put these questions, and many others, to Richard's eldest daughter, Abigail. She acknowledged that she and the rest of her family often asked themselves the same questions. No one would ever know the answers, but they did know that, since his death, hardly a day goes by without someone getting in touch to talk about how Richard affected them. The family has boxes of such testimonials, Abigail reported, people for whom a conversation with Richard was a life-changing experience. For all his willingness to talk on our way to and from Lenox that day in the summer of 2000, Richard was also a very good listener, and the tributes that have reached the family come from many different sources: young people who went to see him for job information interviews, adults who chanced to sit beside him on other, happier flights than his last, and to whom he listened with great care and fellow feeling.

Abigail links her father's effect on others to the Jewish notion of "acts of loving-kindness," though she is not convinced that he engaged in them for specifically religious reasons. These "acts" included hospital visits that were sometimes hours long, she said, contributing to his invariable lateness for all his engagements. He was always trying to reach one more person, in whatever brief respite from his busy schedule he could find. As with his personal life, so with his professional life. During the time I knew Richard, he was constantly in search of clients for a consultative process that would plumb the souls of the corporation and the executive teams that ran it. He never despaired: he was convinced that he would ultimately tap the market for an institutionalized and profitable version of what he gave equally to casual acquaintances and those closest to him.

In that search, Richard left a legacy to fulfill. "He and I were best friends," Abigail says. "He wanted me to join and ultimately take over the business, but I couldn't—we were too much alike." Over time, she believes, he would have wanted her sister, Alison, or her brother, Franklin, to join the business as well. The Ross Group is now all but shuttered, a phone number with an inbox. Still, having graduated from Brown University in art history, today Abigail runs her mother's art gallery on Newbury Street in Boston. She credits her father with helping her to master the basic concepts of business: "When I was growing up, he would bring home situations he had encountered during the day—disguised, you know—and we would sort them out around the dinner table."

That, too, is business in search of the good society.

Coming to Terms with Our Selves

So what do we learn about faith and aspiration from this gathering of principled men: the Apostle E. F., Martin Luther King, Jr., Sir Thomas More, and Richard Ross? I went in search of a story like Sonny's in *The Apostle* because I wanted to focus the relation of faith to business ethics to leadership. I did so in part because I thought that people were feeling the need of spiritual support at a time of massive societal stress, regardless of their national affiliation or their professional focus. And I did so because I had made the acquaintance of a man, Richard Ross, determined to make the connection among those three notions, whose life story had had a particularly poignant ending—here, I believed, there had to be a lesson for me and others.

In *The Apostle*, I discovered a story that conveys some of the contradictions of America's role in the world: the missionary urge, the self-satisfaction, the commercialism, the degradation of the spiritual to the merely material, and an occasionally criminal indifference to others' well-being; but also the will to help out, to improve people's lives, to believe that, as a community, we can do great things, and that our divinity lies in that collaboration. These are the ingredients of Sonny's personality in *The Apostle*, and they are the ingredients of an American national profile thrown into strong relief by the events of September 11, 2001. As such, they contributed to Richard Ross's untimely end, but they also capture some of his great strengths.

Given its earth-bound focus, can we say that *The Apostle* is even remotely about faith? To the extent that it portrays how we as individuals can rise above our own failings and the failings of others to do good, it certainly does invoke faith, in part because Sonny is so clearly at risk. The film then asks us whether we can forgive him for who he is, in the name of what he has done on the positive side of the ledger. This is a very secular take on faith, more ritual than mystical union, more the form than the sub-stance of worship. It is probably the best model for those of us who seek to introduce values into the work we do in organiza-tions, and the work of the organizations themselves. Business is not, despite Sonny's conflation of faith and entrepreneurship, an otherworldly occupation. Even at its most altruistic, it is about the generation of wealth, and the application of wealth to meet customer needs or desires.

Perhaps that is why, in the abstract, the models of Martin Luther King, Jr. and Sir Thomas More appeal so much more strongly to us. Their absolutism, whether willed or suffered, suggests something higher than any bargain one might strike on earth. As critics of More make clear, though, his powerful example also reflects an extreme of daily practice, whether in business or in politics. King's analogous invocation of "extremists...for love" (p. 77) sets a standard most of us will not equal, though we have it there as a goad and a consolation. These two texts show that we as readers and followers can arrive at very different understandings of what it means to have faith, and that social unrest may well ensue. Having understood that risk, both authors ask us to think about how we can fairly exercise our commitment to a set of beliefs in a way that protects our own and our fellows' interests, even as we promote our values.

All three stories challenge us as individuals to judge what we as a society will tolerate in the name of community, and how we will judge the mistakes that get made along the way. That judgment—testing for truth—may be the only aspect of the good society that matters in the end, and that survives any given version of it. Richard Ross believed that people were the substance of corporations, and he stressed business ethics as a way of protecting them; he tested for truth by listening to his clients and helping them listen to themselves. King asked only that his fellow citizens and co-religionists apply their standards to themselves, and showed them in the "Letter" what those standards were. More claimed that he could be true to the society as a whole only by being true to himself. His actions in *A Man for All Seasons* showed in what that self consists, as he honored his pledge to the same God worshiped by his fellow citizens and his king.

Again, it is possible to find flaws in these men; certainly many have done so with the historical figures. Yet they rise above their own limitations by looking to us and asking us to examine ourselves, to seek out and develop our qualities in the name of shared values. For all of these men, that is the good society: the good that each of us carries, and that we can husband and extend to others not as a grand scheme, but as a one-on-one relation that will ripple across our whole society. That is the power of Richard Ross's example. It is also the power of Martin Luther King, Jr.'s rhetoric. He spoke to all Americans as if he were speaking to one person, with the intimacy and fellow feeling and impact that such a conversation would allow.

In this version of the good society, the flaws borne by the leader do not diminish the effect of their stories on us. If anything, their value for the society as a whole lies in their permanent instigation of disagreement, pushing us to debate, shape, and reshape our dreams, and society itself. This model has the feel of the market, the give and take of the deal, the recognition that we will occasionally fail in our negotiations and our respect for one another, but that we will continue to work to create wealth because wealth comes in many forms and for many players. We continue to generate it because we believe in the possibility of bettering ourselves, a faith that brings business and (even reticent!) businesspeople into the good society.

CHAPTER 7

Mastering Mather

Ethical Practice, Leaderless Leadership, and Our Collective Future

The Best and the Brightest

In April 2001, the journalist, editor, columnist, and television commentator David Brooks published an essay in the *Atlantic Monthly* titled "The Organization Kid." Brooks had already established his reputation as an astute observer of American society in his book on the Baby Boomer generation, *Bobos in Paradise*; now, he was taking on the bobos' children. This was a topic of much interest to my wife and me since, as co-masters of one of the Harvard undergraduate houses, we had lived among undergraduates for close to a decade by the time Brooks's piece appeared. Moreover, we were two of the "bobos" that Brooks had alternately skewered and praised in his earlier book, and we, too, had children.

Brooks did most of his research for the piece at Princeton, where he talked to faculty and administrators and interviewed selected undergraduates. Despite cultural differences across institutions, the portrait that emerges in "The Organization Kid" accurately describes certain aspects of the student populations at all of the Ivies and

beyond. Brooks found the new generation—labeled on the cover
of that issue of the *Atlantic* "The Next Ruling Class"—eager to
please and disinclined to the resistance, rebellion, and theater
that many of their parents had practiced during the 1960s. They
were, moreover, actually quite fond of those parents, accepting
of their mores and happy to have their supervision. They had no
qualms about reaching for the levers of success, and knew with
great accuracy where to find them. For them, building résumés
well before college had become a matter of course.

Partly as a result, Brooks argues, the new generation of
students at elite schools lacks the inner rather than externally motivated drive that their parents once demonstrated. In the end, perhaps as a result of that internal void, they also lack a moral life. To
put his argument in terms I introduced in an earlier chapter, they
lack a moral compass, for which Brooks uses the terms *character*
and *self-mastery*. Brooks sees these terms as representative of an
older, more conservative time, one that was aware of adversity and
evil in a way that we as a society no longer are. In fact, the young
people Brooks describes seem not to have a social conscience, or
even to be socially aware, focused as they are on putting together
their successful individual lives. They are—and Brooks's title
makes the connection clear—latter-day versions of William H.
Whyte's *The Organization Man* (1956), willing corporate bees even
when they aren't literally working in corporations. The literary reference suggests this is a new silent majority in the making, even
once individual members rise to positions of great influence.

In the course of his discussion, Brooks gives as much time or
more to the parents of these new organizational individuals, effectively following the natural flow of his earlier commentary on
the Boomer generation. The connection is logical, and entertain-
ing.We recognize the stereotype of the parent in New York,

Washington, or Boston, lining up the right day-care center for the child destined—at least in the parents' minds—for Harvard. But in satirizing the status-consciousness of Boomer parents and their offspring, Brooks misses a chance to document a different side of this apparently well-adjusted, efficient generation. College administrators report that the level of psychological dysfunction among current undergraduates is high. Brooks sees parental reliance on psychotropic drugs such as Ritalin and Prozac to control their children in primary and secondary school as an alarming trend. But that only begins to cover the array of individual distress we and our colleagues witness after these accomplished young men and women move out from under their parents' watchful eyes.

Binge drinking is the most obvious and common manifestation of a need to let off steam, to escape the pressure to which many of our students subject themselves in pursuit of Brooks's goal of social success. It is usually coupled with an at least Harvard-specific desire to be "just like students at all the other [state] schools." We also routinely see, mostly among women, eating disorders and self-mutilation on a minor scale. Date rape and sexual assault are infrequent, but probably underreported; they are often tied to alcohol consumption. Gay and lesbian students continue to face significant stigmatization.

Many students suffer from the routine anxiety that goes with operating in a highly competitive environment. They are victims of the now time-honored fear that they are the one individual whose candidacy the admissions committee misjudged. Many want to please their parents, but can't do it in terms their parents will accept: some students really don't want to be doctors or lawyers. Finally, for all the affection in which many students of this generation hold their parents, a good number have horrendous home lives, the consequences of which occasionally get spelled out in academic and disciplinary procedures, but also in reports from concerned friends or tutors in whom students confide, even when they are to all appearances coping splendidly.

So, are these students the best and brightest? Absolutely—they are enormously talented, accomplished, and decent. As Brooks argues, they are gifted in every imaginable way. At Harvard's Mather House we have had Olympic athletes and athletes who go professional even before they graduate; Rhodes, Truman, and other major scholarship winners; television and film actors; authors of published scientific papers; public service entrepreneurs who have their own start-up organizations, or routinely give twenty to thirty hours a week to campus-run soup kitchens, or arrange for the purchase and liberation of Sudanese slaves, or run yearly model U.N. and model Congress organizations sometimes involving thousands of people from around the globe; musicians who have already launched concert careers, and theater people who write, direct, and act in major college productions, sometimes half a dozen a year—all the while maintaining full academic lives.

More often than not, despite the popular and intermittently accurate view of Harvard students as self-absorbed and self-aggrandizing, you would never know that many of them do all the things they do unless you asked them. Moreover, one could argue—and some college administrators do—that the rising rate of reported distress simply reflects the fact that universities have gotten better at addressing late adolescent angst. It is no longer uncool to reveal you're unhappy, at least in the psychologist's office, and the universities make it easy to find your way there. At some level, too, this is just a version of the efficiency Brooks sees in organization kids: they know when they've got a problem, and they seek out the resources they need to deal with it.

Yet the phrase "the best and the brightest," enshrined in the ironic title of David Halberstam's 1973 book about the leaders who launched and directed America's Vietnam War, is ambiguous in this generation, too. For all the accomplishment, for all the good sense, for all the alignment of values with the larger society that this generation of college students has demonstrated, it seems very unlikely that they will bring us any closer to the good society than their parents have, in part because of their parents, in part because of themselves. Despite the apparently free hand that the organization kids have earned by cooperating with—Brooks might say, willingly being coopted by—their doting parents, they still need to choose among competing goods. To judge from what my wife and I see at the ground level of the organization kids, their judgments will prove fallible because they are still human, and because, in spite of all of the advantages that some of them have had as sons and daughters of the Boomer generation, others with similar parents have had fewer or still more. These inequalities will inevitably play out in the social solutions that they craft for themselves and their peers.

For good or ill, these facts mean that the adults in the lives of the current college generation, in the classroom and beyond, still have a potentially positive role to play. This is as true for the adults who teach or employ them after they graduate as it is for those of us who work with them now. The question is, as always, how best to do so: that is what we have spent our years sorting out, while mastering Mather.

A Little Institutional History

Mather House opened in 1970, the newest of the twelve undergraduate residential complexes in Harvard College, coming forty

years after then-President A. Lawrence Lowell completed his
drive to democratize the economically stratified student experience at the school. At the turn of the twentieth century, wealthy
students lived in expensive and comfortable digs along Mt.
Auburn Street, separated from less well-to-do peers living at
home or in budget accommodations. Lowell wanted to distin-
guish students on intellectual merit rather than property. He
mandated a dormitory experience for first-year students, and
later did the same for the upperclassmen; the residential houses
are the result. Mather House is named for three generations of
the Mather family: Richard, who settled in the Massachusetts Bay
Colony in 1635, following religious troubles in England; his son,
Increase, a Harvard graduate and sixth president of the college,
from 1685 to 1701; and his grandson, Cotton, Harvard class of
1678. When my wife, Sandra, and I took over as master and co-
master in the winter of 1993, a descendant of Richard Mather was
among the students in the house.

Like Richard before them, Increase and Cotton were minis-
ters, leaders in the Boston religious community of the time.
Moreover, as part of the Puritan theocracy that governed the
colony under charter from the British Crown, they had a broader
sphere of influence and responsibility than a church appoint-
ment narrowly defined might today suggest. After the Glorious
Revolution in Britain and related civil unrest in Massachusetts
had led to a suspension of the first colonial charter, Increase
spent four years in England, 1688–1692, negotiating a new one.
He then returned to Boston, only to plunge into the midst of the
public response to the Salem witch trials of 1692, in which his son
also played a major role.

In *Cases of Conscience Concerning Evil Spirits Personating Men*
(1693), Increase counseled prudence and principle in the judicial

process that had been set in motion at Salem: "It were better that ten suspected Witches should escape, than that one innocent Person should be Condemned. . . . The Word of God directs men not to proceed to the execution of the most capital offenders, until such time as upon searching diligently, the matter is *found to be a Truth, and the thing certain*," Deut. 13. 14, 15, (p. 283). His published views are credited with speeding the release of many of the accused as the furor at Salem subsided, though disagreement continues among historians about his motives, the degree to which he fed or moderated the hysteria, and the nature of his commitment to what we now call the rules of evidence, since he did apparently believe in witches and demons.

Throughout this period, Increase was also deeply involved in the affairs of Harvard College. The first generation of Puritan settlers in the Massachusetts Bay Colony had founded it in 1636 to ensure that the Colony had an educated clergy. Increase enrolled there at the age of twelve, as did Cotton in his own time. Yet despite Increase's deep engagement with the school through much of his life, he twice turned down the presidency, torn between the college and the congregation he served as pastor at the North Church in Boston. He was acting president, then rector, and then became president of the college, only finally to give up the office over a requirement that he live in Cambridge; his church was waiting for him in Boston.

Still, modern-day Mather residents love to quote the more brooding and admonitory lines from his sermons and other writings, in which he perceives the wages of New Englanders' sins in everything from inclement weather to smallpox to the colonists' sufferings at the hands of the native Wampanoag and other tribes, as the English settlers encroached on their lands. This last struggle, called King Philip's War (1675–76), is little known, but by all accounts the bloodiest conflict per capita in American history. Increase turned out *A Brief History of the War with the Indians* (1676) with a speed and journalistic quality that we reserve today for the wars in Afghanistan and Iraq. Here, as in all his other work, he seems to have been driven by concern for the welfare of the polity, the importance of capturing and recording events to guide governance as well as individual behavior.

Our undergraduates, meanwhile, invoke the pastor's name for everything from sly sexual references to the phallic nineteen-story tower that dominates the house to more innocent student government exhortations to "Increase Mather Spirit" through beer consumption, Dutch auctions, dating games, and large-scale house parties, most notably the Cancun-style Mather Lather foam dance. At a purely local level, the boosterism is meant in part to counter the lore abroad in the rest of the university that Mather was designed by a prison architect, or that it was explicitly conceived to withstand the student riots of the 1960s. More importantly, the students' spirited use of Mather addresses the question of organizational and specifically Harvard culture, for which Increase is a plausible symbol, and it lends a quasi-political, 1960s-like quality to the students' ribaldry, at least for those of us who experienced it the first time around.

Sometimes, architecture is destiny. The so-called River Houses erected under President Lowell in the early 1930s are neo-Georgian structures of brick, with wood paneling and fireplaces in a comfortably antique look that today's untrained eye might date to 1636, not 1936. At Mather, the architect used a different vernacular: concrete, steel, and large expanses of glass. Even now, after years of hard-living students and architectural adjustments to city codes, it is still all edges. In the spring of 2003, our house council released yet another in a steady stream of house T-shirts.

This one, bright red and done up with a graphic of heroes of so-
cialist realism on the back, said, "Mathergrad—The Kremlin on
the Charles/34 years of Soviet bloc housing," a cunningly brief
blend of political and architectural self-mockery.

Students who are assigned to Mather long for the "real Harvard experience," and one can see why they might. The house
epitomizes brutalist modernism. It is not easy to look at, and it is
not easy to live in. But that is why, in a curious way, it may foster
the "real Harvard experience" better than the other houses. As a
living space, it is as uncompromising as the Puritans who created
the college: it is all about transparency, visibility, accountability.
Every student has his or her own bedroom—a luxury even
today—but the bedrooms are just big enough, in most cases, for
a bed, a desk, and a bookshelf. However they actually get used by
their residents, they are cells made for composing oneself and
one's thoughts before reentering the communal space. That
space consists of the common rooms in the low-rise suites, and
the common spaces for the house as a whole, clearly identified
from the outside in the materials used for those parts of the
house. Even as it recognizes the need for individual space, Mather
enforces and codes sociability—that, too, is a Puritan legacy.

It should be said that Carlhian, the architect, refuses to discuss
his design purposes at this level of cultural abstraction. About
ten years after my wife and I became co-masters, we invited Carlhian back to the house. He accepted readily, and his visit drew
more students than any other in our time, aside from appearances by baseball great Hank Aaron and the current university
president and former U.S. Treasury Secretary Larry Summers.
Carlhian took many questions, and answered them with charm
and humor, yet he refused to be drawn into the subject of his reasons for designing the complex as he had, beyond references to

the larger urban landscape in which it had to take its place, the size and shape of the lot, and the university's specifications for internal accommodations.

We do know from earlier testimony that Carlhian had hoped to have the university's Fogg Art Museum provide objects to engage and entertain the students as they moved about the house. Even he felt there was room for aesthetic repose and renewal in his hard-edged scheme. Budget constraints and curatorial concerns dictated otherwise; so instead, we have the cheery irreverence that has become characteristic of the Mather community—definitely not party headquarters, not quite party central, but all in all a good place to have a good time. The students' commitment to maintaining that reputation softens the edges of a building and an institution that are not known for their warmth and supportiveness, in spite of all the systems that the college and university administrations have put in place to foster a cozier atmosphere. It is hard fully to understand the persistence of the culture, except that it represents the competitive reality of being and striving at Harvard, and it extends beyond the university through its far-flung alumni, who know—and this, too, aligns with the Puritan worldview—that one can and should do well while doing good.

First Commitments

When Sandra and I took the job at Mather, we didn't think much about Puritans and organizational culture. We had been acting masters at Cabot House for a semester, replacing a colleague who was on sabbatical. We loved being back at the Radcliffe Quadrangle, where we had met as undergraduates. We dealt successfully at the start of our tenure with a complicated racial situation that had carried over from the previous year, and we realized that our children, then six and two years old, very much enjoyed a life with hundreds of surrogate older siblings, foosball and ping-pong in easy reach, and soft drinks and French fries on tap daily in the house dining hall.

Because we had simply to hold the fort at Cabot until the regular masters returned, it didn't dawn on us until we moved to Mather that it was a full-scale, full-time managerial position, and that we might actually have to head the community, rather than simply throw parties for it. Yet I have now lived at Mather for twelve years, longer than I have lived anywhere else in my life, and during those years, for all Mather's hard edges and the history they transmit, it has become my version of the good society, for reasons that I have been able to articulate only by being in it, by becoming a part of it.

My first memory of Harvard predates Mather, and even Carlhian's conception of Mather. In the mid-1950s, my parents, my older sister, and I came to Boston to visit family friends. Like so many tourists then and now, we visited Harvard Yard as a major stop on our route. Years later, I returned to Harvard as an undergraduate, and walked or ran almost daily through the Yard, on my way to class or into Widener Library to research a paper, to go to my part-time job shelving documents in the bowels of the stacks, or to meet a friend. Years after that, I brought our sons, Nathaniel and Ben, from our apartment just a few blocks away so that they could chase the Yard's ever-elusive squirrels. And then have come the years when, as co-masters, we lead Mather's seniors into the Yard each Commencement morning to enter the "fellowship of educated men and women."

Commencement is a carefully orchestrated, yet on its surface, totally chaotic event. With a bagpiper at the head of the line, we march up from the house through Cambridge city streets, where, for a few hours on this one morning of the year, pedestrians really do have the right of way. We stop first at Memorial Church so that the university chaplain can bless the graduating seniors, then line up on either side of the sidewalk past University Hall to applaud reunion classes going back fifty years and more, as well as faculty and other dignitaries. After the elders pass through the gauntlet, the students themselves march in two's amid the bright banners and the university band playing and the thousands of family and friends cheering, snapping pictures, maneuvering for a better view of the stage where the president and fellows of Harvard College, the Harvard Corporation, the sheriff of Middlesex County, the faculty, and distinguished honorary degree recipients gather. One more time, we enter the Yard, for this morning known by its other, more formal name of Tercentary Theater.

It has all been planned out, yet when Sandra and I, like the other masters, go into the Yard on those Thursday mornings in early June, we are followed by 150 sleepy (sometimes hung-over), excited, nervous 22-year-olds, and surrounded by thousands of equally sleepy, excited, nervous family and friends, all waiting for the ceremony to begin, and wondering a little when and how it will end. For us, it is always a thrilling moment, and so I was surprised when an alumna came back a year or two after she graduated and commented that the two of us had been figures of calm amid all the jitters on that morning.

Even at the celebratory end of their college years, it seems, students welcome a steadying hand. Knowing that frames our responsibility to help our students survive and thrive, even when they don't need much help, even when no one in particular is responsible for the difficulties they face. In some small way, it seems to me, each senior who graduates contributes to that effort, too; that is what excellence and determination and consideration and completion are about. If we have done our job of escorting them properly, they will do it ever better and more consciously as they move forward in their lives; but we have to connect with them sufficiently to make that happen. That is where mastery begins.

Gathering in the Pieces

When I was almost ten, my father left journalism to join the United States Information Agency. He had come to the United States in 1940, leaving Latvia two weeks before the Soviets invaded. His family was sending him to study at New York University, after which he was expected to return home to Latvia to help manage the family timber business. Instead, he spent four months on Ellis Island, the holder of a passport issued by a country that no longer existed. When he was finally released from his relatively pleasant incarceration—he once told me he had become the ping-pong king of Ellis Island, since there was nothing else to do—he went to work sweeping shavings in a silverware factory in the Bronx under the assumed name of "Charlie Potter"; he never remembered who he was supposed to be when the shop foreman called out to him.

Though a resident alien, my father was eventually drafted into the U.S. military and served in Army Intelligence. He met my mother after the end of hostilities in a small village in Normandy, where she had spent the latter part of the war on a farm with her parents. Her stories were of hunger and difficult times and frequent fear: working in the fields; raising and then eating large numbers of pet rabbits; burying Allied fliers who had been shot down in dogfights over the village; and once threatening the German SS officer billeted on the family farm with his own pistol—

an act she herself doubts actually occurred, though it was perfectly in her character. She married my father in the late 1940s,
and after a year in London they settled for a sunny decade in the
Midwest. Family photo albums show them in the Badlands of
South Dakota, looking very American as they gaze out from a
bluff over the surrounding landscape.

The picture is deceptive, of course, a fantasy concocted of the
scenery and the clothes they wore. Yet they themselves believed
very much in this particular dream, and it seemed natural for
them to go back out into the world to represent the country that
had rescued them from tyranny of the left and of the right, even
though they hardly knew that country. They had a story to tell
the world, and understood viscerally, if not in the daily specifics,
what America was about. Ironically, the transfer of information
ran only one way: my parents quickly discovered the Foreign Service truism that no one at home had much interest in the stories
you brought back from overseas. It was taken for granted that
one didn't try to discuss life "over there" with family and friends,
even though in my parents' case, "over there" was actually home,
where they had lived the bulk of their still young lives and from
which they derived their very identity.

From them, I learned very quickly to listen, to ask questions,
and to be circumspect in retailing my own experiences. For me,
the good stories were always other people's stories, from worlds
of which I had only an imperfect grasp. Like most diplomats'
kids, my background and experience quickly made me that bane
of Western civilization, the rootless cosmopolitan who knows
customs everywhere, yet practices none of them with the easy
self-confidence that a native would, even at home, and who has
discovered the truth we all ought to and would admit, if it didn't
threaten our daily ability to function—that there is no single

right way to do anything. Years later, knowing friends and colleagues would laugh when I stumbled over the choice of "immigrate" or "emigrate," uncertain from which perspective to look at such global transfers of individual bodies, or used the phrase "... or however you pronounce it," a preemptive recognition that local tongues have probably reincarnated names you know from other places in very different forms.

The questioning approach my parents taught me is still valuable today, in that it has taken me a long way toward mastering the art of moderated discussion, the format for most of the debates presented in this book. Over time, though, I have come to realize that my parents and their colleagues, like many people in positions of authority, actually had a very good idea of the background to their interrogative exchanges with other people, in and out of the workplace. They had acceded to their positions in large part because of that expertise, and asked questions simply as a means of applying it more effectively. It was an important discovery: if speaking up and speaking out is essential to ethical practice, if telling good stories is essential to ethical practice, asking questions won't get you there. At some point, the stories elicited by those questions require a story in response, a fair trade that will both establish your authority and acknowledge the validity of the other person's experience. At some point, the interlocutor usually has to step in to keep the conversation going as a conversation, rather than an interview. That is his or her enterprise.

Fortunately for me, the cosmopolitan environment that I experienced as a child has increasingly become the world that we know in America today and recognize in the globalization process occurring around the world. I have the daily expertise to share that knowledge with the various constituencies we serve at Mather: visiting scholars and faculty from many other countries, parents who are bicoastal business people or recent immigrants from across much of the economic spectrum, and the thoroughly diversified student body that fills the Mather dining hall and every other part of the university, just as it does many other schools across the country, at all age levels.

Moreover, the students' cosmopolitanism reflects the importance of story as we have developed it in this book. Late last spring, to take one example, Sandra and I joined four women students whiling away a long lunch break in the Mather dining hall. One, an American, had a hyphenated name, like our own boys. A Korean woman in the group commented that that simply wasn't done in Korea. Then she mentioned her grandparents' complaint that no one knew any longer how to prepare *kimchee*—Korean pickled vegetables. Then the conversation drifted to *Bend It Like Beckham*, the recent film release in which a British Indian family experiences a similar generational conflict over food, and then to *Monsoon Wedding*, Mira Nair's film about the clash and conflation of Indian and Western cultures in India proper. The last leap was a short one, because one of the American students had recently spent five weeks in India, and attended just such a wedding.

We understood our students' drift because of my background and because Sandra grew up in a Lebanese-American family, where her mother distinguished between good behavior and "American" behavior, and Sandra learned how to cook traditional Lebanese dishes even as she refused the family's church for our wedding. We understood it, too, because we shared the cultural totems the young women had introduced; these are easy conversations to have. Yet global literacy isn't enough. We also need to implement policies in the house that make such exchanges possible, and that make it possible for everyone to feel comfortable regardless of their background, with others of very different backgrounds. The security net that I knew by virtue of membership in the diplomatic community doesn't apply at Mather House, or in most of the transnational and transethnic situations we encounter in today's globalizing societies. Knowing isn't enough; we need to apply specific administrative solutions to make knowing, or the acquisition of knowledge, a real possibility for our students.

Telling One Story

When we joined Mather, it was far more uniformly Caucasian than some of the other houses; moving across campus from our acting mastership at Cabot House was like moving from Jesse Jackson's Rainbow Coalition of the 1990s to the Harvard of the 1950s. That felt wrong for everyone concerned, given how the college population had changed in the interim. The first two Mather classes we graduated were also two-thirds male when the college ratio at the time was 1.3 to 1. Like many of our colleagues, we pushed hard to change the system of assignment to the houses, so that the individual house populations would be as diverse as the overall college population. It was a controversial stance to take. Minority students felt that a random assignment system would deprive them of the critical mass they had achieved in a few of the houses, and everyone was worried that they would be separated from their like-minded friends. One of our faculty affiliates, the Anglo-Ghanaian philosopher Anthony Appiah, commented during the debate over random assignment: "Only in America would you throw together a bunch of teenagers from completely different backgrounds and expect them to get along."

In 1994 the house experienced a spate of racist graffiti that distressed everyone, threatened to pit black against Hispanic students, and showed no signs of resolving itself through the identification of a culprit or culprits, despite an anonymous tip line set up by the university police. One Asian student voiced the feelings of many: "I don't want to believe it could happen here." But it did happen at Mather, just as most of the things that happen outside the walls of the university happen at some point on the inside, too. Then you have to find the story that will persuade people that change is in order, and that the particular change you have in mind will work best for all parties, even when you know that some disagree.

As discussed in Chapter 6, the matter of controlling for faith surfaces here, too. You may know that you are right, but for those whose positions are threatened as the system evolves, saving face matters. With a population that was heavily athletic, we argued simply that we wanted to have more of our students around more of the week and on weekends, instead of on the road for games away or working out at the athletic complex on demanding team schedules. We argued that it was good for people to integrate across areas of interest, an initiative that seemed much less controversial than forced integration across ethnic lines. We made the case for community, a specific kind of community, which was in line with our function in the college and the house.

Most importantly, though, we believed in that community, having lived and benefited from a version of it all our lives. At a certain point during the debate over random assignment, I realized that you do need to declare what you believe, why you believe it, and if at all possible—for purposes of veracity and entertainment—where, when, with or through whom, and how. This may seem obvious to most people, but given my wandering background, it wasn't to me. Rooting practices in a culture and organizational setting is essential, if they are to have an effect. The fact of choice based on broad exposure doesn't alter the need to choose; it simply imposes the obligation to analyze efficiently, and to tell the story that emerges.

In this case, the story was one of policies gradually introduced at all of the Ivies in the late 1950s and 1960s, that turn fundraising alumni phonathons in the University Development Office from an all-male, gray-suited, silver-haired affair for classes up to about 1965 into something far more diverse thereafter. We were simply arguing to take these policies one step further, in the face of student arguments that what the college did in the classroom was its business, but shouldn't extend to their living space and limit their right to choose with whom they lived. The distinction between learning and living was one that the college rejected from its very earliest days, and though the terms of that combination have changed substantially since Harvard's Puritan founders set to work, the principle remains, and prevailed in this case. Our first random class entered Mather in the fall of 1996, a mix of athletes and theater types and lab rats and a group of sixteen jazz musicians. Mather's common spaces have been busy with groups rehearsing, meeting, and celebrating ever since.

At the same time, we know that it usually works best to take a cue from the constituency we wish to represent, and to steer for more or less universal values across the diversity that we have now created. During Commencement ceremonies at the house in June 1999—again, our first random class—I suggested to our graduating seniors that they might someday come back to witness their grandchildren graduating from the college, just as their grandparents were standing by as witnesses on that day. I meant the line to punctuate that moment in the speech by bringing the generations together, but it met with absolutely no response from the graduates. Then, looking down at all those expectant faces, I heard them silently say, as much as I heard myself say out loud, "Perhaps you'll come back to collect an honorary degree, like the honorees we witnessed this morning." The response, still silent, was almost palpable: though the ratio of honorees to the global population from which they are drawn is impossibly small, earning the recognition implicit in an honorary degree was a more plausible ambition to this group of 22-year-olds than grandchildren, and I should have known that. Now that I had heard and voiced their silent message, the speech could go on.

In short, mastering at Mather has consisted in recognizing our own beliefs, recognizing the validity of other people's stories, and building them into the big story that we can then tell back to the community in a form that offers some assurance it will be heard. Despite all the systems—and the college systems have mattered enormously in our work—we have found that we have to make the community personal in this way, if our presence is to matter at all. For us, at least, mastery lies in the give-and-take of all parties, not in any one individual or group of individuals. It generates a community personality that transcends all the individual parties to it, even as it requires us to model it, enact it, make its truth manifest.

Spring Cleaning

In our second year in Mather House, we took down the curtains in the breakfast room to the master's residence. We did this, not out of a fit of spring cleaning madness, but because of the architecture and because, by then, we had a much better sense of why the houses have masters, and how we might best respond to our assigned role.

The master's residence occupies one corner of the lot on which the house sits. As with much of the rest of the house, the prevalence of glass and the relative shallowness of the space behind it mean that much of what goes on inside is readily visible to anyone outside. Students have occasionally commented to us on the highly visible quality of life in the low-rise, an almost-closed U of four to five stories, with everyone's suites available for inspection from similar spaces across the main courtyard. In the master's residence, the breakfast room and kitchen give directly onto a smaller, private courtyard, which is private only in the sense that we alone have access to it; a dozen student bedrooms and common rooms look from the upper stories directly into the ground-level space where we routinely eat our meals and convene as a family. Regardless of the curtains that screened us when we first arrived, we soon realized we were in a goldfish bowl, our every move and interaction always potentially visible to some portion of the community of which we were the heads; and since sound travels well through glass and raw concrete, our daily family life was audible to the students, too.

So, why take down the curtains? Partly, of course, our decision was aesthetic: if you live in a glass house, it makes sense to enjoy the glass—or rather, the world outside the glass that was designed to be a part of the experience of living in that space. With floor-to-ceiling windows looking onto an enclosed courtyard, it was hard to imagine simply drawing a curtain on the courtyard and severing the link between the natural setting of the residence and the residence itself. Partly, too, we were doing psychological guesswork: it stood to reason that if the curtains were closed some of the time, students would be much more interested in watching what went on in the residence when the curtains were open. If we went through the routine of opening the curtains during the daylight hours and closing them at night, we would be issuing a daily invitation to our neighbors to check on progress since the last opening. Removing the curtains, we reasoned, would remove that interest altogether.

And yet, one or another casual emissary from the various rooming groups that have occupied those suites over the years will routinely comment on how nice it would be to have dinner in the residence, based on their observations of our family dinners. One group of women commented, late in the fall of their first year in the house, that they had decided on observation that our family was a matriarchy. How much time had they spent watching through the breakfast room window, to come up with that analysis? So in the end, we took down the curtains not because we thought we could outsmart anyone, but because we realized it was easier and smarter to go with the public role than fight or try to minimize it. If we were to be leaders of the house, if, as adults, we were to model behavior for the students for whom we were responsible, we might just as well begin the modeling at ground level—in the nitty-gritty of daily life. If we wanted them to behave in a certain way, we might as well let them see that we practiced what we preached: we had to be good spouses, good parents who brought up good kids, and thoughtful individuals with careers that might eventually appeal to casual spectators in search of a future.

Having made that theoretical commitment, of course, we had to practice it. If taking down the curtains put less external psychological pressure on us—"no one is really looking now, since they can look anytime"—it distinctly heightened the internal pressure. Over the years, testing for appropriateness has become second nature: this could be a version of "what would the neighbors say?" but it goes beyond maintaining social status to the larger question of setting standards, not simply abiding by them. Needless to say, it feels sometimes as though, like our students, we are living in the Puritan shadow of Increase Mather, only we have an age- and role-appropriate obligation to act to his standard, not flout it.

Appropriateness is certainly defined here in part by most people's base-level expectations for civilized behavior: no drunken brawls, no child-beating, and so on. But it goes beyond those minimal standards to human interaction that fosters a happy and productive environment through a balanced existence: the life of the mind, sociability, community engagement— in short, what the "House Master's Manual" requires of us. We had the advantage of two young children when we started. In those early years, we strolled out into the main courtyard after day care or elementary school smack into the flow of students returning from afternoon classes for dinner. Invariably, one or two were looking for distraction after a long day, and informal whiffle ball or foursquare or touch football or Frisbee seemed just the thing. Sometimes, they stopped because they missed younger siblings, or needed a quick fix of family. With others we might trade just a few words, and with still others a greeting, but even in the latter cases it was one of the most effective and enjoyable ways of walking the shop floor that I can imagine, a way of showing that we were present, eager to keep in touch with the rest of the house, and having a good time as a family.

We have missed the casual contact since our boys outgrew those pick-up games, but as I write this, our elder son has begun his undergraduate years at Harvard, and we find we have already begun to draw a different but equally effective line of access to our students as a result. Opening the curtains at Mather seems to have revealed truths going both ways, if his decision to stay on in

Cambridge is any indication. The games are getting more serious, but he has been eager to join the community outside our
window.

"Leaderless Leadership"?

At the end of a recent Aspen Institute Executive Seminar, an eight-
day affair with twenty-three business executives and other professionals, one of the participants approached me with a grin and,
instead of saying good-bye, simply said, "Leaderless leadership."

Over close to two decades, he had been a senior executive
with several of the major players in the asset management business. He had recently gone out on his own, leaving New York for
a more relaxed setting. He was also teaching part-time, had just
started a master's degree program, and was very involved in an
international nonprofit organization. It seemed a very good and
full life to live.

I asked him, "Is that the next step?"

"No," he replied. "It's what you've just done."

The phrase "leaderless leadership" has been in the air for some
time now, advanced with variations in books by management
gurus and other observers of organizations. At one level, it is
very much what my co-moderator and I had hoped to accomplish in those sessions at Aspen: to ask questions of the participants, each as talented and accomplished as this particular man.
As they answered the questions we put to them, we hoped each
member would learn from the others, and they might also discover new and previously unsuspected qualities in themselves,
new aspects of their expertise.

At the same time, these discussions aim at more than the improvement of a small group of talented and curious executives. They are also intended as a model for leadership, placing at the center of organizations a public discussion of topics that should matter to all of us—human nature, the origins and development of rights, distributive justice, liberty and democracy, the role of science and technology, and responsibility for the good society. One needn't be an undergraduate to take an interest in such things. Indeed, the participants showed abundantly that, even in the midst of successful careers in diverse fields, they were eager to think about, and take a hand in, improving the society that we all share. They are the men and women that the undergraduates at Mather and in college dorms across the country will become.

Like their older counterparts at Aspen, the students with whom my wife, my sons, and I have lived know too much, and are too skillful, to be told simply what to do. Yet we are preparing them to enter a world where decisions get made and someone does remain in charge, if only by virtue of the expertise that he or she brings to the table. And so, we come back to the notion of mastery introduced early in this book and built into our title and our role at Mather. Without veering into cynicism or starry-eyed idealism, we need to recognize the obligation that comes with expertise and the importance of engaging in an ongoing process of education or training that will make others equally expert, so that they can at some point succeed us. We need to enjoy what we do enough, and have sufficient confidence in ourselves and others and our discipline, to let people find their way, not fuss too much when they make mistakes, and then be ready to articulate the solutions—tell the stories—that recognize multiple interests and still set the community on a single, plausible path to success.

That is the good society: five short steps to ethical practice that every one of us can and must take, story by story, if we are to secure our collective future. The businesspeople I have cited here—Bobby, Richard Grubman, Jack Rennie, Abigail Ross Goodman—have demonstrated this combination of skills in their professional lives, setting an example of principled engagement in their organizations and with their colleagues, subordinates, and the larger public. Many others like them have gone unnamed here, but their spirit made this book possible, too. Numbers, as any good businessperson will tell you, don't lie; you can use them or abuse them, but they will do the ethical work you require if you let other people stand up, tell their stories, and be counted. It is a heartening experience to see it happen, one that each of us can manage if we have the courage to model our best guess as to what makes life worth living.

That is the story of success, for the individual, the organizations in which we lead, and the society to which we owe a measure of our opportunities and abilities. Will you tell it?

Cambridge, Massachusetts
March 2005

Annotated Bibliography/ Filmography
105 Steps to Mastering Ethics in Business

The following annotated list includes materials I have used in ethics seminars in varying combinations, either as background to or the subject of moderated discussion. I have also included entries for all materials cited in *The Story of Success*. Entries are organized by primary relevance to individual chapters of this study; however, many of them can be used to explore more than one category.

Chapter 1: The Importance of Story

Aristotle, *Nicomachean Ethics*. (350 BCE). Trans. D.P. Chase, 1911. Mineola, NY: Dover, 1998; republication of Aristotle's *Ethics*, London: J.M. Dent & Sons, 1911. One of the fathers of Western philosophy lays out the terms on which man may achieve happiness.

Aristotle, "Politics" (350 BCE). Trans. Benjamin Jowett, 1886. In *The Basic Works of Aristotle*, New York: Random House, 1941, pp. 1127–1316. In a continuation of the *Ethics*, Aristotle assesses the relation of the individual to society.

Robert Brawer, *Fictions of Business: Insights on Management from Great Literature*. New York: John Wiley & Sons, 1998. Once a professor of English and then the CEO of Maidenform, Brawer uses classics of Western fiction to talk about typical business challenges.

Joel Coen, dir., *O Brother, Where Art Thou?* (2000). The Coen brothers produce a version of Homer's *Odyssey* set in the American South of the early twentieth century, where "old-timey music" is the vocabulary of people's lives and a latter-day Ulysses talks his way out of jail and back to his less-than-forgiving wife.

Robert Coles, *Children of Crisis: Selections from the Pulitzer Prize-winning Five-Volume Children of Crisis Series.* Boston: Back Bay Books, 2003. In interviews and commentaries originally published in five volumes from 1967 to 1977, Coles captures the effects of segregation and the struggle for civil rights on children in the American South.

Confucius, *The Analects.* (circa 500 BCE). Trans. Simon Leys, New York: W.W. Norton & Co., 1997. Compiled by the followers of Confucius, *The Analects* captures the teachings of China's greatest sage, focusing on the values of humanity, reciprocity, and the role of the gentleman in society.

Rebecca Goldstein, "The Legacy of Raizel Kaidish." In *Strange Attractors,* New York: Penguin Books, 1993, pp. 227–240. A young woman finds the stories her mother tells her of life in Buchenwald, one of the Nazis' death camps, more real than her own life after the war. Then her mother tells her the truth about her experience in the camp.

Richard Grubman discussed in Zeke Ashton, "Cree's Conference Call Blues," *The MotleyFool/Fool.com,* Oct. 24, 2003; "Microphone Mishap: Watching Your Ps and Qs," Dale Spencer, *I Financial Marketing;* "Enron Fails to Smooth Things Over," Peter Eavis, *TheStreet.com,* Oct. 23, 2001; "The High-Wire Act," Joe Hagan, *Folio,* June 1, 2002; Steve Bailey, "My Favorite Troublemakers," *Boston Globe,* January 7, 2004; "Investing on the Edge," John Pulley, *Chronicle of Higher Education,* May 10, 2002.

Thomas Hobbes, *Leviathan.* (1651). New York: Pelican Books, 1968. Hobbes draws from his mechanistic, scientific view of man a notion of the sovereign state, or Leviathan, that he believes will save us from a chaotic state of nature "through the mutual relation between protection and obedience."

John Locke, *Second Treatise of Government*. (1690). Indianapolis/Cambridge: Hackett Publishing, 1980. Locke defends a liberal state, refuting Hobbes's grim notion of the state of nature, challenging the divine right of kings, and setting forth civil liberties as part of a limited social contract.

Alasdair MacIntyre, *After Virtue*. London: Gerald Duckworth & Co., Ltd., 1981. In this study of the failure of contemporary moral theory, MacIntyre develops notions of practice and narrative or story as they enable ethics in the modern world.

Karl Marx and Friedrich Engels, *The Communist Manifesto*. (1848). New York: Signet Classic, 1998. Marx and Engels set forth the historical circumstances that have generated the need for new social and economic relations. See also, Karl Marx, "The Economic and Philosophical Manuscripts of 1844" (written 1844, first published 1932), in *The Marx-Engels Reader*, 2nd Edition. New York: W.W. Norton, 1978.

Arthur M. Okun, *Equality and Efficiency: The Big Tradeoff*. (1974). Washington, DC: Brookings Institution Press, 1975. Okun explores the tradeoff between social policies promoting greater equality through rights and economic policies focused on efficiency.

Douglas Ready, "How Storytelling Builds Next-Generation Leaders." In *MIT Sloan Management Review*, Summer 2002, Vol. 43, #4, pp. 63–69. Ready explores how corporations can use story to develop successors for top management in large organizations.

Royal Dutch/Shell, "Global Scenarios: 1995–2020." Public Scenarios PX 96-2. Designed and produced by Publicity Services, May 1996. One installment in the triennial series of scenarios articulated by strategic planners at Royal Dutch/Shell, focusing on the potential for competition between American and East Asian models in the coming decades.

Donald Schön, *The Reflective Practitioner*. New York: Basic Books, 1983.

The late MIT professor of urban studies and education discusses how professionals "name and frame" problems in order to solve them, and assesses the change during the latter part of the twentieth century in how society at large views professional activity.

Gordon Shaw, Robert Brown, Philip Bromiley, "Strategic Stories: How 3M Is Rewriting Business Planning." In *Harvard Business Review,* May–June 1998, reprint # 98310. 3M discovers that the principles of story—setting the stage, introducing conflict, providing a resolution—work as well in business planning as they do in fiction.

Annette Simmons, *The Story Factor: Secrets of Influence from the Art of Storytelling.* Cambridge, MA: Perseus Publishing, 2001. Simmons discusses the key components to successful stories in the workplace.

U.N. Universal Declaration of Human Rights (1948). Available on-line. The Declaration has served as the main template for global ethical standards during the past half-century.

Chapter 2: Speak Up, Speak Out

Pearl Buck, "The Enemy." In *Far and Near: Stories of Japan, China, and America.* New York: The John Day Co., 1947, pp. 1–21. A Japanese doctor in wartime Japan has to decide whether or not to save the life of an escaped, but wounded, American prisoner of war.

Aaron Feuerstein, interviewed in "Malden Mills," CBS *Sixty Minutes,* Sunday, March 24, 2002; and "The Mensch of Malden Mills," *CBSNEWS.com,* July 6, 2003. The President and CEO of Malden Mills, the manufacturer of Polartec® fleece, explains why he decided to rebuild after his plant burned to the ground in 1995 and pay his 3,000 employees while they waited to return to work.

Frank Gilbreth, Jr. and Ernestine Gilbreth Carey, *Cheaper by the Dozen.* (1948). New York: Bantam Books, 1975. Also, *Belles on Their Toes.* (1950). New York: Bantam Books, 1984. Memoirs of growing up with two of America's most successful early twentieth-century management gurus.

Andrew S. Grove, *Only the Paranoid Survive: How to Exploit the Crisis Points That Challenge Every Company and Career*. New York: Currency/Doubleday, 1996, 1999. The former CEO and current chairman of the board of microprocessor manufacturer Intel discusses strategies for survival in a highly competitive market.

Du Bose Heyward, *The Country Bunny and the Little Gold Shoes*. Boston: Houghton Mifflin, 1939. A little girl bunny decides to become one of the Easter bunnies, but has to fight prejudice and make a virtue of single motherhood to succeed.

Immanuel Kant, "The Metaphysical Elements of Justice," Part I of *The Metaphysics of Morals*. (1797). Trans. John Ladd. New York: Bobbs-Merrill, 1965. Against the background of Kant's quest for the rational basis of morality, Part I places rights under law or justice, while Part II focuses on virtue in the realm of ethics, a distinction central to discussions later in *The Story of Success.*

Timothy Mo, *The Monkey King*. Boston/London: Faber and Faber, 1978. A Western-influenced son-in-law discovers what it means to do business in a Hong Kong family enterprise.

Bharati Mukherjee, *Jasmine*. New York: Fawcett Crest, 1989. A Punjabi woman makes her way from India to the United States, then finds the heartland of her adoptive country and her own self.

Bharati Mukherjee, "The Management of Grief." In *The Middleman and Other Stories*. New York: Grove Press, 1988, pp. 177–197. An Indian immigrant to Canada finds herself mediating between her birth culture and her adoptive culture in the wake of a plane crash.

Harry Mulisch, *The Assault*. (1982). Trans. Claire Nicolas White. New York: Pantheon Books, 1985; also a film—*De Aanslag*, dir. Fons Rademakers (1986). Twelve-year-old Anton must pick up the pieces of his life after his parents and brother are executed in a reprisal raid by German occupiers in 1944 Holland.

Chapter 3: See the Big Picture

Alan Bennett, *The Madness of George III.* (1992). Boston/London: Faber & Faber, 1995. Also a film—*The Madness of King George,* dir. Nicholas Hytner (1994). George III, the British king who lost the American colonies, also seems briefly to lose his mind; however, his role as king and leader means he can't ever be seen to be less than fully himself.

Angel Cabrera, "The Proposed 'Hippocratic Oath' for Business," in collaboration with the faculty of the Instituto de Empresa and the Global Leaders for Tomorrow of the World Economic Forum. Madrid, October, 2002. The proposed oath offers a set of professional standards for business based on Hippocrates' ancient code for physicians.

Angel Cabrera, "A Hippocratic Oath for Business?" *Handelsblatt,* July 18, 2003. See discussion in text for a description. Cabrera's op-ed piece generated a series of responses running into October 2003 on Handelsblatt.com. See: http://www.handelsblatt.com/hbiwwwangebot/fn/relhbi/SH/0/de pot/0/sfn/buildhbi/strucid/200014/bmc/cn_bild_basket/bmc/cn_ schlagzeilen_basket_ext!400,100,0,teaser,1/basketID/727767/bmc/ cn_firmenkasten/index.html

E.M. Forster, *A Passage to India.* (1924). New York: Harvest Books, 1965. In early twentieth-century India, a trio of English citizens befriends a well-educated representative of the local—and subject—populace. A moment of mystery makes clear that cross-racial friendships are still a thing of the future, and that the British Raj may not last forever.

Robert W. Gordon, "Professionals and Professionalism: An

Overview." Unpublished manuscript. A professor of law and legal history at Yale, Gordon gives an account of the evolution of the professions in the West, the various perspectives we currently hold on professional activity, and the way in which the professions respond to needs that market forces can't or won't.

Kazuo Ishiguro, *The Remains of the Day*. (1989). New York: Vintage International, 1990. A butler who served his master to the exclusion of all else realizes, late in life, that he may have missed something important.

Thomas Kuhn, *The Structure of Scientific Revolutions*. (1962). Chicago: University of Chicago Press, 1970. The late MIT physicist, philosopher, and historian of science explores how our scientific understanding of the world periodically undergoes what he calls "paradigm shifts," radical reassessments of what we know and how we should see the world.

Ang Lee, dir., *Crouching Tiger, Hidden Dragon* (2000). Also, Ang Lee and James Schamus, *Crouching Tiger, Hidden Dragon: Portrait of the Ang Lee Film*. New York: Newmarket Press, 2000. Ang Lee's film about a famous sword and the lives it affects won an Academy Award for Best Foreign Picture. Beyond its lush imagery and fanciful martial arts displays, the film explores competing social codes in Qing Dynasty society, with echoes for the China of today.

James Madison, "Federalist X." In Alexander Hamilton, James Madison, and John Jay, *The Federalist Papers*. (1787–1788). New York: Mentor, 1999, pp. 45–52. James Madison argues that a republican form of government will protect the new United States against the ills of faction, thus guaranteeing the Union articulated in an as-yet-unratified U.S. Constitution.

W. Somerset Maugham, "The Outstation." (1953). In *Collected Short Stories, Vol. IV*. New York: Penguin Books, 1978, pp. 338–365. A veteran colonial administrator has to deal with an impertinent young assistant who doesn't understand the local customs.

Herman Melville, *Billy Budd*. (1924). New York: Pocket Books, 1972. Also a film—*Billy Budd*, dir. Peter Ustinov (1962). Capt. Vere must decide the fate of Billy Budd, seaman, after Budd inadvertently kills an officer on board Vere's ship.

Antoine de Saint-Exupéry, *Night Flight*. (1931). Trans. Stuart Gilbert. New York: Harvest/Harcourt Brace Jovanovich, 1932. An aviator sets forth on a mission that he quickly realizes can only end in death.

Roger Moore, dir., *Roger and Me* (1989) and *Fahrenheit 9/11* (2004). As described in the text.

Peter Schneider, *The Wall Jumper*. (1982). Trans. Leigh Hafrey. New York: Pantheon Books, 1983. West German writer and Berlin chronicler Schneider recounts the stories of Germans East and West who cross the Berlin Wall, more often than not simply because it is there.

Peter Schneider, "Scenes from a Marriage." In *The New York Times Magazine*, Aug. 12, 2001, pp. 44 ff. Schneider examines the 1998 merger of Daimler-Benz and the Chrysler Corporation, comparing corporate cultures in the two companies and speculating on the future of the merged company.

Peter Senge, *The Fifth Discipline*. (1990). New York: Currency/Doubleday, 1994. In his landmark book on organizational theory, Senge explores the importance of systems thinking for building the learning organization. Key concepts related to *The Story of Success* include "personal mastery," the "leader as teacher," and the "purpose story."

William Shakespeare, *King Lear*. (1607–1608). New York: Penguin, 1958. When Lear decides to divide his kingdom among his three daughters, he discovers that love is hard to measure, and authority a fleeting possession.

Noel M. Tichy, with Nancy Cardwell, *The Cycle of Leadership: How Great Teachers Teach Their Companies to Win*. (2002, 2004). New York: HarperBusiness, 2004.

Alexis de Tocqueville, *Democracy in America*. (1835, 1840). Trans. Henry

Reeve, with corrections by Francis Bowen and Phillips Bradley. New York: Alfred A. Knopf, 1966. A young French aristocrat tours America in the early 1830s and composes his observations in a book on one nation's version of democracy.

United Nations, "What is the Global Compact?" and "The Nine Principles" of the Global Compact. Available on-line. Launched in 1999, the UN Global Compact partners governments, nongovernmental agencies, and corporations in encouraging a respect for human rights, fair labor practices, and sustainable development.

John Updike, "Made in Heaven." In *Trust Me: Short Stories*. New York: Fawcett, 1988, pp. 190–207. A young businessman falls in love with a secretary who declares her highest value is the salvation of her soul.

Virginia Woolf, *Three Guineas*. (1938). New York: Harvest/Harcourt Brace Jovanovich, 1966. Woolf explains the conditions on which she will donate a guinea to three causes: the employment of professional women, an end to war, and the building of a women's college.

Fred Zinnemann, dir., *High Noon* (1952). A small-town sheriff is about to relinquish his post for married bliss, but learns that a gunman is coming to town in search of revenge. The sheriff tries to build support among the townspeople, but discovers he will have to solve the problem himself.

Chapter 4: Break the Rules, Make the Rules, Absorb the Costs

Jean-Jacques Beineix, dir., *Diva* (1981). A young French postal clerk finds himself caught up in art theft and a prostitution ring as a result of his passion for an American opera singer. Only a mysterious man-about-town can save him.

Cameron Crowe, dir., *Jerry Maguire* (1996). Sports agent Jerry Maguire decides he needs to reframe his professional life, and finds that adhering to higher principles means he will have to do it his way.

F. Scott Fitzgerald, *The Great Gatsby*. (1925). New York: Collier Books, 1992. Gatsby has the charm of quick success, but can't quite leave his past behind him, as a doting disciple soon learns.

Henry King, dir., *Twelve O'Clock High* (1949). Faced with a bomber group suffering from catastrophically low morale during WWII, a desk officer takes over and applies tough love to get them back on track.

Sinclair Lewis, *Babbitt*. (1922). New York: Bantam Classics, 1998. Lewis skewered American middle-class values in this novel of a businessman who wants to belong, but knows he hasn't found the key to happiness.

Thomas Mann, *Buddenbrooks: the Decline of a Family*. (1900). Trans. John E. Woods. New York: Vintage Books, 1994. Mann scandalized his hometown with this semiautobiographical account of a merchant family's decline.

Liam O'Flaherty, "Two Lovely Beasts." In *Two Lovely Beasts and Other Stories*. New York: the Devin-Adair Company, 1948, pp. 3–32. A poor villager on the coast of Ireland suddenly decides he wants to become an entrepreneur. He succeeds, but we are left asking at what price.

Jack Rennie, discussed in *Massachusetts Board of Education, 2000 Annual Report*, March 2001; and in "SBA Presents Mayor Menino with Award for Outstanding Leadership," Mayor's Office Press Release, *City of Boston* (on-line), Sept. 12, 2003. Jack Rennie, a successful entrepreneur, also exemplified social enterprise in his devotion to improving education in Massachusetts.

David Russell, dir., *Three Kings* (1999). During the Gulf War, three GIs and a Special Forces officer steal the gold Saddam Hussein stole from the Kuwaitis, but find they have taken more than they bargained for.

Jane Smiley, *Good Will*. In *Ordinary Love and Good Will*. New York: Ivy Books, 1989, pp. 105–218. A Vietnam veteran retires to the mountains of Pennsylvania with his wife and son, only to discover that his many talents are not enough to forge an existence strictly on his terms.

Adam Smith, *The Wealth of Nations.* (1776). New York: Modern Library, 1937. Smith's study laid the conceptual groundwork for laissez-faire economics, with an emphasis on free markets and a distrust of government intervention that are still widely preached today.

Wole Soyinka, *Death and the King's Horseman.* (1975). New York: W.W. Norton & Co., 2003. Yoruba tradition and British administrative cultures clash, negating a more encompassing definition of what it means to have a self and a role in society.

Oliver Stone, dir., *Wall Street* (1987). A young Wall Street trader wants to emulate financier Gordon Gekko, who believes that "greed...is good."

Max Weber, *The Protestant Ethic and the Spirit of Capitalism.* (1904–1905). Trans. Talcott Parsons. New York: Charles Scribner's Sons, 1958. Weber traces the emergence of capitalism to the rise of Protestantism, in which the pursuit and accumulation of wealth becomes a duty or calling, enhanced by a thrifty focus on the work itself, not the expenditure of wealth that the work allows.

Tom Wolfe, *The Bonfire of the Vanities.* New York: Farrar, Straus & Giroux, 1987. Investment banker Sherman McCoy discovers the full spectacle of New York City after an accident upends his carefully crafted world.

Emile Zola, *Germinal.* Trans. Leonard Tancock. (1885). New York: Penguin Books, 1954. Capital and labor clash in a mid-nineteenth-century French coalfield.

Chapter 5: Tell Good Stories

Horatio Alger, Jr., *Ragged Dick: or, Street Life in New York with the Boot Blacks.* (1868). New York: Signet Classic/Penguin, 1990. A classic Horatio Alger tale, not so much of rags to riches, but rags to respectability.

Charles Dickens, *A Christmas Carol*. (1843). London: Penguin Books, 1984. The much-read, much-enacted story of how well-to-do Scrooge discovers the importance of giving as well as getting, after seeing the Ghosts of Christmas Past, Present, and Yet to Come.

Michael Frayn, *Copenhagen*. (1998). London: Methuen Publishing, 2000. Physicists Nils Bohr and Werner Heisenberg and Bohr's wife, Margrethe, come back from the dead to ponder guilt and innocence after the design and use of the atom bomb at the end of World War II.

Johann Wolfgang von Goethe, *Elective Affinities*. (1809). Trans. David Constantine. Oxford: Oxford University Press, 1994. A nobleman and his wife try to create a world unto themselves on their estate, but find that larger, natural forces intervene to disrupt their plans.

Ashutosh Gowariker, dir., *Lagaan: Once Upon a Time in India* (2001). A village in India under British rule stakes its future on a game of cricket against local British forces. The film demonstrates multiple models of leadership.

Vaclav Havel, *Summer Meditations*. (1991). Trans. Paul Wilson. New York: Vintage Books, 1992, 1993. The former Czech dissident and first president of the Czech Republic muses on the demands of leadership and the importance of values in politics.

James Hilton, *Lost Horizon*. (1933). New York: Pocket Books, 1939. Also a film—*Lost Horizon*, dir. Frank Capra (1937). A hijacked planeload of Westerners find themselves in a mysterious utopia, run by a former priest; in Shangri-La, it seems, immortality is within reach.

Norman Jewison, dir., *Other People's Money* (1991). Larry the Liquidator has made a fortune on leveraged buyouts. His latest target, however, won't give up without a fight.

Lao Tze, *Tao te Ching (The Book of the Way and Its Virtue)*. (600–300 BCE). Trans. James Legge, 1891. Mineola, NY: Dover, 1997. Lao Tze, or

"Old Master," is the founder of Taoism and the putative author of this book of eighty-one sayings advocating nonaggression, stoicism, and simplicity.

David Lodge, *Nice Work*. (1988). New York: Penguin Books, 1990. The CEO of a manufacturing company gets entangled with a literary critic who deconstructs his vision of the world, even as he constructs hers.

Penny Marshall, dir., *Big* (1988). By dint of magic, 13-year-old Josh becomes an executive in a toy company. He knows the product, but he has to learn about corporate politics.

Gloria Naylor, *Linden Hills*. New York: Penguin Books, 1985. A community of blacks in the American Midwest has achieved material success, but lost their collective soul.

Masayuki Suo, dir., *Shall We Dance?* (1997). A Japanese *salaryman* discovers that dutiful behavior doesn't make a happy life, but teamwork and leadership may.

Virginia Woolf, *Mrs. Dalloway*. New York: Harcourt Brace Jovanovich, 1925. In the wake of the Great War, Mrs. Dalloway stages a party that will symbolize a return to peacetime normalcy, even as Septimus Warren Smith, a shell-shocked veteran, slowly moves toward suicide.

Chapter 6: Test for Truth

Robert Bolt, *A Man for All Seasons*. (1960). New York: Vintage International, 1962. Bolt's play captures the dilemma at the heart of Sir Thomas More's confrontation with Henry VIII of England. Henry wants More to surrender his faith in the authority of the Church for obedience to Henry; More clings to both his faith and his professional practice as a gifted lawyer.

Joseph Conrad, *Heart of Darkness*. (1902). London: Penguin Books, 1989. In equatorial Africa, Conrad's narrator journeys upriver in search of a company agent who has gone mad with power.

Costa-Gavras, dir., Z. (1969). Costa-Gavras's film recounts the real-life assassination, in 1963, of a liberal deputy to the Greek parliament, and the investigation and cover-up that it generated. A study in leadership styles and the importance of professional standards, Z is a modern Greek tragedy.

Robert Duvall, dir., *The Apostle* (1997) and *The Apostle: A Screenplay*. New York: October/Boulevard Books, 1998. Robert Duvall's "Holy Ghost" preacher, Sonny Dewey, kills a man in a jealous rage, and then builds a new church and congregation by way of atonement.

Milton Friedman, *Capitalism and Freedom*. (1962). Chicago: University of Chicago Press, 1982. Friedman's now classic statement of the virtues of private enterprise and the free market points the way to a successful liberal society.

Bill Joy, "Why the Future Doesn't Need Us." In *Wired Magazine*, 8.04, April 2000, pp. 238 ff. The chief scientist at Sun Microsystems reflects on the threats posed to life as we know it by robotics, bioengineering, and nanotechnologies.

Martin Luther King, Jr., "Letter from Birmingham Jail." In *Why We Can't Wait*. 1963, 1964. New York: Signet Classic, 2000, pp. 64–84. One of King's best-known essays, the "Letter" directly addresses the white moderates who urged King and his movement to bide their time in securing civil rights for American blacks.

Ursula K. LeGuin, "The Ones Who Walk Away from Omelas." In *The Wind's Twelve Quarters*. (1975). New York: HarperPrism, 1995, pp. 345–357. LeGuin posits a utopian community in which everyone leads a happy life thanks to one child sequestered in vile conditions in a basement closet.

Alan Lightman, "Progress." In *Dance for Two*. New York: Pantheon Books, 1996, pp. 87–93. Lightman builds an essay around his refusal to acquire an e-mail account, questioning our apparently instinctual assumption that technological innovation is a good thing.

Luis Puenzo, dir., *La Historia Oficial (The Official Story)* (1985). An afflu-ent schoolteacher comes to terms with the political realities of Ar-gentina under the junta of the late 1970s and early 1980s, and learns what it means to fight for human rights and the truth.

Alain Resnais, dir., *Mon Oncle d'Amérique* (1980). Built around the theo-ries of behavioral scientist Henri Laborit, Resnais's film explores how we acquire a self, and how easily that identity can both cause us trouble and collapse under the pressure of daily events.

Ridley Scott, dir., *Blade Runner* (1982; "Director's Cut," 1993). In twenty-first-century Los Angeles, a company manufactures "replicants," robots so sophisticated they develop their own emo-tions and values.

Sophocles, *Antigone*. (circa 442 BCE). Trans. Paul Woodruff. Indianapo-lis/Cambridge: Hackett Publishing, 2001. Antigone, daughter to Oedipus, insists on burying her brother Polyneices, despite King Creon's edict that, as a traitor to Thebes, Polyneices should not be granted such rites.

Chapter 7: Mastering Mather

Bertolt Brecht, *Galileo*. (1940, 1952). Trans. Charles Laughton. New York: Grove Press, 1952, 1966. The German playwright explores the life of physicist and astronomer Galileo Galilei. The scientist recanted his teaching that the earth orbits the sun, in order either to save his own neck or to finish his *Discorsi*, which laid the groundwork for even greater discoveries.

David Brooks, *Bobos in Paradise: The New Upper Class and How They Got There*. (2000). New York: Touchstone/Simon & Schuster, 2001. Brooks explores the means by which members of the baby boom generation have grown into establishment figures in their own right, but still on rather countercultural terms.

David Brooks, "The Organization Kid." In *The Atlantic Monthly*, April 2001, pp. 40 ff. The *New York Times* columnist explores the current generation of top-tier college students; he finds them well prepared, highly motivated, but wanting in character.

Gurinder Chadha, *Bend It Like Beckham* (2003). Jess wants to play soccer as well as David Beckham, but her traditional Indian family believes girls must attend to other matters. With help from an English friend, and a change of heart on her family's part, she finds the means to pursue her ambition.

Charles Dickens, *Hard Times*. (1854). New York: W.W. Norton & Co., 1990. Dickens's novel satirizes utilitarian philosophy in the classroom and in life, as it depicts the fate of several intertwined families in a British factory town during the Industrial Revolution.

Marleen Gorris, dir., *Antonia's Line* (1995). A woman returns to her ancestral farm in the Dutch countryside and slowly builds a thriving community for herself, her descendants—all women—and the misfits of the neighboring village.

Leigh Hafrey, "What's In a Book?" In *Harvard Review*, Fall 1993, pp. 33–35. Hafrey describes his elder son's learning to speak, and draws conclusions on the relation of basic human drives to story and storytelling.

David Halberstam, *The Best and the Brightest*. (1973). New York: Ballantine Books, 1993. Halberstam chronicles the men and the decisions that led to America's involvement in the Vietnam War.

Hippocrates, "The Hippocratic Oath" (circa 400 BCE). Available online. Professional code for physicians composed in ancient Greece, and still pledged today in modern form at many medical schools.

Increase Mather, "Cases of Conscience Concerning Evil Spirits Personating Men." (1693). In *The Wonders of the Invisible World: Being an Account of the Tryals of Several Witches Lately Executed in New-England*, by Cotton Mather. London: John Russell Smith, 1862, pp. 219–291.

One of America's founding Puritans, the Rev. Increase Mather explores aspects of the Salem witch trials, then in full spate, and warns against imprudent reliance on spectral evidence.

Increase Mather, A Brief History of the War with the Indians in New-England. London: Printed for Richard Chiswell, 1676. Mather chronicles the bloody clash between English colonists and the Wampanoag and other native American groups in what has since become known as King Philip's War.

Mira Nair, Monsoon Wedding (2001). As described in the text.

Peter Schneider, "Saving Konrad Latte." In The New York Times Magazine, Feb. 13, 2000, pp. 52 ff. Schneider, a West German novelist and political commentator, recounts the story of one German Jew who lived out World War II in Berlin, thanks to the concerted efforts of his Gentile fellow citizens.

Henry David Thoreau, "Walden." In Walden and Civil Disobedience. (1854). New York: Penguin, 1983. In the first chapter of his classic text on the importance of living simply and thinking clearly, the sage of Concord lays out the nature of his experiment in the woods by Walden Pond.

William H. Whyte, The Organization Man. New York: Simon and Schuster, 1956. In his best-selling book, Whyte argues that organizational culture is fast becoming the principal determinant of American social behavior, even as Americans continue to proclaim their essential individualism.